Printed on recycled paper.

S0-ACL-852

SOCIAL STUDIES

Anthology

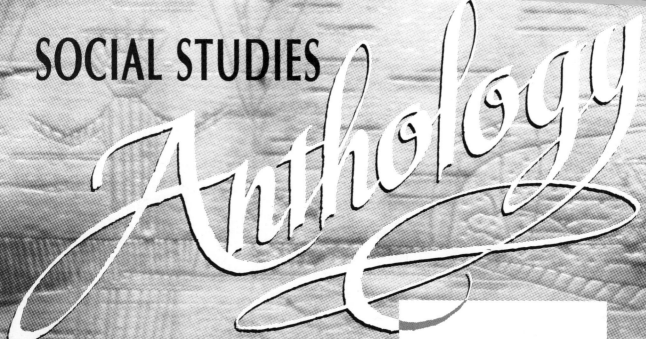

THE WORLD AROUND US

The cover photos of the Statue of Liberty, the Constitution, and the sacred scrolls of the southern Ojibwa all help to tell the story of the United States. They are symbols of some of the ideals which have shaped our country.

MACMILLAN/McGRAW-HILL SCHOOL PUBLISHING COMPANY
NEW YORK   CHICAGO   COLUMBUS

PROGRAM AUTHORS •

Dr. James A. Banks
Professor of Education and Director of the Center for
   Multicultural Education
University of Washington
Seattle, Washington

Dr. Barry K. Beyer
Professor of Education and American Studies
George Mason University
Fairfax, Virginia

Dr. Gloria Contreras
Professor of Education and Director of the Office of
   Multicultural Affairs
University of North Texas
Denton, Texas

Jean Craven
District Coordinator of Curriculum Development
Albuquerque Public Schools
Albuquerque, New Mexico

Dr. Gloria Ladson-Billings
Assistant Professor of Education
University of Wisconsin
Madison, Wisconsin

Dr. Mary A. McFarland
Director of Staff Development and Instructional
   Coordinator of Social Studies, K-12
Parkway School District
Chesterfield, Missouri

Dr. Walter C. Parker
Associate Professor of Social Studies Education and
   Director of the Center for the Study of Civic
   Intelligence
University of Washington
Seattle, Washington

CONTENT CONSULTANTS •

Yvonne Beamer
Resource Specialist
Native American Education Program
New York, New York

Mario T. Garcia
Professor of History and American Studies
Yale University
New Haven, Connecticut

Héctor Lindo-Fuentes
Associate Professor of History
Fordham University
Bronx, New York

Ruthanne Lum McCunn
Chinese Historical Society of America
San Francisco, California

Valerie Ooka Pang
Associate Professor, School of Teacher Education
San Diego State University
San Diego, California

Clifford E. Trafzer
Professor of Ethnic Studies and Director of Native
   American Studies
University of California
Riverside, California

GRADE-LEVEL CONSULTANTS •

Tavis Hardin
Fifth Grade Teacher
North Birmingham Elementary School
Birmingham, Alabama

Kathy Hellesen
Elementary Teacher
Hoover School
Schaumburg, Illinois

Tarry Lindquist
Fifth Grade Teacher
Lakeridge Elementary School
Mercer Island, Washington

Noreen S. McAndrews
Elementary Social Studies Teacher
Holy Cross School
Deerfield, Illinois

Gerard Moss
Fifth Grade Teacher
Public School 250
Brooklyn, New York

ACKNOWLEDGMENTS •

*The publisher gratefully acknowledges permission to reprint
the following copyrighted material:*

"Lineage" from FOR MY PEOPLE by Margaret Walker.
Copyright 1942 by Yale University Press. Used by
permission of Margaret Walker Alexander.

Excerpt from WAR COMES TO WILLY FREEMAN
by James Lincoln Collier and Christopher Collier.
Copyright © by James Lincoln Collier and Christopher
Collier. Reprinted by permission of Dell Books, a
division of Bantam Doubleday Dell Publishing
Group, Inc.

(continued on page 199)

Macmillan/McGraw-Hill School Division
10 Union Square East
New York, New York 10003

Printed in the United States of America
ISBN 0-02-146127-9
1 2 3 4 5 6 7 8 9   POH   99 98 97 96 95 94 93 92

TABLE OF *Contents*

= audio cassette

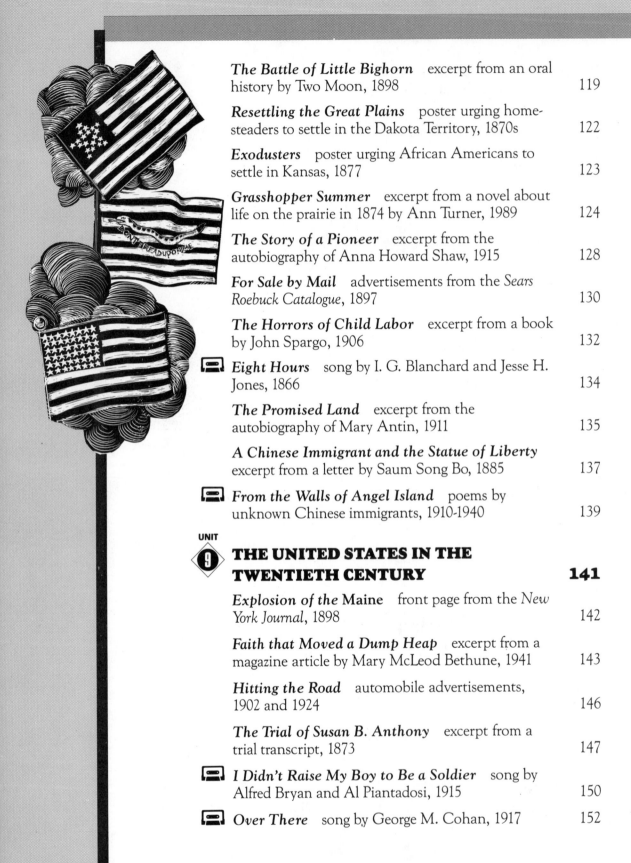

USING YOUR *Anthology*

In *United States and Its Neighbors* you will be reading about many different people, places, and times. This Anthology, or collection of documents created by different people, will make the information in your textbook come to life in a special way. Some of the documents are letters, stories, diaries, songs, poems, and political cartoons. Others are items you might not have thought of as documents, such as old advertisements, posters, illustrations, and even home-made signs and a buffalo hide. As you study these documents, you will be able to see, feel, and hear what it was like to live in other times and places. The documents in this Anthology will all help you to better understand the story of our country and the people who helped to build it.

INTRODUCTION •
Gives you background information about the selection and tells you what kind of document it is. Is it fiction or nonfiction? Is it a poem or a song? The introduction also gives you the dates of the birth and death of the author. At the end, the introduction asks you a question to think about as you read the document.

CONCLUSION •
Tells you what happened next and asks you to think further about the selection

CASSETTE LOGO •
Tells you that the selection appears on the Anthology Cassette

TEXTBOOK LINK •
Tells you which chapter and lesson in your textbook the document is linked to

DEFINITIONS •
Gives you the meanings of difficult words

SOURCE •
Tells you where the selection came from

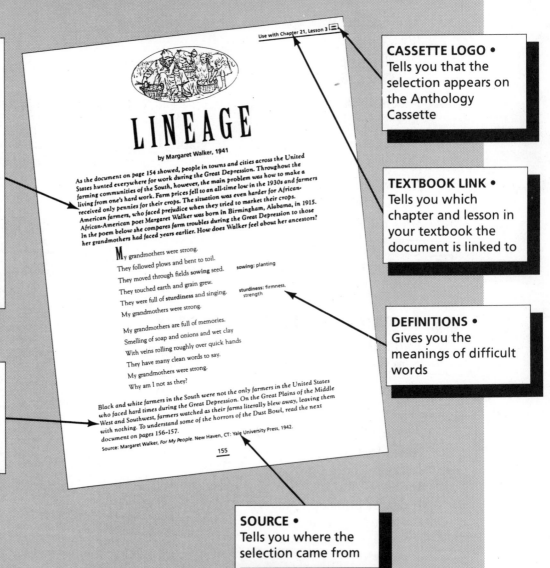

Use with Chapter 21, Lesson 3

LINEAGE
by Margaret Walker, 1941

As the document on page 154 showed, people in towns and cities across the United States hunted everywhere for work during the Great Depression. Throughout the farming communities of the South, however, the main problem was how to make a living from one's hard work. Farm prices fell to an all-time low in the 1930s and farmers received only pennies for their crops. The situation was even harder for African-American farmers, who faced prejudice when they tried to market their crops. African-American poet Margaret Walker was born in Birmingham, Alabama, in 1915. In the poem below she compares farm troubles during the Great Depression to those her grandmothers had faced years earlier. How does Walker feel about her ancestors?

My grandmothers were strong.
They followed plows and bent to toil.
They moved through fields sowing seed.   sowing: planting
They touched earth and grain grew.
They were full of **sturdiness** and singing.   sturdiness: firmness, strength
My grandmothers were strong.

My grandmothers are full of memories.
Smelling of soap and onions and wet clay
With veins rolling roughly over quick hands
They have many clean words to say.
My grandmothers were strong.
Why am I not as they?

Black and white farmers in the South were not the only farmers in the United States who faced hard times during the Great Depression. On the Great Plains of the Middle West and Southwest, farmers watched as their farms literally blew away, leaving them with nothing. To understand some of the horrors of the Dust Bowl, read the next document on pages 156-157.

Source: Margaret Walker, *For My People*. New Haven, CT: Yale University Press, 1942.

155

viii

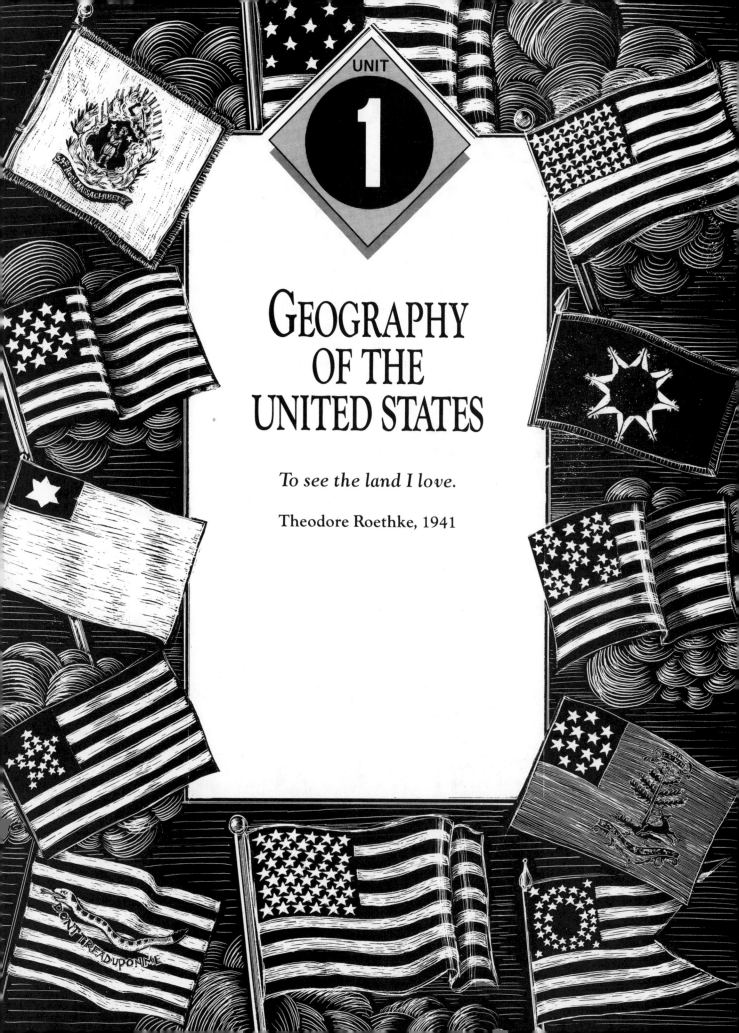

UNIT

1

GEOGRAPHY OF THE UNITED STATES

To see the land I love.

Theodore Roethke, 1941

Night Journey

by Theodore Roethke, 1941

Seeing the United States from an airplane is very different from seeing the country from a train. From a plane, mountains, lakes, and valleys look tiny and almost like toys. Through a train window, however, the geography of the land comes to life—especially when you take a ride with the poet Theodore Roethke (reth' kē, 1908-1963). Born in Michigan, Roethke became one of the leading poets in the United States. In Night Journey, *the poem below, Roethke describes a midnight train ride across the United States. As you read this poem, picture in your mind what Roethke is describing from his train window. Notice the different types of geographical features he passes. How do Roethke's words make you feel the land and the train as well as see them?*

Now as the train **bears** west   **bears:** heads

Its rhythm rocks the earth,

And from my **Pullman berth**   **Pullman berth:**
     bed in a railroad car

I stare into the night

While others take their rest.

Bridges of iron lace,

A suddenness of trees,

A lap of mountain mist

All cross my line of sight,

Then a **bleak** wasted place,   **bleak:** barren

And a lake below my knees.

Full on my neck I feel

The straining at a curve;

My muscles move with steel,

I wake in every nerve.

I watch a **beacon** swing   **beacon:** signal light

From dark to blazing bright;

We thunder through **ravines**   **ravines:** steep valleys

And **gullies** washed with light.   **gullies:** dry riverbeds

Beyond the mountain pass

Mist deepens on the **pane**;   **pane:** window glass

We rush into a rain

That rattles double glass.

Wheels shake the **roadbed stone**,   **roadbed stone:** stone
                                          beneath the tracks

The **pistons** jerk and shove,   **pistons:** engine parts

I stay up half the night

To see the land I love.

Traveling by train is one of the faster ways to see the countryside. But you can also travel more slowly—by bicycle, by skateboard, or on foot. How do the feeling of movement and the look of the countryside change when you use a different form of transportation?

Source: Theodore Roethke, *The Collected Poems of Theodore Roethke*. Garden City, NY: Doubleday and Company, Inc., 1966.

3

Natural Disasters

Newspaper Headlines, 1888–1980

Geography affects how people live and has always played an important role in history. People are most often aware of geography when a natural disaster—such as an earthquake or a hurricane—strikes the region of the country in which they live. Below are newspaper headlines describing four major natural disasters in the history of the United States. What natural disasters are these newspapers reporting? How might these disasters have affected people's lives?

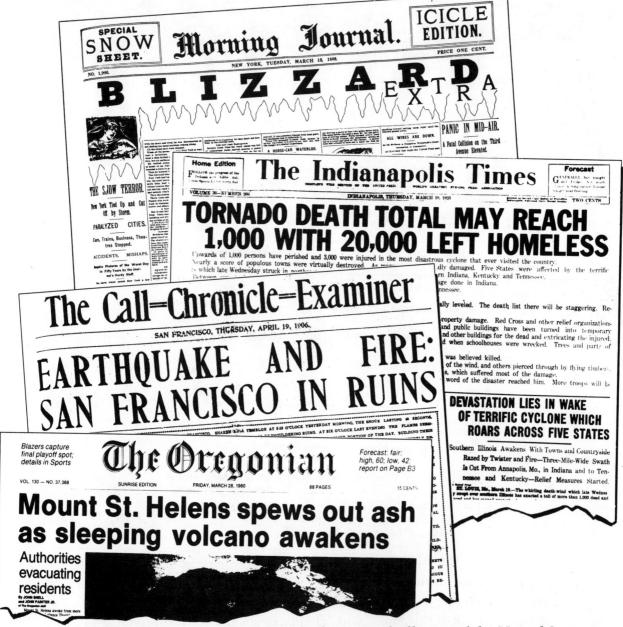

As these headlines show, natural disasters have struck all parts of the United States at different times in history. Has a natural disaster ever occurred in your lifetime, near where you live? How do geography, climate, and weather affect your life?

4

Don't Fence Me In

by Cole Porter, 1944

When people from smaller countries visit the United States, many are amazed by its vast size. Few other nations on earth stretch across an entire continent or border two different oceans. Thus it is not surprising that when people think about the United States, they often imagine wide open spaces and the freedom to move about as one pleases. Songwriter Cole Porter (1893–1964) captured such feelings in this song about a cowhand. Which regions of the country might the cowhand be describing?

Wild Cat Kel-ly, look-ing might-y pale, was stand-ing by the sher-iff's
Wild Cat Kel-ly, back a-gain in town, was sit-ting by his sweet-heart's

side____ and when that she-riff said "I'm send-ing you to jail,"
side____ and when his sweet-heart said "Come on, let's set-tle down,"

Refrain

Wild Cat raised his head and cried: } Oh, give me land, lots of land un-der
Wild Cat raised his head and cried: }

star-ry skies a-bove, don't fence me in.____ Let me ride thru the wide o-pen

5

coun-try that I love, don't fence me in. Let me be by my-self in the

eve-ning breeze,__ lis-ten to the mur-murs of the cot-ton-wood trees.__

Send me off for-ev-er, but I ask you please,__ don't fence me in.__

__ Just turn me loose, let me strad-dle my old sad-dle un-der-neath the west-ern

skies. _____ On my cay-use, let me wan-der o-ver

yon-der till I see the moun-tains rise. _____ I want to

ride to the ridge where the West com-menc-es, gaze at the moon till I

lose my sens-es. Can't look at hob-bles and I can't stand fenc-es,

1. don't fence me in.__ 2. Oh, give me__

Source: Cole Porter, *Don't Fence Me In*. Secaucus, NJ: Warner Bros. Publications, 1944.

6

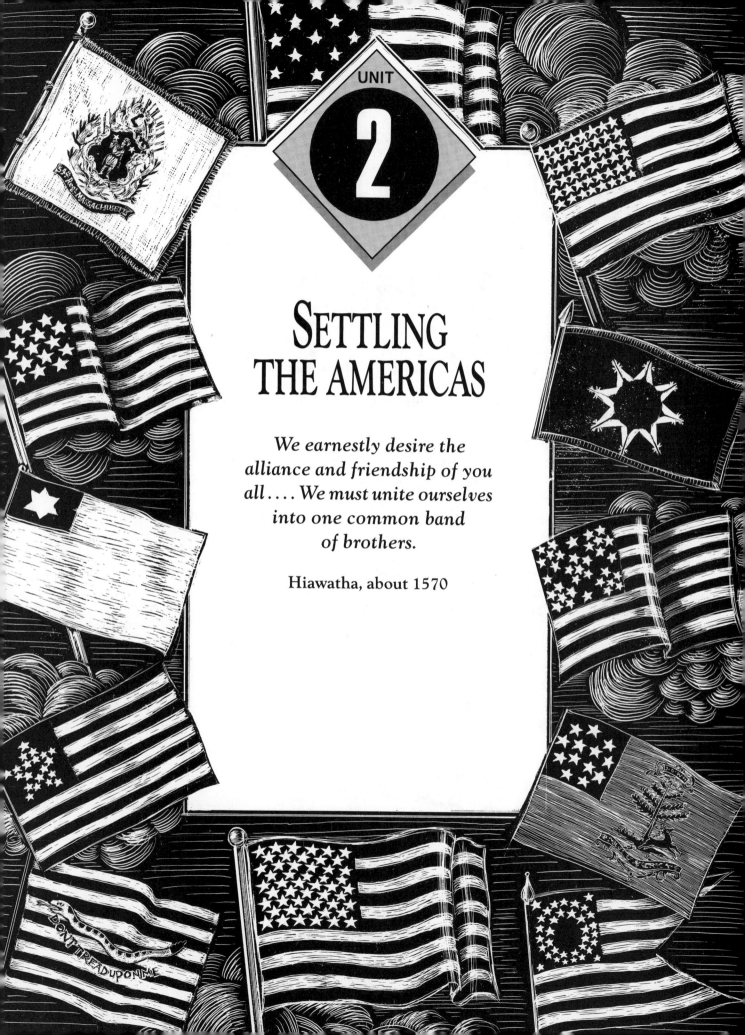

UNIT

2

SETTLING THE AMERICAS

We earnestly desire the
alliance and friendship of you
all.... We must unite ourselves
into one common band
of brothers.

Hiawatha, about 1570

A Dakota Winter Count

by Lone Dog, 1801–1870

How do you keep track of past events that have happened in your life? Do you use a calendar, or perhaps keep a diary? For hundreds of years the Dakota, or Sioux, Indians used a special kind of calendar to keep track of their history. These calendars were called winter counts because each winter the Dakota gathered together and chose an important event of the past year. An artist then recorded this event by drawing a pictograph, or picture, on the hide of an animal.

During the 1800s a Dakota named Lone Dog, who lived in what is today Montana, recorded in red and black on a buffalo hide most of the winter count shown on the next page. The first pictograph in Lone Dog's winter count dates from the winter of 1800-1801. This pictograph, which is highlighted, shows three short columns of 30 parallel lines. These lines stand for the deaths of 30 Dakota who were killed in battle during the past year. You can read each year of the winter count by following the pictographs in a spiral, counterclockwise. Lone Dog wrote the final pictograph in the winter of 1869-1870.

Here is another example of a pictograph and the story it tells:

1840-1841. Two hands are about to grasp one another. This shaking of hands stood for a peace agreement between the Dakota and the Cheyenne. The hands are in two different colors to represent two different nations.

Locate this pictograph in the winter count on the next page. Then study Lone Dog's other pictographs. See if you can figure out their meanings before checking the key on page 10, which explains some of them. How does the winter count show the events and issues that the Dakota considered important? How is Lone Dog a historian of his people?

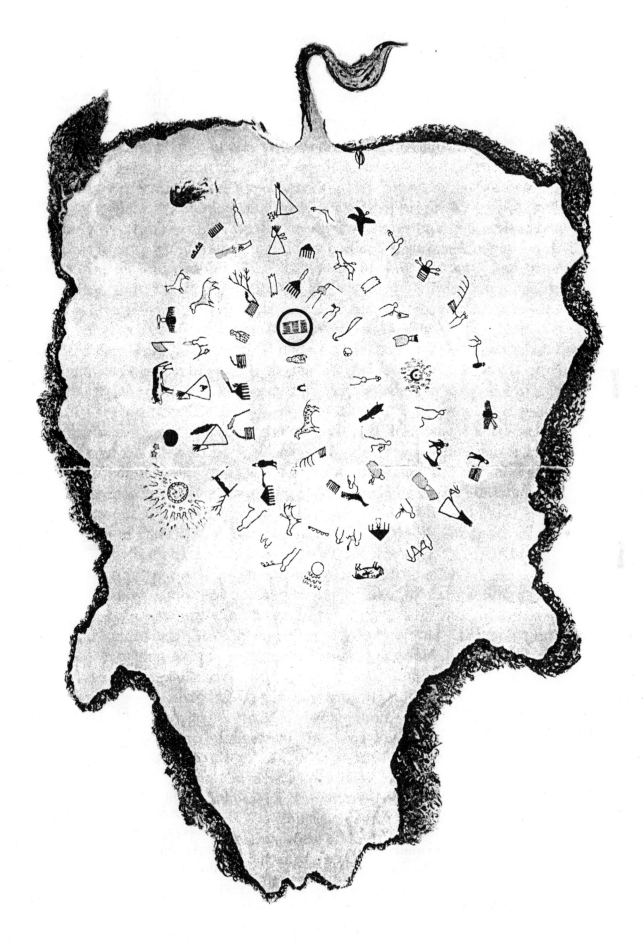

1801-1802. Spots cover the body of a person. These spots represent blotches caused by smallpox. Many Dakota died of smallpox in this year.

1812-1813. A lasso stands for the first year that the Dakota caught and tamed wild horses.

 **1817-1818.** A building with smoke coming out of its chimney is next to a dead tree, which means that the structure was built with dry wood. During this year a Canadian trader built a store near the Dakota in the valley of the Minnesota River. Can you find other pictographs that show trading stores or forts?

1825-1826. Five circles appear above a line. The circles may represent the heads of people trying to stay above water. The Missouri River overflowed its banks in 1825 and caused a major flood, killing many Dakota.

 1833-1834. The moon is surrounded by many falling stars. On November 12, 1833, a great meteor shower fell all over the United States.

1853-1854. A man wearing a hat holds out a striped blanket. The Dakota exchanged many goods this year with traders.

 **1861-1862.** Buffalo tracks appear beside a tepee. Note the cloven, or split, hoofs, characteristic of the buffalo. Food was so plentiful during this year that buffalo seemed to come right up to the Dakota's homes.

1867-1868. A flag stands for a peace conference that Dakota leaders held with officials of the United States government. The two groups met in August 1867 and agreed to a peace treaty during the following year.

Dakota winter counts are one of many written documents that Native Americans made to help preserve their history. If you were to make a winter count of your own life—or that of your school or community or state—what kinds of events might you want to include? Winter counts are one type of historical document that can teach us about the past. To learn about another type, read the next document on page 11.

Source: Garrick Mallery, *Picture-Writing of the American Indians.* Washington, D.C., 1893; reprinted New York: Dover Publications, 1972.

An American History Textbook in the 1800s

by Emma Willard, 1869

Imagine that a special machine has transported you back in time, and you are now sitting in a classroom in the year 1869. You and the other students are asked to read from an American history textbook written by Emma Willard (1787-1870), a leading educator of the 1800s. First published in 1828, Willard's textbook was one of the first—and most popular—American history textbooks in the nineteenth century. Although written at about a junior high school level, the book was used by students of all ages. Look below at the book's opening pages, which focus on history and geography. How do they look compared with your textbook today? Now read the text. How is it different from your 1990s textbook? How is it similar?

Washington's Inauguration.

CHAPTER I.

Definitions, &c.

1. THE subject of this work is the United States CHAP. I. of America; or, as those States are sometimes called, Subject. the Republic or Nation of America.

What constitutes a nation? First, there must be a country, with the natural divisions of land and water; second, there must be men, women, and children to inhabit that country; and third, those inhabitants must be bound together in one, by living Its triple division. under a common government, which extends its protection over all, and which all are bound to obey.

2. To every nation there belongs a *history*: For whenever the inhabitants of any large portion of the Any nation's his earth, are united under one government, *important* tory. *public events* must there have taken place. *The record* of *these events* constitutes the history of that country.

3. The events of history should always be recorded, with the circumstances of *time* and *place*. To tell *when* events happened, is to give their chronology;

1. What is the subject of this work? What three parts compose a nation?—2. What constitutes any nation's history? 3. How should events be recorded? What is it to give their chronology?
13

14   ONE NATION.

CHAP. I. to tell *where* they happened, their geography. The history of a nation, is therefore inseparably con-Connect-nected with its geography and chronology. Chrono ed with its geography nology may properly be called the skeleton of his-and chro-tory, geography the base on which it stands.
nology.
4. First, let us inquire, where is the country of which we desire to know the history? In the vast universe, is a system of planets surrounding a sun, Where hence called the solar system. The third planet from ur coun-try is. the sun is called the earth. On the earth's surface, the UNITED STATES OF AMERICA occupies a northern portion of the smaller of two continents. In extent, it is one of the largest nations of the world.

5. In longitude, the Republic of America ranges through sixty degrees, from the Atlantic ocean to Its lati-the Pacific. In latitude, it reaches from the Cape of tude and iongitude. Florida, in north latitude twenty-five degrees, to British and Russian America in forty-nine. Thus stretching through the greater part of the northern temperate zone, it includes every variety of climate, from the hot unhealthy swamps of Florida, to the Its cli-cold mountainous regions of northern New England, mate. and the north-western territories.

6. The soil and productions of our country are as various as its climate. Compared with other coun-Soil. tries, it contains a large proportion of arable land; and what is of the utmost consequence to the accom-Natural modation of man, it is *well watered*. On the whole, advan-tages. it may be pronounced, one of the most fertile, healthy, and desirable regions of the earth.

3. Their geography? Are chronology and geography connected with history?—4. In regard to the universe where, as astronomy teaches, are the United States? In regard to the earth's surface, or as respects geography, where is this country? What can you say of its extent?—5. What of its longitude? Of its latitude? Climate?—6. Soil and productions? Its natural advantages generally?—7. Does this region seem designed for one great nation, or for several small ones?

Suppose that a special machine transported you 100 years into the future. What might a textbook from the 2090s look like? Why do you think that history textbooks change over time?

Source: Adapted from Emma Willard, *Abridged History of the United States, or Republic of America*. New York and Chicago: A. S. Barnes & Company, 1869.

11

THE BEAUTIFUL DREAM

Navajo Story Told by Lana Semallie, 1976

The Navajo have an oral tradition that helps them to pass down their culture from one generation to the next. This oral tradition includes telling aloud their stories, legends, and history. In 1976 a writer named Byrd Baylor visited Indian schoolchildren in the Southwest and asked them to tell stories they had heard from someone in their tribes. Lana Semallie, a Navajo girl living in Arizona, told the story below. In which ways do the animals in this story act like people?

Many centuries ago Maii, the Coyote, was hanging around.

Coyote always liked to plan something tricky so this day he went walking with Porcupine and Brother Skunk. He was thinking as he walked along.

Ahead of them a wagon was going down the road. They saw a piece of meat fall off. They all ran for it and they all got there about the same time.

But Coyote did not want to share the meat so he said, "That's not fair."

He suggested they all race down a hill and the winner would eat the meat by himself. So that is what they did.

The race started. Porcupine curled up and rolled down the hill. He won.

"That's not fair," Coyote said.

Coyote suggested another plan. He said, "The one who dreams the most beautiful dream will eat that meat."

So that is what they planned.

Coyote and Skunk went to sleep but Porcupine stayed awake. He had a plan of his own.

Finally Coyote and Skunk woke up and told their dreams. They were both good dreams. They were both beautiful dreams.

Then they asked Porcupine what he had dreamed.

Porcupine said, "I dreamed I ate the meat."

They all jumped up and looked in the tree where they had left the meat. The meat was gone and Porcupine was looking fat.

Coyote is a popular character who appears over and over again in stories of the Navajo and other Southwest Indians. He is usually a funny character who gets into mischief when trying to trick his friends. But no matter how clever Coyote is, he often ends up getting fooled. If you were to write a story about Coyote, what adventures would you make up? What kinds of mischief would you have him getting into?

Source: Byrd Baylor, *And It Is Still That Way.* New York: Charles Scribner's Sons, 1976.

Founding of the Iroquois League

by Hiawatha, about 1570

During the 1500s five Native American groups, or nations, known as the Iroquois were living what is today New York State. These five nations—the Onondaga, the Oneida, the Seneca, the Cayuga, and the Mohawk—fought frequently with each other. Around 1570, however, a Mohawk chief named Hiawatha began to spread a message of peace among the Iroquois. In one powerful speech, he urged the five nations to stop fighting and unite into a peaceful league, or union. Hiawatha's words were passed down by Iroquois families for hundreds of years, a tradition known as oral history. Then, in 1881, an Iroquois chief named Elias Johnson wrote an English version of the speech as it had been told to him. This is the version of Hiawatha's speech that you are about to read. Note the different terms Hiawatha uses to refer to the place where each nation believed its creation began. These terms are printed in italics. How does Hiawatha describe the strength of each Iroquois nation?

Friends and Brothers: You being members of many tribes, you have come from a great distance; the voice of war has aroused you up; you are afraid . . . [for] your homes, your wives and your children; you tremble for your safety. Believe me, I am with you. My heart beats with your hearts. We are one. We have one common object. We come to promote our common interest, and to determine how this can be best done.

To oppose those **hordes** of northern tribes, singly and alone, would prove certain destruction. We can make no progress in that way. We must unite ourselves into one common band of brothers. We must have but one voice. Many voices makes confusion. We must have one fire, one pipe [of peace] and one war club. This will give us strength. If our warriors are united they can defeat the enemy and drive them from our land; if we do this, we are safe.

hordes: crowds

13

Onondaga, you are the people sitting under the shadow of the *Great Tree*, whose branches spread far and wide, and whose roots sink deep into the earth. You shall be the first nation, because you are warlike and mighty.

Great Tree: tree of peace, or white pine

Oneida, and you, the people who recline your bodies against the *Everlasting Stone*, that cannot be moved, shall be the second nation, because you always give good **counsel**.

Everlasting Stone: rock near present-day Oneida, New York
counsel: advice

Seneca, and you, the people who have your **habitation** at the foot of the *Great Mountain*, and are overshadowed by its **crags**, shall be the third nation, because you are all greatly gifted in speech.

habitation: home
Great Mountain: hill near Canandaigua Lake
crags: steep cliffs

Cayuga, you, whose dwelling is in the *Dark Forest*, and whose home is everywhere, shall be the fourth nation, because of your superior cunning in hunting.

Dark Forest: forest near Cayuga Lake

Mohawk, and you, the people who live in the open country, and possess much wisdom, shall be the fifth nation, because you understand better the art of raising corn and beans and making cabins.

You five great and powerful nations, with your tribes, must unite and have one common interest, and no **foe** shall disturb or **subdue** you.

foe: enemy
subdue: conquer

And you of the different nations of the south, and you of the west, may place yourselves under our protection, and we will protect you. We earnestly desire the **alliance** and friendship of you all. . . .

alliance: cooperation

If we unite in one band the Great Spirit will smile upon us, and we shall be free, prosperous and happy; but if we shall remain as we are we shall **incur** his displeasure. We shall be enslaved, and perhaps **annihilated** forever.

incur: bring on
annihilated: destroyed

Brothers, these are the words of Hiawatha. Let them sink deep into your hearts. I have done.

Hiawatha's speech helped convince his listeners to put aside their differences and unite. Leaders of the Five Nations formed a new government and called themselves the Iroquois League. A sixth nation, the Tuscarora, joined the league in 1712. The Iroquois soon became one of the most powerful groups in North America. Benjamin Franklin, a leader in the fight for American freedom from Great Britain in the 1700s, admired the league's strength and system of government. He later urged people in the 13 colonies to consider a similar plan of union.

Source: Elias Johnson (A Native Tuscarora Chief), *Legends, Traditions and Laws, of the Iroquois, or Six Nations, and History of the Tuscarora Indians.* Lockport, NY: Union Printing and Publishing Co., 1881.

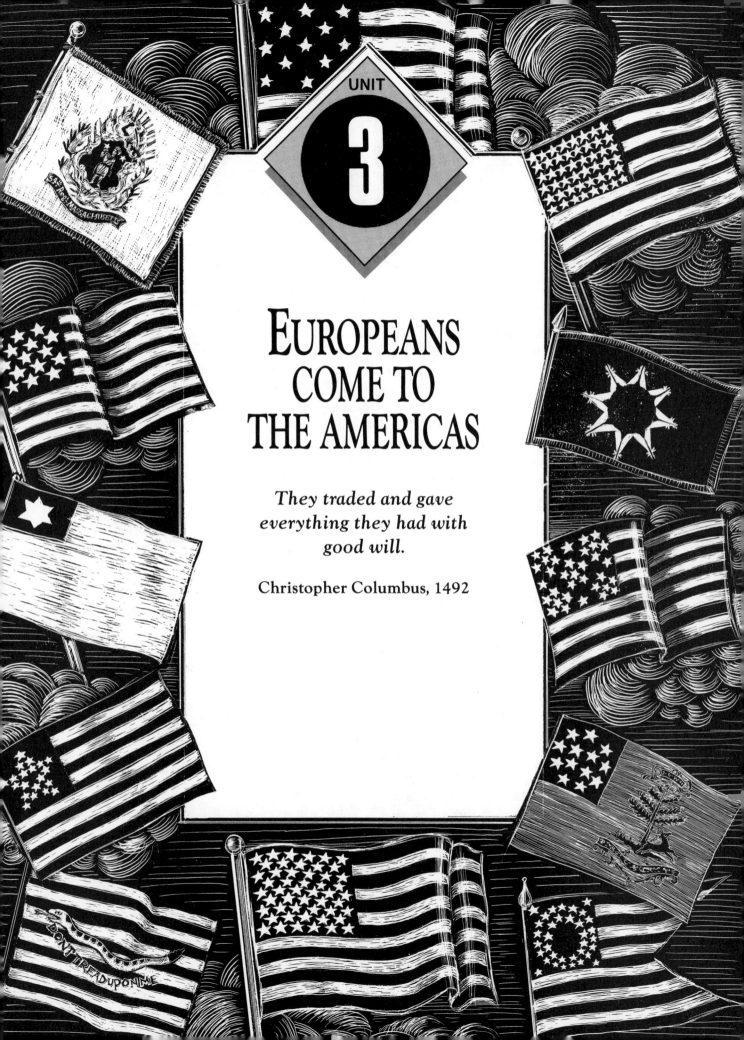

UNIT

3

EUROPEANS COME TO THE AMERICAS

They traded and gave everything they had with good will.

Christopher Columbus, 1492

Reaching the Americas

by Christopher Columbus, 1492

On August 3, 1492, Christopher Columbus (1451-1506) and his crew of 90 sailors set sail from Spain on three ships hoping to find a new route to Asia. After stopping to get supplies in the Canary Islands, the crew sailed west across the Atlantic Ocean—a voyage no European had attempted in hundreds of years. What was this historic voyage like? Fortunately, Columbus kept a journal, or diary, of his trip. In the part of his journal you are about to read, Columbus describes the long, dangerous journey and the first sight of land, a small island in the Caribbean Sea. Notice Columbus's opinion of the Arawak, the first people he meets in the Americas, and how the Arawak treat the Europeans. In what ways does Columbus consider himself a trader and explorer? In what ways does he see himself as a conqueror as well?

September 9

This day we completely lost sight of land, and many men sighed and wept for fear they would not see it again for a long time. I comforted them with great promises of lands and riches. To **sustain** their hope and **dispel** their fears of a long voyage, I decided to **reckon** fewer **leagues** than we actually made. I did this that they might not think themselves so great a distance from Spain as they really were.

For myself I will keep a **confidential** accurate reckoning.

sustain: keep up
dispel: drive away
reckon: count
leagues: units of distance

confidential: secret

September 24

I am having serious trouble with the crew. . . . All day long and all night long those who are awake and able to get together never **cease** to talk to each other [as they gather] in circles, complaining that they will never be able to return home. They have said that it is insanity and **suicidal** on their part to risk their lives following the madness of a **foreigner**. . . . I am told by a few trusted men (and these are few in number!) that if I **persist** in going onward, the best course of action will be to throw me into the sea some night.

cease: stop

suicidal: very dangerous

foreigner: Columbus is called a foreigner because he was born in Italy
persist: continue

October 10

Between day and night I made 177 miles [285 km]. I told the crew 132 miles [212 km], but they could stand it no longer. They grumbled and complained of the long voyage, and I **reproached** them for their lack of spirit, telling them that, for better or worse, they had to complete the **enterprise** on which the **Catholic Sovereigns** had sent them.

October 11

About 10 o'clock at night, while standing on the **sterncastle**, I thought I saw a light to the west. It looked like a little wax candle bobbing up and down. It had the same appearance as a light or torch belonging to fishermen or travelers who **alternately** raised and lowered it, or perhaps were going from house to house. . . .

The moon, in its third quarter, rose in the east shortly before midnight. . . . Then, at two hours after midnight, the *Pinta* fired a cannon, my **prearranged** signal for the sighting of land.

I now believe that the light I saw earlier was a sign from God and that it was truly the first positive **indication** of land. When we caught up with the *Pinta*, which was always running ahead because she was a swift sailor, I learned that the first man to sight land was Rodrigo de Triana, a seaman from Lepe.

October 12

At dawn we saw . . . people, and I went ashore in the ship's boat, **armed**. . . . I **unfurled** the royal banner and the captains brought the flags which displayed a large green cross with the letters **F** and **Y** at the left and right side of the cross. . . .

No sooner had we concluded the **formalities** of taking possession of the island than people began to come to the beach. . . . All those that I saw were young people, none of whom was over 30 years old. They are very well-built people, with handsome bodies and very fine faces. . . . Their eyes are large and very pretty. . . . These are tall people and their legs, with no exceptions, are quite straight, and none of them has a **paunch**. They are, in fact, **well proportioned**. Their hair is . . . straight, and **coarse** like horsehair. They wear it short over the eyebrows, but they have a long **hank** in the back that they never cut. Many of the natives paint their faces; others paint their whole bodies; some, only the eyes or nose. Some are painted black, some white, some red; others are of different colors.

reproached: scolded

enterprise: task
Catholic Sovereigns: Queen Isabella and King Ferdinand

sterncastle: rear part of a boat

alternately: taking turns

prearranged: set up before

indication: sign

armed: carrying weapons
unfurled: unfolded

F: for Ferdinand
Y: for Ysabella, Isabella
formalities: ceremonies

paunch: big belly
well proportioned: well built
coarse: rough
hank: coil

The people here called this island *Guanahani* in their language, and their speech is very **fluent**, although I do not understand any of it. They are friendly and **well-dispositioned** people who **bear no arms** except for small spears, and they have no iron. I showed one my sword, and through **ignorance** he grabbed it by the blade and cut himself. Their spears are made of wood, to which they attach a fish tooth at one end, or some other sharp thing. . . .

fluent: smooth and rapid

well-dispositioned: easygoing

bear no arms: carry no weapons

ignorance: not knowing

They traded and gave everything they had with good will, but it seems to me that they have very little and are poor in everything. . . .

This afternoon the people . . . came swimming to our ships and in boats made from one log. They brought us parrots, balls of cotton thread, spears, and many other things. . . . For these items we **swapped** them little glass beads and **hawks' bells**. . . .

swapped: traded

hawks' bells: small bells that attach to the leg of a hawk

They ought to make good and skilled servants, for they repeat very quickly whatever we say to them. . . . I will take six of them to Your Highnesses when I depart. . . .

October 13

After sunrise people . . . again began to come to our ships in boats **fashioned** in one piece from the trunks of trees. These boats are wonderfully made . . . and every bit as fine as those I have seen in **Guinea**. They come in all sizes. Some can carry 40 or 50 men; some are so small that only one man rides in it. . . .

fashioned: built

Guinea: region of western Africa

I have been very **attentive** and have tried very hard to find out if there is any gold here.

attentive: alert

Columbus left the Caribbean on January 15, 1493, with six Arawak prisoners and arrived in Spain in March. News of his voyage spread quickly through Europe and changed the world forever. Columbus's journey had joined two "worlds"—the continents of North and South America and the continents of Europe, Asia, and Africa—that had been separated for thousands of years. European explorers, conquerors, and treasure hunters soon began streaming across the Atlantic Ocean in search of gold and other riches. Columbus returned to the Americas three more times. On his later voyages he enslaved thousands of Native Americans and forced them to dig for gold. The harsh treatment and diseases brought by European explorers soon caused the death of all the Arawak. To learn about the Europeans' hunger for gold, read the next document on pages 19-20.

Source: Robert H. Fuson, translator, *The Log of Christopher Columbus*. Camden, ME: International Marine Publishing Company, 1987.

THE CONQUISTADORS SEARCH FOR GOLD

by an Aztec Eyewitness, 1550s

In the early 1500s Spanish conquerors, known as conquistadors, explored both North and South America. One of these conquistadors was 34-year-old Hernando Cortés. Like Christopher Columbus, whose journal you read on pages 16-18, Cortés hoped to find gold and other riches. In 1519 Cortés and about 500 Spanish soldiers marched through present-day Mexico and conquered one of the largest empires in the world— the Aztec empire. In the 1550s an historian interviewed an Aztec eyewitness who had seen the Spanish conquest. This witness described how Cortés and his men acted when they seized the fabulous treasures of the empire's capital city, Tenochtitlán. As you read this account, notice what the eyewitness sometimes compares the conquistadors to. Why do you suppose the eyewitness chose to make such comparisons?

When the Spaniards were **installed** in the palace, they asked **Motecuhzoma** about the city's resources and **reserves** and about the warriors' **ensigns** and shields. They questioned him closely and then demanded gold.

Motecuhzoma guided them to it. They surrounded him and crowded close with their weapons. He walked in the center, while they formed a circle around him.

When they arrived at the treasure house . . . the riches of gold and feathers were brought out to them: ornaments made of **quetzal** feathers, richly worked shields, disks of gold, the necklaces of the **idols**, . . . gold **greaves** and bracelets and crowns. . . .

The Spaniards burst into smiles; [and] their eyes shone with pleasure; they were delighted by them. They picked up the gold and fingered it like monkeys; they seemed to be **transported** by joy, as if their hearts were **illumined** and made new.

The truth is that they longed and **lusted for** gold. Their bodies swelled with greed, and their hunger was **ravenous**; they hungered like pigs for that gold. They snatched at the golden ensigns, waved them from side to side and examined every inch of them. . . .

The Spaniards immediately stripped the feathers from the gold shields and ensigns. They gathered all the gold into a great mound and set fire to everything else, regardless of its value. Then they

installed: settled

Motecuhzoma
(mô tä kwä sõ' mä): Aztec emperor, also called Moctezuma and Montezuma

reserves: valuables

ensigns: flags

quetzal: a kind of bird

idols: statues of gods
greaves: leg armor

transported: carried away
illumined: lit up
lusted for: wanted strongly
ravenous: intense

melted down the gold into **ingots**. As for the precious green stones, they took only the best of them. . . .

ingots: bars

Next they went to Motecuhzoma's storehouse . . . where his personal treasures were kept. The Spaniards grinned like little beasts and patted each other with delight.

When they entered the hall of treasures, it was as if they had arrived in **Paradise**. They searched everywhere and **coveted** everything; they were slaves to their own greed. All of Motecuhzoma's possessions were brought out: fine bracelets, necklaces with large stones, ankle rings with little gold bells, the royal crowns and all the royal **finery**—everything that belonged to the king and was reserved to him only. They seized these treasures as if they were their own, as if this **plunder** were merely a stroke of good luck. And when they had taken all the gold, they heaped up everything else in the middle of the **patio**.

Paradise: heaven
coveted: wanted

finery: jewels and fancy clothing

plunder: fortune

patio: courtyard

By 1570, 50 years after the Spanish conquest, over 1 million Aztecs had been killed by foreign diseases, warfare, and the effects of forced labor. By this time Cortés and other Spaniards had carried much of the Aztecs' gold back to Europe.

Source: Miguel Leon-Portilla, ed., *The Broken Spears: The Aztec Account of the Conquest of Mexico.* Boston: Beacon Press, 1962.

A European Describes an Indian Religion

by Paul Le Jeune, 1634

In the early 1600s Christian missionaries began coming to the colony of New France. Father Paul Le Jeune (lə zhən, 1591-1664), a Catholic priest, arrived in Quebec in 1632 with the goal of converting the Huron. Like most Europeans of that time, Le Jeune felt he was superior to Native Americans, and he used hate-filled words such as "savages" to describe them. As you read this excerpt of a report Le Jeune wrote in 1634, note how he failed to understand or respect the Huron's religion. What examples of unfairness and lack of knowledge about Indian culture can you find? When you are done, compare Le Jeune's account with Tatanga Mani's description of an Indian religion on page 22.

Their Religion, or rather their **superstition**, includes prayer; but O, my God, what prayers they make! In the morning, when the little children come out from their Cabins, they shout, *Cacouakhi, Pakhais Amiscouakhi, Pakhais Mousouakhi, Pakhais,* "Come, Porcupines; come, Beavers; come, Elk"; and this is all of their prayers.

superstition: false belief

When the Savages sneeze, and sometimes even at other times, during the Winter, they cry out in a loud voice, *Etouctaian miraouinam an Mirouscamikhi,* "I shall be very glad to see the Spring."

At other times, I have heard them pray for the Spring, or for rescue from evils and other similar things; and they express all these things in the form of desires, crying out as loudly as they can, "I would be very glad if this day would continue, if the wind would change," and so forth. I could not say to whom these wishes are addressed, for they themselves do not know, at least those whom I have asked have not been able to **enlighten** me. . . .

enlighten: instruct

These are some of their superstitions. How much dust there is in their eyes, and how much trouble there will be to remove it that they may see the beautiful light of truth!

After 17 years, Le Jeune returned to France without ever truly understanding Huron beliefs. Most Europeans who arrived after him also looked down on Native Americans and made fun of their different religions. This unfairness and lack of knowledge about Indian cultures remained the attitude of many white settlers for years to come—and had tragic results. These white settlers, feeling they were superior, often found nothing wrong with killing Native Americans or taking their lands or trying to change their ways of life. For a description of an Indian group's religious beliefs by a Native American, read the document on the next page.

Source: Adapted from Reuben Gold Thwaites, ed., *The Jesuit Relations and Allied Documents: Travels and Explorations of the Jesuit Missionaries in New France, 1610–1791,* Vol. VI. Cleveland: The Burrows Brothers Company, 1897.

An Indian Describes an Indian Religion

by Tatanga Mani, 1969

Long after Father Paul Le Jeune left Quebec in 1649, many people in North America continued to call Native Americans "savages" and to say their beliefs were "superstitions." In the 1960s a Native American leader responded to these harsh and unfair views. Tatanga Mani (1871-1967), also known as Chief Walking Buffalo, was the leader of the Stoney Indians of western Canada. A biography of Tatanga Mani written in 1969 included many passages from interviews he had given. As you read the Stoney chief's words in the excerpt from this biography, think back to Father Le Jeune's description of Indian religious beliefs on page 21. How do Tatanga Mani's words bring a whole new meaning to the Huron prayers that Father Le Jeune did not understand?

We [Indians] were on pretty good terms with the Great Spirit, creator and ruler of all. You whites assumed we were savages. You didn't understand our prayers. You didn't try to understand. When we sang our praises to the sun or moon or wind, you said we were worshiping idols. Without understanding, you condemned us as lost souls just because our form of worship was different from yours.

We saw the Great Spirit's work in almost everything: sun, moon, trees, wind, and mountains. Sometimes we approached him through these things. Was that so bad? I think we have a true belief in the supreme being, a stronger faith than that of most whites who have called us **pagans**. . . .

pagans: people without religious beliefs

Oh yes, I went to the white man's schools. I learned to read from school books, newspapers, and the Bible. But in time I found that these were not enough. Civilized people depend too much on man-made printed pages. I turn to the Great Spirit's book which is the whole of his creation. . . . You know, if you take all your books, lay them out under the sun, and let the snow and rain and insects work on them for a while, there will be nothing left. But the Great Spirit has provided you and me with an opportunity for study in nature's university, the forests, the rivers, the mountains, and the animals, which include us. . . .

Do you know that trees talk? Well, they do. They talk to each other, and they'll talk to you if you listen. Trouble is, white people don't listen. They never listened to the Indians, and so I don't suppose they'll listen to other voices in nature.

For hundreds of years many people in the United States and Canada did not understand or respect the religious beliefs of Native Americans, and they tried to convert them to Christianity. Indians resisted these changes and fought to preserve their ways of life.

Source: Grant MacEwan, *Tatanga Mani, Walking Buffalo of the Stonies.* Edmonton: M.G. Hurtig Ltd., 1969.

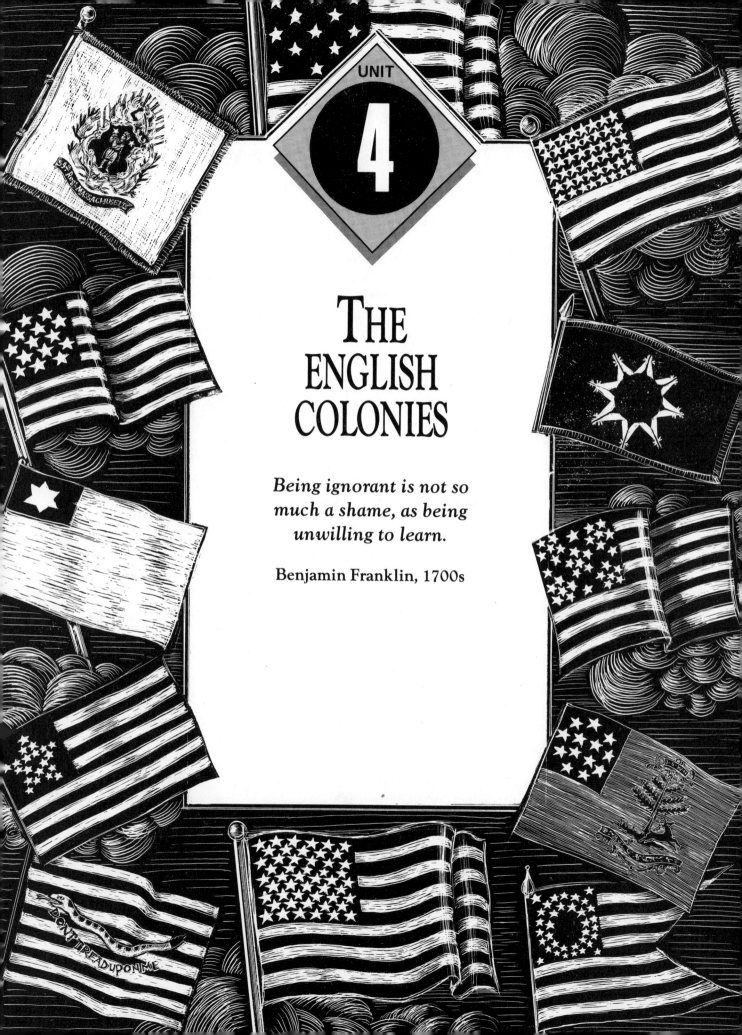

UNIT

4

THE ENGLISH COLONIES

Being ignorant is not so much a shame, as being unwilling to learn.

Benjamin Franklin, 1700s

AN INDENTURED SERVANT IN VIRGINIA

by Richard Frethorne, 1623

In the early 1600s many poor people in England longed to go to Virginia but could not afford the voyage. They solved this problem by coming as indentured servants. Under this arrangement, the person agreed to work without pay for several years for a colonist who paid for his or her trip. One of these early indentured servants was a young Englishman named Richard Frethorne. The following excerpt is from a letter he wrote home to his parents in England in 1623. How does this letter show that life in Virginia was far different from what he had expected? Why do you think that Frethorne wrote this letter?

[March 20, 1623]

Loving and kind father and mother:

This is to let you understand that I your child am in a most **heavy case** by reason of the nature of the country, [which] is such that it causeth much sickness . . . and . . . diseases, which maketh the body very poor and weak. And when we are sick there is nothing to comfort us; for since I came out of the ship, I never ate anything but peas and loblollie (that is, water **gruel**). As for deer or **venison** I never saw any since I came into this land. There is indeed some **fowl**, but we are not allowed to go and get it, but must work hard both early and late for a mess of water gruel and a mouthful of bread and beef. A mouthful of bread for a penny loaf must serve for 4 men which is most pitiful. [You would be sad] if you did know as much as I [do], when people cry out day and night—Oh, that they were in England without their **limbs**! And [they] would not **care to lose** any limb to be in England again [even if] they [had to] beg from door to door. . . .

I have nothing to comfort me, nor is there nothing to be gotten here but sickness and death. . . . I have nothing at all; no, not a shirt to my back, but two rags nor no clothes, but one poor suit, nor but one pair of shoes, but one pair of stockings, but one cap, [and] but two **bands**. My cloak is stolen by one of my own **fellows**, and to his dying hour [he] would not tell me what he did with it. But some of my fellows saw him have butter and beef out of a ship, which my cloak, I doubt [not] paid for, so that I have not a penny, nor a penny

heavy case: sad condition

gruel: thin porridge
venison: deer meat
fowl: birds

limbs: arms or legs
care to lose: mind losing

bands: belts
fellows: friends

worth to help me. . . . I am not half [of] a quarter so strong as I was in England, and all is for want of **victuals**, for I do protest unto you that I have eaten more in [one] day at home than I have . . . here for a week. . . .

    I find [myself in] . . . great grief and misery, and [I] saith, that if you love me you will **redeem me** suddenly, for which I do **entreat** and beg. And if you cannot get the merchants to redeem me for some little money, then for God's sake . . . entreat some good folks to lay out some little sum of money, in **meal** and cheese and butter and beef. Any eating meat will yield great profit. . . . Good father, do not forget me, but have mercy and pity my miserable case. I know if you did but see me you would weep to see me, for I have but one suit. . . . For God's sake, pity me. I pray you to remember my love . . . to all my friends and **kindred**. I hope all my brothers and sisters are in good health, and as for my part I have set down my **resolution** that . . . the answer of this letter will be life or death to me. Therefore, good father, send as soon as you can. . . .

Richard Frethorne

victuals: food

redeem me: buy back my period of service
entreat: plead

meal: grains

kindred: family

resolution: belief

What became of Richard Frethorne remains a mystery. Whether he returned to England, stayed in Virginia, or died young is unknown. Life in Virginia remained full of hunger, hardships, and disease throughout the 1600s. Still, indentured servants continued to pour into the colony in hopes of a better life. Many completed the long period of service and gained their freedom. Not only whites were indentured servants. Most of the first Africans in Virginia—although brought by force to America—were treated like indentured servants in the early and middle 1600s. Many of these Africans also gained their freedom. Altogether, more than half of the people who came to Virginia between 1607 and 1776 came, like Richard Frethorne, as indentured servants.

Source: Adapted from Susan Myra Kingsbury, ed., *The Records of the Virginia Company of London*, Vol. IV. Washington, D.C.: Government Printing Office, 1935.

The Mayflower Compact

Pilgrim Agreement, 1620

When the passengers aboard the Mayflower saw that they had reached New England instead of Virginia in 1620, they quickly realized that their new home was not subject to any European laws. How would this new colony govern itself? To answer this question, Pilgrim leaders drew up a compact, or agreement, and 41 of the ship's 101 passengers signed it before they went ashore. As you read the Mayflower Compact below and the rewritten modern version on the next page, think about what the signers are agreeing to do. Why do they believe it is important to set up a government? Note the names of the people who signed the compact. Why do you think there are no women's names?

In the Name of God, Amen. We, whose names are underwritten, the Loyal Subjects of our dread Sovereign Lord King *James*, by the Grace of God, of *Great Britain, France,* and *Ireland,* King, *Defender of the Faith,* etc. Having undertaken for the Glory of God, and Advancement of the Christian Faith, and the Honour of our King and Country, a Voyage to plant the first Colony in the northern Parts of *Virginia*; Do by these Presents, solemnly and mutually, in the Presence of God and one another, covenant and combine ourselves together into a civil Body Politick, for our better Ordering and Preservation, and Furtherance of the Ends aforesaid; And by Virtue hereof do enact, constitute, and frame, such just and equal Laws, Ordinances, Acts, Constitutions, and Officers, from time to time, as shall be thought most meet and convenient for the general Good of the Colony; unto which we promise all due Submission and Obedience. IN WITNESS whereof we have hereunto subscribed our names at *Cape-Cod* the eleventh of *November,* in the Reign of our Sovereign Lord King *James,* of *England, France,* and *Ireland,* the eighteenth, and of *Scotland,* the fifty-fourth, *Anno Domini,* 1620.

Mr. John Carver	Mr. Samuel Fuller	Edward Tilly
Mr. William Bradford	Mr. Christopher Martin	John Tilly
Mr. Edward Winslow	Mr. William Mullins	Francis Cooke
Mr. William Brewster	Mr. William White	Thomas Rogers
Isaac Allerton	Mr. Richard Warren	Thomas Tinker
Miles Standish	John Howland	John Ridgale
John Alden	Mr. Steven Hopkins	Edward Fuller
John Turner	Digery Priest	Richard Clark
Francis Eaton	Thomas Williams	Richard Gardiner
James Chilton	Gilbert Winslow	Mr. John Allerton
John Craxton	Edmund Margesson	Thomas English
John Billington	Peter Brown	Edward Doten
Joses Fletcher	Richard Bitteridge	Edward Liester
John Goodman	George Soule	

In the name of God, Amen. We, who have signed our names below, are the loyal subjects of King James of Great Britain. In honor of God, our Christian religion, our king, and our country, we took a voyage to build the first colony in northern Virginia. To keep order in this colony, we agree in this document to join together under one government. We promise to make laws and rules that are fair and will apply equally to everyone. We also promise to obey these laws and rules. We hope that the laws, rules, and leaders we choose will both improve and help preserve the colony.

Having read and agreed to this compact, we have signed our names at Cape Cod on November 11, 1620.

In addition to helping Plymouth colony grow, the Mayflower Compact helped to establish the idea of self-government among European settlers in North America. Over 150 years later, this idea would be clearly expressed in another important document— the Declaration of Independence. You can read this document on pages 40-44.

Source: Ben. Perley Poore, *The Federal and State Constitutions*, Part 1. New York: Burt Franklin, 1924.

27

Life on a New England Farm

by Ruth Belknap, 1782

What was life like on a farm in colonial New England? For most people it meant hard work, especially for women. The following poem, written in 1782, gives an idea of some of the many chores performed by farm women. The poet, Ruth Belknap, was the wife of a minister and lived in Dover, New Hampshire. Why do you think she titled her poem "The Pleasures of a Country Life"?

The Pleasures of a Country Life

Up in the morning I must rise

Before I've time to rub my eyes.

With half-**pin'd** gown, unbuckled shoe,   **pin'd:** pinned

I haste to milk my **lowing** cow.   **lowing:** mooing

But, Oh! it makes my heart to ache,

I have no bread till I can bake,

And then, alas! it makes me sputter,

For I must **churn** or have no butter.   **churn:** stir milk into butter

The hogs with **swill** too I must serve;   **swill:** garbage fed to pigs

For hogs must eat or men will starve.

Besides, my **spouse** can get no clothes   **spouse:** mate; husband or wife

Unless I much offend my nose.

28

For all that try it know it's true

There is no smell like **coloring blue.**

coloring blue: bleach

Then round the **parish** I must ride

And **make enquiry** far and wide

To find some girl that is a **spinner,**

Then hurry home to get my dinner. . . .

parish: area served by a minister

make enquiry: ask questions

spinner: person who makes yarn on a spinning wheel

All summer long I toil & sweat,

Blister my hands, and scold & **fret.**

And when the summer's work is **o'er,**

New **toils** arise from Autumn's store.

Corn must be **husk'd,** and pork be kill'd,

The house with all confusion fill'd.

O could you see the grand display

Upon our annual butchering day. . . .

fret: worry

o'er: over

toils: jobs

husk'd: stripped of its outer covering

parson: minister

Ye starch'd up folks that live in town,

That lounge upon your beds till noon,

That never tire yourselves with work,

Unless with handling knife & fork,

Come, see the sweets of country life,

Display'd in **Parson** B[elknap's] wife.

Although most women, like Ruth Belknap, worked on farms in colonial New England, many held other jobs as well. Some colonial women worked as printers, doctors, and merchants. Others ran inns, restaurants, and owned their own businesses. For both women and men, there was never a lack of work in colonial New England.

Source: Laurel Thatcher Ulrich, *Good Wives: Image and Reality in the Lives of Women in Northern New England, 1650–1750.* New York: Oxford University Press, 1982.

Poor Richard's Almanac

by Benjamin Franklin, 1732–1757

In colonial America there were no television or radio news shows to tell people what the weather would be like each day, or when community events such as fairs would take place. Instead, people depended on little booklets called almanacs for such information. Because almanacs were so popular among the colonists, many printers wrote their own versions and competed with one another for buyers. When Benjamin Franklin (1706-1790) first printed his Poor Richard's Almanac *in 1732, there were at least six other almanacs on sale in Philadelphia alone. Yet Franklin's almanac quickly became the most popular in the English colonies because he included many clever and funny sayings. How do the sayings below help us to understand some of the ideas and values that colonists considered important?*

When the well's dry, we know the worth of water.

Keep conscience clear, Then never fear.

Three may keep a secret, if two of them are dead.

He that is of opinion money will do every thing may
well be suspected of doing every thing for money.

Wish not so much to live long,
as to live well.

If your head is wax, don't walk
in the sun.

Plough deep while sluggards sleep; and
you shall have corn to sell and to keep.

30

Genius without education
 is like silver in the mine.

Well done, is twice done.

The family of fools is ancient.

Men and melons are hard to know.

Lost time is never found again.

An empty bag cannot stand upright.

Glass, china, and reputation, are easily
 crack'd, and never well mended.

Dost thou love life? Then do not squander
 time; for that's the stuff life is made of.

There are three things extremely hard, steel,
 a diamond and to know one's self.

Being ignorant is not so much a shame,
 as being unwilling to learn.

Don't throw stones at your neighbors', if
 your own windows are glass.

The honey is sweet, but the bee has a sting.

Where there is hunger, law is not regarded; and where
 law is not regarded, there will be hunger.

A slip of the foot you may soon recover, but a slip
 of the tongue you may never get over.

Little strokes, Fell great oaks.

Paintings and fightings are best seen at a distance.

Ben Franklin continued to publish **Poor Richard's Almanac** *until 1757. From then until he died in 1790, Franklin was an important leader in the colonies and in the struggle for American independence.*

Source: Benjamin Franklin, *Poor Richard's Almanack*. Mount Vernon, NY: The Peter Pauper Press, n.d.

31

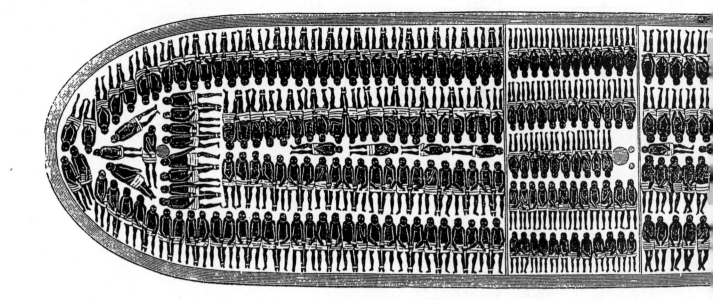

SHIP OF HORRORS

by Olaudah Equiano, 1789

By the late 1600s, slavery existed throughout the English colonies. For the slave traders, buying and selling human beings was a money-making business. But for the Africans kidnapped from their homeland, the forced ocean voyage to the Americas involved some of the greatest horrors that human beings have ever endured. In the excerpt below, adapted from his autobiography written in 1789, Olaudah Equiano (1745-1797) describes some of these horrors. Olaudah was an 11-year-old boy living in West Africa in 1756 when slave traders kidnapped him in order to take him to North America. The excerpt begins just as Olaudah arrives at the coast of Africa, about to begin the overseas voyage. What are some of the reactions of Olaudah and the other prisoners to the way in which they are treated? What are some of the things Olaudah wishes for?

The first thing I saw when I arrived at the coast was the sea and a slave ship waiting to pick up its cargo. The sight of the slave ship amazed me. This amazement turned into terror when I was carried on board. The crew immediately grabbed me and tossed me in the air to see if I was healthy. I was now convinced that I had gotten into a world of bad spirits and that they were going to kill me. The fact that their skin color differed so much from ours, that their hair was so long, and that the language they spoke was unlike any I had ever heard, strengthened my belief that they planned to kill me. I was so filled with horror and fear at that moment that if I had possessed 10,000 worlds, I would have given them all away to trade places with the poorest slave in my own country.

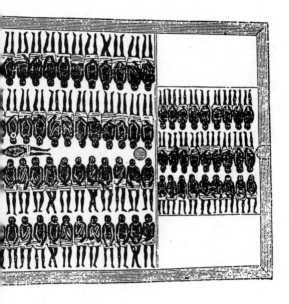

THE
INTERESTING NARRATIVE
OF
THE LIFE
OF
OLAUDAH EQUIANO,
OR
GUSTAVUS VASSA,
THE AFRICAN.
WRITTEN BY HIMSELF.

VOL. I.

Behold, God is my salvation · I will trust and not
be afraid, for the Lord Jehovah is my strength
and my song : he also is become my salvation.
And in that day shall ye say, Praise the Lord, call
upon his name, declare his doings among the people.
Isaiah xii. 2, 4.

FIRST AMERICAN EDITION.

NEW-YORK:
Printed and Sold by W. DURELL, at his
Book-Store and Printing-Office, No. 19, Q. Street.
M,DCC,XCI.

When I looked around the ship and saw large numbers of black people chained together—every one of them looking sad and unhappy—I no longer doubted my fate. Overpowered by horror and fright, I fell on the deck and fainted. When I woke up I was surrounded by black people. I asked them if these white men with their long hair and horrible looks were going to eat us up. They told me no. They tried to cheer me up, but I still felt miserable.

I now realized I would never again return to my native country. Never again would I see the shores of Africa. As I was realizing all of this, the crew sent me to the lower decks of the ship. Everybody down there was crying and the smell was worse than anything I had ever smelled in my life. It was so bad I became sick and could not eat. I did not feel like tasting a thing. I now wished only for death. At that moment two white men offered me food. When I refused they grabbed my hands, stretched me across a barrel, tied my feet, and whipped me.

Never in my life had I been treated in this way. As much as I feared drowning, I thought of jumping overboard. But the ship had nets all around it to prevent people from jumping into the ocean. Also, those prisoners who were not chained down were watched very closely by the crew to keep them from jumping overboard. Some prisoners who tried were beaten, and those who refused to eat were whipped every hour. This was often the case with myself.

A little later I came across some people from my own nation. Although we were all in chains, seeing them made me feel better. I asked them what was going to happen to us. They told me we were being carried to the white people's country to work for them. This cheered me up a little. After all, if all I had to do was work then things could not be so bad. But I still feared I would be put to death. The white people, I thought, looked and acted like savages. I had never seen such brutal cruelty in my life. They acted this way not only toward us blacks but toward each other. I saw them whip one white man so cruelly with a large rope that he died as a result. Then they tossed him over the side of the boat like an animal. This made me fear these people all the more, for I expected to be treated in the same manner.

After all the cargo was loaded, the smell in the lower decks became even worse. Everybody dripped with sweat and the air became unfit for breathing. We were packed together in chains so tightly we could hardly move or turn over. The cramped surroundings and the deadly heat almost suffocated us. Many slaves fell sick and died—a result of being packed so closely. The only reason they were packed so closely was to increase the profits of the slave dealers. This wretched situation was made even worse by the scraping of the chains. Children often fell into the tubs used for bathrooms and almost choked to death. The shrieks of the women and the groans of the dying made this scene a horror beyond belief.

One day the crew caught a large number of fish and feasted upon them. We begged and prayed for some of the fish that were left over. But to our amazement, they refused to give us any. Instead, they threw the fish overboard! Before they did this, however, some of my countrymen who were starving tried to grab some of the fish when they thought no one was looking. But they were discovered and whipped horribly.

One day, when the sea was smooth and the wind mild, two prisoners decided they would rather die than endure such a life of misery. Although they were chained together, they somehow managed to jump beyond the nets and into the sea. Immediately, another prisoner also jumped overboard. I believe many more would have done the same thing if the crew had not prevented them. The boat stopped at once to pick up the three prisioners who had jumped into the sea. The first two had drowned but they rescued the last one. They later whipped him extra cruelly for preferring death to slavery. In this manner we continued to undergo more hardships than I can now describe. These hardships were all caused by the wretched and terrible slave trade.

Olaudah Equiano was one of hundreds of thousands of Africans kidnapped and brought by force to North America at the hands of slave traders in the 1600s and 1700s. Roughly 200,000 more died on the ocean voyage. Equiano survived the voyage and worked as a slave in both Barbados, an island in the Caribbean, and the colony of Virginia. A British sea captain soon bought him and made him a sailor. Although enslaved, Equiano managed to earn money and bought his freedom in 1766. As a free man, he traveled the world and explored the northern Arctic. Years later he settled in England and wrote his autobiography. The book was widely read in the 1790s and contributed to the growth of the anti-slavery movement.

Source: Adapted from Olaudah Equiano, *The Interesting Narrative of the Life of Olaudah Equiano, or Gustavus Vassa, the African. Written by Himself.* New York: W. Durell, 1791.

SLAVE SALES

Advertisements, 1700s

During the 1700s European and American merchants forcibly transported more Africans to American shores than in any other century. Once these Africans arrived they were sold as slaves—and they could be resold at any time. As a result, slave sales were common events in the New England, Middle, and Southern colonies. Below is a selection of advertisements from newspapers and posters that appeared in colonial America. (Note that the letter s sometimes appeared as ſ.) How do these advertisements attempt to deprive Africans and African Americans of their humanity? How did one of these African Americans try to escape slavery?

TO BE SOLD on board the Ship *Bance-Yland*, on tuesday the 6th of *May* next, at *Aſhley-Ferry* ; a choice cargo of about 250 fine healthy

NEGROES,

juſt arrived from the Windward & Rice Coaſt. —The utmoſt care has already been taken, and ſhall be continued, to keep them free from the leaſt danger of being infected with the SMALL-POX, no boat having been on board, and all other communication with people from *Charles-Town* prevented.

Auſtin, Laurens, & Appleby.

N. B. Full one Half of the above Negroes have had the SMALL-POX in their own Country.

RUN away, on the 3d Day of *May* laſt, a young Negro Boy, named *Joe*, this Country born, formerly be longed to Capt. *Hugh Heſt*. Whoever brings the ſaid Boy the Subſcriber at *Ediſto*, or to the Work Houſe in *Charles Town*, ſhall have 3 l. reward. On the contrary who-ever harbours the ſaid Boy, may depend upon being ſeverely proſecuted, by

Thomas Chiſbam.

TO BE SOLD *by* William Yeomans, (in *Charles Town Merchant*,) a parcel of good Plantation Slaves. Encouragement will be given by taking Rice in Payment, or any Time Credit, Security to be given if required There's likewiſe to be ſold, very good Troop-leg ſaddles and Furniture, choice Barbados and Boſton *Rum*, alſo Cordial Waters and Limejuice, as well as a parcel of extraordinary Indian trading Goods, and many of other ſorts ſuitable for the Seaſon.

TO BE SOLD,

A Likely negro Man, his Wife and Child ; the negro Man capable of doing all ſorts of Plantation Work, and a good Miller : The Woman exceeding fit for a Farmer, being capable of doing any Work, belonging to a Houſe in the Country, at reaſonable Rates, inquire of the Printer hereof.

In the late 1700s slavery slowly began to die out in the North. Sales of enslaved people, however, continued to be daily events in the South until after the Civil War.

35

LIFE UNDER SLAVERY

by Martha Showvely, 1937

During the 1700s and 1800s about one out of three people living in the South were enslaved African Americans. These slaves had no rights. They could be sold at any time—away from their parents and away from their families. In 1846, nine-year-old Martha Showvely was separated from her family in Powhatan County, Virginia. In 1937, when she was a very old woman, she told an interviewer about this separation. What do you think Martha Showvely felt was the most unjust part of slavery?

When I was nine years old, they took me from my mother and sold me and two of my cousins to a slave trader. The slave trader was **carrying** us to Richmond to sell us [farther] down South. When we got to Richmond, we went in a store. Some men were in there and they asked the trader if those Negroes were for sale. He told them yes. One of the men looked at me and said to Ben Tinsley, "Here is a nice little Negro girl for you to take home and wait on you around the house." After they talked a long time, he said he wanted me. I thought when they were talking that he was going to take all of us. When he bought me and started to take me off, I asked him if he was going to take all of us. He said no. The trader said he was going to carry them down to Georgia. I started crying. Master Tinsley asked what I was crying for. I said I didn't want to leave my cousins. He said he didn't want them and then he carried me on off. I never did see my cousins anymore. . . .

carrying: taking

Master Tinsley made me the house girl. I had to make the beds, clean the house and other things. After I finished my regular work, I would go to the mistress's room, bow to her, and stand there until she noticed me. Then she would say, "Martha, are you through with your work?" I would say, "Yes ma'am." She would say, "No you aren't; you haven't lowered the shades." I would then lower the shades, fill the water pitcher, arrange the towels on the washstand and anything else mistress wanted me to do. . . . We had to be doing something all day. Whenever we were in the presence of any of the white folks, we had to stand up.

When slavery finally ended in 1865, Martha Showvely was an adult. She and her husband and children moved away from the Tinsley house and set up their own home. She tried to find her other family members, but she never saw any of them again.

Source: Adapted from Charles L. Perdue, Jr., Thomas Barden, and Robert K. Phillips, eds., *Weevils in the Wheat: Interviews with Virginia Ex-Slaves*. Charlottesville, VA: University Press of Virginia, 1976.

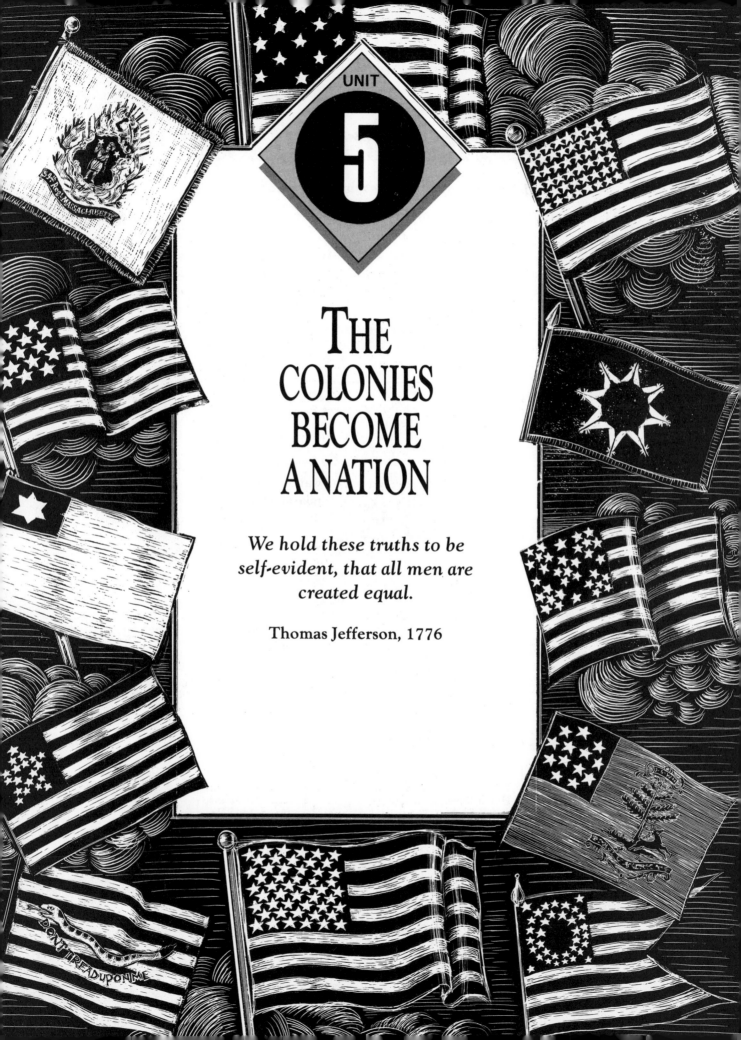

UNIT

5

THE
COLONIES
BECOME
A NATION

We hold these truths to be
self-evident, that all men are
created equal.

Thomas Jefferson, 1776

The Boston Massacre

from the Boston *Gazette and Country Journal*, 1770

On March 5, 1770, a crowd of colonists gathered in Boston and began hurling rocks at a group of British soldiers. Angered, the soldiers fired into the crowd—instantly killing four people. Outraged colonists called this a massacre, and three days later thousands turned out for the funeral. The following newspaper article appeared in the Boston Gazette and Country Journal. Look at the original version below and then read the modern translation on the next page. (Notice that in the original article, the letter ſ is often used in place of an s.) In what ways does the newspaper article try to shape the reader's opinions?

Laſt Thurſday, agreeable to a general Requeſt of the Inhabitants, and by the Conſent of Parents and Friends, were carried to their *Grave* in Succeſſion, the Bodies of *Samuel Gray, Samuel Maverick, James Caldwell,* and *Criſpus Attucks*, the unhappy Victims who fell in the bloody Maſſacre of theMonday Evening preceeding !

On this Occaſion moſt of the Shops in Town were ſhut, all the Bells were ordered to toll a ſolemn Peal, as were alſo thoſe in the neighboring Towns of Charleſtown Roxbury, &c. The Proceſſion began to move between the Hours of 4 and 5 in the Afternoon ; two of the unfortunate Sufferers, viz. Meſſ. *JamesCaldwell* and *Criſpus Attucks*, who were Strangers, borne from Faneuil-Hall, attended by a numerous Train of Perſons of all Ranks ; and the other two, viz. Mr. *Samuel Gray*, from the Houſe of Mr. Benjamin Gray, (his Brother) on the North-ſide the Exchange, and Mr. *Maverick*, from the Houſe of his diſtreſſed Mother Mrs. *Mary Maverick*, in Union-Street, each followed by their reſpective Relations and Friends : The ſeveral Hearſes forming a Junction in King-Street, the Theatre of that inhuman Tragedy ! proceeded from thence thro' the Main-Street, lengthened by an immenſe Concourſe of People, ſo numerous as to be obliged to follow in Ranks of ſix, and brought up by a long Train of Carriages belonging to the principal Gentry of theTown. The Bodies were depoſited in one Vault in the middle Burying-ground : The aggravated Circumſtances of their Death, the Diſtreſs and Sorrow viſible in every Countenance, together with the peculiar Solemnity with which the whole Funeral was conducted, ſurpaſs Deſcription.

Last Thursday, the bodies of Samuel Gray, Samuel Maverick, James Caldwell, and Crispus Attucks were carried to their graves. All four had died the unhappy victims of the bloody massacre three days earlier! Local citizens had requested a public funeral, and the victims' parents and friends agreed to it.

The funeral procession began between 4:00 and 5:00 in the afternoon. Most of the stores in town were closed, and all the bells in Boston, Charlestown, Roxbury, and elsewhere rang solemnly in honor of the dead. Two of the unfortunate sufferers, James Caldwell and Crispus Attucks, were both unknown in Boston. Beginning at Faneuil (fan′ yəl) Hall, a group made up of all kinds of people marched behind their coffins. A second group of people marched from the house of Samuel Gray's brother, and a third from the house of Samuel Maverick's very sad mother. The three groups came together at King Street, where the terrible tragedy had taken place! The procession then continued down Main Street. Huge crowds of people joined the march—so many, in fact, that they had to walk in rows of six people across. The procession was completed by a long train of carriages owned by the town's wealthier people. The bodies were at last buried in the ground. The alarming way in which the victims died, the sadness visible on everyone's faces, and the seriousness of the entire funeral are beyond description.

About 10,000 of Boston's 16,000 people turned out for the funeral. This heavy turnout was very surprising because two of those killed—a pair of sailors named James Caldwell and Crispus Attucks, a former slave—knew very few people in Boston. Newspapers all over the colonies reported the funeral, and the event that became known as the Boston Massacre increased colonists' anger against the British. As tensions between Britain and the American colonies grew during the next few years, many newspapers printed articles in favor of independence.

Source: Boston *Gazette and Country Journal*, March 12, 1770.

Declaration of Independence

by Thomas Jefferson, 1776

By the summer of 1776, American colonists had been at war with Britain for 14 months. During that time colonists debated whether they were fighting for more rights from Britain or for total independence. As the fighting went on, more and more colonists argued that peace with Britain was no longer possible. In June 1776 members of the Second Continental Congress asked 33-year-old Thomas Jefferson (1743-1826) of Virginia to write a statement explaining why the colonies ought to be independent. Read the Declaration of Independence that Jefferson wrote and the notes of explanation beside it. Notice Jefferson's ideas about government, rebellion, and people's rights. Notice also what injustices he accuses King George III of Great Britain of having committed against the colonists. How do King George's actions take away the rights that Jefferson believes people and governments should have?

When in the Course of human events,

it becomes necessary for one people to dissolve the political bands which have connected them with another, and to assume, among the Powers of the earth, the separate and equal station to which the Laws of Nature and of Nature's God entitle them, a decent respect to the opinions of mankind requires that they should declare the causes which impel them to the separation.

At certain times in history, it is necessary for a group of people to break away from the government that has ruled them and to form a new, independent nation. At such a time, their reasons for separation and independence should be clearly stated.

We hold these truths to be self-evident, that all men are created equal, that they are endowed by their Creator with certain unalienable Rights, that among these are Life, Liberty, and the pursuit of Happiness.

We believe that everyone agrees on certain basic ideas: All people are created equal and they have basic rights that can never be taken away. People have the right to live, the right to be free, and the right to seek happiness.

40

That, to secure these rights, Governments are instituted among Men, deriving their just Powers from the consent of the governed.

That, whenever any Form of Government becomes destructive of these ends, it is the Right of the People to alter or to abolish it, and to institute new Government, laying its foundation on such Principles, and organizing its powers in such form, as to them shall seem most likely to effect their Safety and Happiness.

Prudence, indeed, will dictate that Governments long established should not be changed for light and transient causes; and, accordingly all experience hath shown, that mankind are more disposed to suffer, while evils are sufferable, than to right themselves by abolishing the forms to which they are accustomed. But, when a long train of abuses and usurpations, pursuing invariably the same Object, evinces a design to reduce them under absolute Despotism, it is their right, it is their duty, to throw off such Government, and to provide new Guards for their future security.

Such has been the patient sufferance of these Colonies; and such is now the necessity which constrains them to alter their former Systems of Government. The history of the present King of Great Britain is a history of repeated injuries and usurpations, all having in direct object the establishment of an absolute Tyranny over these States.

To prove this, let Facts be submitted to a candid world.

He has refused his Assent to Laws the most wholesome and necessary for the public good.

He has forbidden his Governors to pass Laws of immediate and pressing importance, unless suspended in their operation till his Assent should be obtained; and when so suspended, he has utterly neglected to attend to them.

He has refused to pass other Laws for the accommodation of large districts of People, unless those People would relinquish the right of Representation in the Legislature, a right inestimable to them and formidable to tyrants only.

He has called together legislative bodies at places unusual, uncomfortable, and distant from the depository of their Public Records, for the sole purpose of fatiguing them into compliance with his measures.

To preserve these rights, people create governments. Every government must have the support of the people it governs.

If a government loses this support or tries to take away basic freedoms, people have the right to change their government or to get rid of it and form a new government that will protect their rights.

However, people should not change governments that have long been in power for minor or temporary problems. We have learned from history that people are usually more willing to put up with a bad government than to get rid of it. But when people see their government misusing its power and mistreating its people time after time, it is the right and duty of the people to get rid of their government and to form a new one.

The colonies have suffered patiently long enough, and it is now time to change our government. King George III of Great Britain has ruled badly for many years. His main goal has been to establish total control over the colonies.

These statements are proven by the following facts:

King George III has rejected much-needed laws passed by the colonists.

He has not permitted important laws to be passed by his governors in America.

He has refused to redraw the borders of large voting districts unless the people living there agreed to give up their right to be represented in the legislature.

He has ordered lawmakers in the colonies to meet far from their homes and offices in places that are unusual and difficult to get to. His only reason for doing this has been to tire out the lawmakers so that they will accept his rule.

41

He has dissolved Representative Houses repeatedly, for opposing, with manly firmness, his invasions on the rights of the people.	When lawmakers have criticized the king for attacking their rights, he has broken up the legislature's meetings.
He has refused for a long time, after such dissolutions, to cause others to be elected; whereby the Legislative Powers, incapable of Annihilation, have returned to the People at large for their exercise; the State remaining in the mean time exposed to all the dangers of invasion from without, and convulsions within.	After breaking up their meetings, the king has refused to allow new elections. As a result, colonists have been living in danger, unable to protect themselves or pass new laws.
He has endeavoured to prevent the Population of these States; for that purpose obstructing the Laws of Naturalization of Foreigners; refusing to pass others to encourage their migration hither, and raising the conditions of new Appropriations of Lands.	He has tried to stop colonists from moving west and settling in new lands. He has also tried to prevent people from foreign countries from settling in America by making it hard for newcomers to become citizens.
He has obstructed the Administration of Justice, by refusing his Assent to Laws for establishing Judiciary Powers.	In some places, he has not let colonists set up a system of courts.
He has made Judges dependent on his Will alone, for the tenure of their offices, and the amount and payment of their salaries.	He has forced colonial judges to obey him by deciding how long they can serve and how much they are paid.
He has erected a multitude of New Offices, and sent hither swarms of Officers to harass our People, and eat out their substance.	He has sent officials from Britain to fill new government offices in the colonies. These officials have mistreated people and demanded unfair taxes.
He has kept among us, in times of Peace, Standing Armies, without the Consent of our legislature.	In times of peace, he has kept soldiers in the colonies even though Americans did not want them.
He has affected to render the Military independent of and superior to the Civil Power.	He has tried to give soldiers power over colonial legislatures.
He has combined with others to subject us to a jurisdiction foreign to our constitution, and unacknowledged by our laws; giving his Assent to their Acts of pretended Legislation:	He and other leaders in Great Britain have passed laws for the colonies that Americans did not want. In these laws the British government has:
For quartering large bodies of armed troops among us:	forced colonists to house and feed British soldiers;
For protecting them, by a mock Trial, from Punishment for any Murders which they should commit on the Inhabitants of these States:	protected these soldiers by giving them phony trials and not punishing them for murdering colonists;
For cutting off our Trade with all parts of the world:	cut off trade between Americans and people in other parts of the world;

42

For imposing Taxes on us without our Consent:

demanded taxes that colonists never agreed to;

For depriving us, in many cases, of the benefits of Trial by Jury:

prevented colonists accused of crimes from having their trials decided fairly by a jury;

For transporting us beyond Seas to be tried for pretended offences:

brought colonists falsely accused of crimes to Great Britain to be put on trial;

For abolishing the free System of English Laws in a neighbouring Province, establishing therein an Arbitrary government, and enlarging its Boundaries, so as to render it at once an example and fit instrument for introducing the same absolute rule into these Colonies:

extended the borders of the neighboring province of Quebec to include lands stretching to the Ohio River, thus forcing colonists in this region to obey harsh French laws rather than English laws. The goal of the British government is to force all colonists to obey these harsh laws;

For taking away our Charters, abolishing our most valuable Laws, and altering fundamentally the Forms of our Governments:

taken away our charters, or documents that make governments legal, canceled important laws, and completely changed our forms of government;

For suspending our own Legislatures, and declaring themselves invested with Power to legislate for us in all cases whatsoever.

broken up our legislatures and claimed that Great Britain has the right to pass all laws for the colonies.

He has abdicated Government here, by declaring us out of his Protection and waging War against us.

King George III has ended government in the colonies by waging war against us and not protecting us.

He has plundered our seas, ravaged our Coasts, burnt our towns, and destroyed the Lives of our People.

He has robbed American ships at sea, burned down our towns, and ruined people's lives.

He is at this time transporting large Armies of foreign Mercenaries to compleat the works of death, desolation and tyranny, already begun with circumstances of Cruelty & perfidy scarcely paralleled in the most barbarous ages, and totally unworthy the Head of a civilized nation.

He is right now bringing foreign soldiers to the colonies to commit horrible and brutal deeds. These actions by the king are some of the cruelest ever committed in the history of the world.

He has constrained our fellow Citizens taken Captive on the high Seas to bear Arms against their Country, to become the executioners of their friends and Brethren, or to fall themselves by their Hands.

He has forced colonists captured at sea to join the British navy and to fight and kill Americans.

He has excited domestic insurrections amongst us, and has endeavoured to bring on the inhabitants of our frontiers, the merciless Indian Savages, whose known rule of warfare, is an undistinguished destruction of all ages, sexes and conditions.

He has urged enslaved people in the colonies to rebel, and he has tried to get Native Americans to fight against colonists.

In every stage of these Oppressions We have Petitioned for Redress in the most humble terms: Our repeated Petitions have been answered only by repeated injury. A Prince, whose character is thus marked by every act which may define a Tyrant, is unfit to be the ruler of a free People.	For years we have asked King George III to correct these probems and safeguard our rights. Unfortunately, the king has refused to listen to our complaints and he continues to treat us badly. The king is such an unfair ruler that he is not fit to rule the free people of America.
Nor have We been wanting in attention to our British brethren. We have warned them from time to time of attempts by their legislature to extend an unwarrantable jurisdiction over us. We have reminded them of the circumstances of our emigration and settlement here. We have appealed to their native justice and magnanimity, and we have conjured them by the ties of our common kindred to disavow these usurpations, which, would inevitably interrupt our connections and correspondence. They too have been deaf to the voice of justice and of consanguinity. We must, therefore, acquiesce in the necessity, which denounces our Separation, and hold them, as we hold the rest of mankind, Enemies in War, in Peace Friends.	We have also asked the British people for help. We have told them many times of our problems and pointed out the unfair laws passed by their government. We hoped they would listen to us because they believed in reason and justice. We hoped they would listen to us because we are related to each other and have much in common. But we were wrong: The British people have not listened to us at all. They have ignored our pleas for justice. We must, therefore, break away from Great Britain and become a separate nation.
We, therefore, the Representatives of the United States of America, in General Congress Assembled, appealing to the Supreme Judge of the world for the rectitude of our intentions, do, in the Name, and by Authority of the good People of these Colonies, solemnly publish and declare, That these United Colonies are, and of Right ought to be Free and Independent States; that they are Absolved from all Allegiance to the British Crown, and that all political connection between them and the State of Great Britain, is and ought to be totally dissolved; and that as Free and Independent States, they have full Power to levy War, conclude Peace, contract Alliances, establish Commerce, and to do all other Acts and Things which Independent States may of right do. And for the support of this Declaration, with a firm reliance on the protection of divine Providence, we mutually pledge to each other our Lives, our Fortunes and our sacred Honour.	In the name of the American people, we members of the Continental Congress declare that the United States of America is no longer a colony of Great Britain but is, instead, a free and independent nation. The United States now cuts all its relations with Great Britain. As a free nation, the United States has the right and power to make war and peace, make agreements with other nations, conduct trade, and do all the things that independent nations have the right to do. To support this Declaration of Independence, we promise to each other our lives, our fortunes, and our personal honor.

On July 4, 1776, the members of the Second Continental Congress approved the Declaration of Independence. This action made it clear that Americans were no longer colonists, but rather citizens of a new country called the United States of America. For more than 200 years, Jefferson's words have inspired people all over the world in their struggle for liberty and independence. To learn how African Americans applied some of the ideas in the Declaration of Independence to their own struggle for freedom, read the next document on pages 45-46.

A Petition for Freedom

by African Americans of Massachusetts, 1777

When the American Revolution began, slavery was legal in all 13 colonies. However, the aims and ideals of the Revolution—independence and freedom—were important to all Americans. During the 1770s African Americans in Massachusetts wrote many petitions to colonial leaders, seeking an end to slavery. The following 1777 petition to the new Massachusetts state government was signed by Prince Hall, a leading Boston minister, and seven other African Americans. As you read this excerpt, notice how the writers compare their struggle for freedom to the American struggle for independence from Great Britain. Which words and ideas in the petition can also be found in the Declaration of Independence, which you read on pages 40-44?

To the Honorable Counsel and House of Representatives for the State of Massachusetts Bay in General Court assembled, January 13, 1777

The petition of a great number of Blacks detained in a state of slavery in the **bowels** of a free and Christian country humbly show that your petitioners **apprehend** that they have in common with all other men a natural and **unalienable** right to that freedom which the Great Parent of the Universe hath **bestowed** equally on all mankind and which they have never **forfeited** by any compact or agreement whatever. But they were unjustly dragged by the hand of cruel power from their dearest friends and some of them even torn from the embraces of their tender parents—from a **populous**, pleasant, and plentiful country and in violation of laws of nature and of nations and in **defiance of** all the tender feelings of humanity brought here [to America] . . . to be sold like beasts of burden and like them condemned to slavery for life. . . . A life of slavery like that of your petitioners deprived of every social privilege of everything **requisite** to **render** life tolerable is far worse than **nonexistence**. . . .

Your petitioners have long and patiently waited the event of petition after petition by them presented to the legislative body

bowels: deepest parts
apprehend: understand
unalienable: incapable of being taken away
bestowed: given
forfeited: given up

populous: filled with people
defiance of: opposition to

requisite: necessary
render: make
nonexistence: death

of this state and [they] . . . **cannot but** express their astonishment

cannot but: can only

that it has never been considered that every principle from which America has acted in the course of their unhappy difficulties with Great Britain pleads stronger than a thousand arguments in favor of your petitioners. They therefore humbly **beseech** your honors to give this petition its due weight and

beseech: beg

consideration and cause an act of the Legislature to be passed whereby they may be restored to the enjoyments of that which is the natural right of all men—and [that] their children who were born in this land of liberty may not to be held as slaves. . . .

And your petitioners, as in duty bound shall ever pray.

Lancaster Hill	Jack Purpont
Peter Bess	Nero Suneto
Brister Slenten	Newport Symner
Prince Hall	Job Lock

Lawmakers in Massachusetts ignored this petition for freedom just as they had ignored earlier petitions. Continued pressure by African Americans during the Revolutionary War, however, along with the ideals of the Revolution itself, led people in Massachusetts to end slavery in the 1780s. By 1800 most states in the North had outlawed slavery.

Source: *Collections of the Massachusetts Historical Society*, Vol. III, Fifth Series. Boston, 1877.

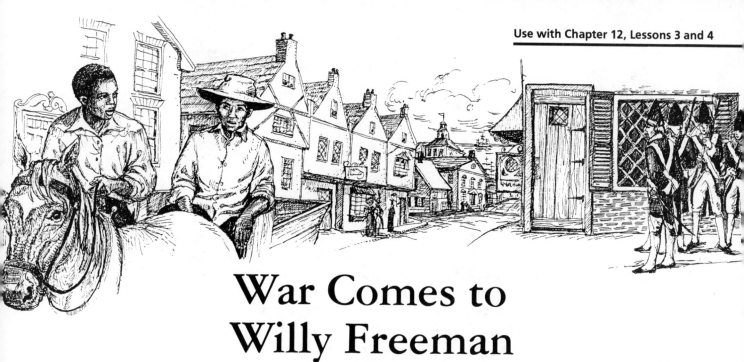

War Comes to Willy Freeman

by James Lincoln Collier and Christopher Collier, 1983

The American Revolution affected the lives of everybody in the United States, whether they were rich or poor, male or female, black or white. As the two documents you read on pages 40-46 showed, the ideas of independence and liberty were on the minds of many people during the Revolutionary War. But choosing sides—between the British and the Patriots—often meant risking your life.

The novel War Comes to Willy Freeman *tells the story of a free, 13-year-old African-American girl during the American Revolution. After seeing her father, a Patriot soldier, killed by the British, Willy Freeman races home to tell her mother. But her mother is gone, carried off by British soldiers. All alone, Willy walks to Stratford, Connecticut, where her enslaved Uncle Jack Arabus lives. Uncle Jack is a Patriot soldier off fighting, and Willy stays with his family. At first Willy feels safe, but then she begins to fear that her uncle's owner is planning to enslave and sell her. Willy decides to run away to New York City to try and find her mother. She disguises herself as a boy and races off. Along the way she meets a boy named Horace who works for Samuel Fraunces, the owner of an important tavern in New York City.*

In the excerpt you are about to read, Willy is hiding in Horace's wagon as they are just arriving in New York City. Notice some of the dangers Willy faces during the American Revolution. Should she tell Samuel Fraunces which side she is on? Should she reveal her identity as a girl? How does the war affect Willy's life?

We rode along a little ways, until we turned a corner. Then Horace told me to come out, and I climbed out and sat up on the seat beside him again, and we went along to Black Sam Fraunces' tavern.

It was a big building, bigger than anything in **New London** for sure. It was brick, four stories high, and four or five chimneys sticking out of the roof. There was big windows everywhere and a fancy door with windows over it, too. Horace read the sign out front. It said THE

New London: town in Connecticut

47

QUEEN'S HEAD, which was to suit the British while they was **occupying** New York.

We swung around back. There was a barn here for the horses and some sheds and a well, and such. I was beginning to feel nervous, and wondered what to do. What I ought to do, I knew, was get introduced to Mr. Fraunces, and ask him about Ma. He was a big man in New York and would know how to find out if there was a black woman captured by the British somewhere. Besides, Uncle Jack knew him—**leastwise** he said he did—and Mr. Fraunces was likely to help me **on account** of that.

But it was pretty bold for somebody low as me to go marching up to somebody as high up as Mr. Fraunces and ask for help. Most probably he'd tell me he never heard of Jack Arabus, go away and stop bothering me. But even so, I knew I had to try and it made me scared to think about it.

I helped Horace unload the **cordwood** and stack it alongside one of the sheds. Then he said, "You still ain't had nothing to eat."

"I'm pretty hungry," I said.

"Well, all right," he said. "You come on into the kitchen and I'll get you something."

"Will Mr. Fraunces mind?" I said.

"Mind? Mr. Fraunces? Why, I don't have to ask Mr. Fraunces about nothing like that. We're this close. He always says, 'Horace, you just go ahead to do what you think best.' He trusts me that much."

Well, I wondered about it: the story didn't seem to lower Horace none. But I didn't say anything.

We went into the kitchen. It was a big room, with a huge fireplace at one end and big pots hanging there steaming away. A couple of cooks was slicing apples at a big table. There was barrels of sugar and flour and molasses and such around, too, but I noticed they was pretty empty. "It was different before the war," Horace said. "Then we'd have a whole side of beef on a **spit** over the fire and apple pies and puddings and spice cakes and everything. But food's scarce now."

He grabbed up a couple of wooden plates from off a shelf and went down to the fireplace where the stew pots was, with me following along, getting hungrier by the minute from the smells. I hadn't had a proper meal for nearly four days. Just staring down at that stew bubbling away made me swallow hard. Horace grabbed up a ladle that was hooked over the edge of one of the stew pots.

Just then one of the cooks jumped over to us and snatched the ladle out of his hand. "Here, you boy, what do you think you're doing?"

"Hey," Horace shouted. "Mr. Fraunces says I was to help myself when I wanted."

Then a voice from behind us said, "Mr. Fraunces says you're to do what, Horace?"

We spun around. Standing at the door was a tall black man dressed in a blue suit with a silver buckle at his belt and ruffles on

occupying: in control of
leastwise: at least
on account of: because of

cordwood: wood for burning

spit: metal pole on which meat is roasted

48

his chest. I knew right away it must be Mr. Fraunces, and my heart jumped.

I looked at Horace and back at Mr. Fraunces and then at Horace again.

Horace was wrapping his long self up and unwrapping himself a mile a minute. "Well, sir—well—I—sir," he said, and stopped there.

Mr. Fraunces looked at me. "Who's this?" he asked.

"He helped me unload the wood," Horace said. "He's hungry."

"I see," Mr. Fraunces said. "But we can't be feeding the entire **populace**, Horace. Food's scarce."

populace: population; people living in an area

I was feeling mighty nervous, like I'd done something wrong, and I didn't know whether I ought to speak up about Uncle Jack or just scoot on out of there. I knew I shouldn't ought to miss my chance, but I was scared.

Mr. Fraunces didn't give me no time to think about it, for he walked over, took a look at me, and said, "When was the last time you had a meal, son?"

"I ain't had nothing much but a couple of roast potatoes the past two days."

"I see," he said. "Where are you from?"

It was now or never. "Sir, my uncle says he knows you. He's a soldier with General Washington. His name is Jack Arabus."

"Jack Arabus?" he said. "Why, I know Jack. Where is he now?"

"In camp. Up on the **Hudson Highlands** somewhere."

"And you're his nephew?"

Hudson Highlands: land and cliffs overlooking the Hudson River north of New York City

It still took me by surprise when people called me a nephew instead of a niece, and I knew I'd better get used to it. "Yes, sir," I said.

I didn't know what to tell him. Was he on the American side or the British? Here he was running a tavern right in the middle of New York, which was owned by the British. On the other side of it, Uncle Jack would sure have told me if he was for the British. Unless maybe he'd changed over to the British side and Uncle Jack didn't know. A lot of people did that during the war—changed sides.

I decided to be cautious. So I said, "Well, I been staying with Uncle Jack up at Newfield in Stratford. My Ma, she was taken off by the British. Well, maybe she ran off with them, but I don't know. I figure she's down here in New York somewheres and I came down to find her."

"Your Ma went off with the British? How did that happen?"

I was getting into it more than I wanted, and I began to sweat a little. I figured I'd better be careful about telling lies: Mr. Fraunces was likely to be smarter about it than Horace. "We had some **skirmishing** up around where I'm from and I went and hid out and when I came back she was gone, and they said she went off with the British."

"Where was that?"

"**Groton**," I said.

He nodded his head. "That was a very sad business up there," he said.

skirmishing: fighting

Groton: town in Connecticut

"Yes, sir," I said. "I know it was. I saw some of it."

"I suppose you did," he said. He didn't say nothing for a moment. Then he said, "What's your name?"

"Willy." Then I said, "Willy Freeman," so's he knows I wasn't no slave. . . .

"You know, Willy," he said, "a lot of black people favor the British. They believe that the British will free them if they fight for them. Did you think you'd be better off with the British here in New York?"

Seeing as he'd asked me **point blank**, I was stuck. There wasn't no way out of it. I remembered what Horace said about lying—to make it ordinary, and lower myself. But I didn't know what kind of lie to tell and I decided I might as well tell the truth. "Sir, my Pa got killed by the British at **Fort Griswold**. I saw it myself. They stabbed him with their **bayonets**, and he flung his arms back like so—" I started to cry again and couldn't finish and stood there sobbing away like a fool. He didn't say anything and finally I got a hold of myself and stopped crying and wiped my face off with my sleeve.

"What was a young boy like you doing up there?"

"I ain't even a boy, sir," I blurted out. "I'm a girl."

He gave a kind of a jump. "A girl?"

"Yes, sir."

He stared into my face. "Why, I suppose you are," he said. "How on earth did you land in that battle?"

So I told him the whole story, about the British coming and me going to the fort to bring the horse back and the fighting and going down to Stratford and the rest of it. He just sat there listening. When I got done he didn't say anything for a minute, but thought about it all. Then he said, "Well, I guess you've had enough trouble for a while, Willy. We'll manage to put you up for a bit, until you can get settled."

"Thank you, sir," I said. "I'll work hard, I promise."

"I'm sure you will," he said.

"The main thing is, I got to find Ma." Once more I got the image of her coming along the street and us seeing each other and hugging.

He shook his head. "You don't even know she's in New York."

It was true. I looked at him, feeling discouraged. I guess it showed on my face, for he said, "Well, there are a couple of places you could try. And, Willy," he said, "I think it best that you stay a boy for a while."

point blank: directly

Fort Griswold: fort in Groton, Connecticut

bayonets: steel blades on the ends of rifles

Both Samuel Fraunces and Jack Arabus were real people who played an important role in the American Revolution. Samuel Fraunces secretly helped the Patriots and later worked for George Washington. Today Fraunces Tavern is a museum. Jack Arabus served as a soldier in the Patriot army. He played a key role in gaining the freedom of about 300 Connecticut slaves who fought in the war.

Source: James Lincoln Collier and Christopher Collier, *War Comes to Willy Freeman*. New York: Delacorte Press, 1983.

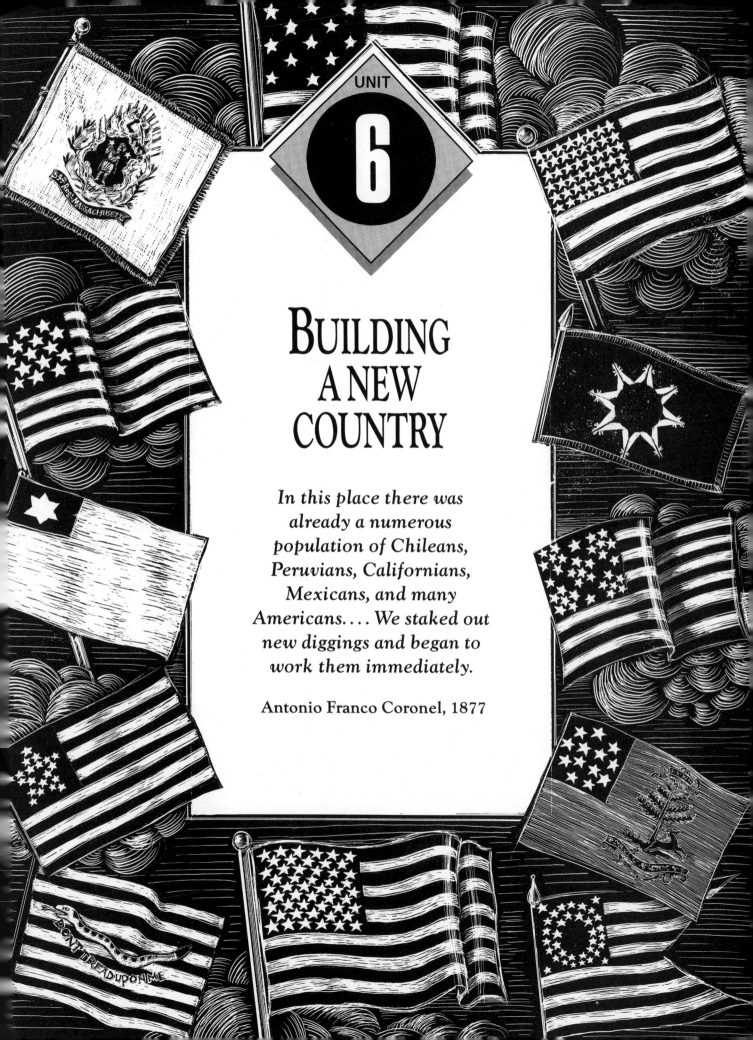

UNIT

6

BUILDING A NEW COUNTRY

In this place there was already a numerous population of Chileans, Peruvians, Californians, Mexicans, and many Americans.... We staked out new diggings and began to work them immediately.

Antonio Franco Coronel, 1877

Two Views on Women's Rights

by Abigail Adams and John Adams, 1776

In the spring of 1776, many Americans were expecting the 13 colonies to declare their independence from Britain. Once independence was achieved, some people hoped that the new government would treat women and men as equals under the law. One of these people was Abigail Adams (1744-1818), the 31-year-old wife of colonial leader John Adams (1735-1826). At the time, American women had few legal rights or powers. The Adamses were a close couple, and Abigail called John her "dearest friend" and "beloved partner." On the issue of women's rights, however, the Adamses had very different opinions. The excerpts below are from three letters that were written in 1776 while Abigail was in Massachusetts running the family farm and John was in Philadelphia serving in the Continental Congress. How do their views differ on women's rights and equality?

Abigail to John, March 31, 1776

I long to hear that you have declared **an independency**—and by the way in the new code of laws which I suppose it will be necessary for you to make I desire you would remember the ladies, and be more generous and favorable to them than your ancestors. Do not put such unlimited power into the hands of the husbands. Remember all men would be **tyrants** if they could. If particular care and attention is not paid to the ladies we are determined to **foment** a rebellion, and will not hold ourselves bound by any laws in which we have no voice, or representation.

That your sex are naturally tyrannical is a truth so thoroughly established as to **admit** of no **dispute**, but such of you as wish to be happy willingly give up the harsh title of master for the more tender and endearing one of friend. Why then, not put it out of the power of the vicious and the lawless to use us with cruelty and indignity. . . . Men of sense in all ages **abhor** those customs which treat us only as the **vassals** of your sex. Regard us then as beings placed by **providence** under your protection and in imitation of the Supreme Being make use of that power only for our happiness.

an independency: independence

tyrants: oppressive rulers

foment: stir up

admit: be
dispute: disagreement

abhor: hate
vassals: servants
providence: God

John to Abigail, April 14, 1776

As to Declarations of Independency, be patient. . . .

As to your extraordinary code of laws, I cannot but laugh. We have been told that our struggle has loosened the **bands** of government every where. That children and **apprentices** were disobedient—that schools and colleges were grown **turbulent**—that Indians **slighted** their guardians and Negroes grew **insolent** to their masters. But your letter was the first **intimation** that another tribe more numerous and powerful than all the rest were grown discontented. . . .

Depend upon it, we know better than to **repeal** our masculine systems. Although they are in full force, you know that they are little more than **theory**. We dare not exert our power in its full **latitude**. We are obliged to go fair, and softly, and in practice you know we are the **subjects**. We have only the name of masters, and rather than give up this, which would completely subject us to the **despotism** of the **petticoat**, I hope General Washington, and all our brave heroes would fight.

bands: ties

apprentices: workers learning a trade

turbulent: stormy

slighted: showed disrespect to

insolent: disrespectful

intimation: clue

repeal: undo

theory: unsure belief

latitude: strength

subjects: ones who obey

despotism: oppressive rule

petticoat: woman's skirt; old symbol for a woman

Abigail to John, May 7, 1776

I can not say that I think you very generous to the ladies, for whilst you are **proclaiming** peace and good will to men, **emancipating** all nations, you insist upon retaining an absolute power over wives. But you must remember that **arbitrary** power is like most other things which are very hard, very **liable** to be broken—and notwithstanding all your wise laws and **maxims** we have it in our power not only to free ourselves but to **subdue** our masters, and without violence throw both your natural and legal authority at our feet. . . .

proclaiming: announcing

emancipating: freeing

arbitrary: unlimited

liable: likely

maxims: truths

subdue: conquer

John Adams later served as second President of the United States from 1797 to 1801. His very limited views of women's rights and equality were similar to those of most American men of his day. As First Lady, Abigail Adams assisted her husband in the White House. It would be many years, however, before women received the same rights as men.

Source: L. H. Butterfield, ed., *Adams Family Correspondence*, Vol. I. Cambridge, MA: The Belknap Press of Harvard University Press, 1963.

The Constitution

Plan for the United States Government Written in 1787

After the American Revolution, many people began to feel that the Articles of Confederation was not working well. To solve this problem, 55 delegates gathered in Philadelphia in May 1787 and hammered out a new plan of government called the Constitution. Since then 27 amendments, or changes, have been added to the Constitution. Below are the entire original Constitution, its amendments, and notes of explanation. The crossed-out sections of the Constitution are no longer in effect. As you read the Constitution, notice the different powers of the three branches of government: the legislative branch, the executive branch, and the judicial branch. How does the Constitution make these three branches work together?

Preamble

We the people of the United States, in order to form a more perfect Union, establish justice, insure domestic tranquility, provide for the common defense, promote the general welfare, and secure the blessings of liberty to ourselves and our posterity, do ordain and establish this Constitution for the United States of America.

The people of the United States make this Constitution for several reasons: to form a stronger and more united nation; to ensure peace, justice, and liberty; to defend its citizens; and to improve the lives of its people.

Article 1. The Legislative Branch

Section 1. The Congress

All legislative powers herein granted shall be vested in a Congress of the United States, which shall consist of a Senate and House of Representatives.

Congress has the power to make laws. Congress is made up of two houses: the Senate and the House of Representatives.

Section 2. The House of Representatives

1. The House of Representatives shall be composed of members chosen every second year by the people of the several states, and the electors in each state shall have the qualifications requisite for electors of the most numerous branch of the state legislature.

1. Members of the House of Representatives are elected every two years by qualified voters in each state.

2. No person shall be a Representative who shall not have attained to the age of twenty-five years, and been seven years a citizen of the United States, and who shall not, when elected, be an inhabitant of that state in which he shall be chosen.

2. To be a member of the House of Representatives, a person must be at least 25 years old, a United States citizen for at least seven years, and live in the state he or she represents.

3. Representatives ~~and direct taxes~~ shall be apportioned among the several states which may be included within this Union, according to their respective numbers, ~~which~~

3. The number of Representatives for each state is based on the population, or number of people, who live in that state. Every ten years a census, or count,

shall be determined by adding to the whole number of free persons, including those bound to service for a term of years, and excluding Indians not taxed, three fifths of all other persons. The actual enumeration shall be made within three years after the first meeting of the Congress of the United States, and within every subsequent term of ten years, in such manner as they shall by law direct. The number of Representatives shall not exceed one for every 30,000, but each state shall have at least one Representative; and until such enumeration shall be made, the state of New Hampshire shall be entitled to choose three, Massachusetts, eight, Rhode Island and Providence Plantations, one, Connecticut, five, New York, six, New Jersey, four, Pennsylvania, eight, Delaware, one, Maryland, six, Virginia, ten, North Carolina, five, South Carolina, five, and Georgia, three.

must be taken to determine the population of each state. At first, this census of the population included indentured servants but not most Native Americans. Each enslaved person was counted as three fifths of a free person. Today all people are counted equally.

4. When vacancies happen in the representation from any state, the executive authority thereof shall issue writs of election to fill such vacancies.

4. Special elections called by the state's governor must be held to fill any empty seat in the House of Representatives.

5. The House of Representatives shall choose their Speaker and other officers; and shall have the sole power of impeachment.

5. Members of the House of Representatives choose their own leaders. House members alone have the power to impeach, or accuse, government officials of crimes in office.

Section 3. The Senate

1. The Senate of the United States shall be composed of two Senators from each state, chosen by the legislature thereof, for six years; and each Senator shall have one vote.

1. Each state has two Senators. Each Senator serves a term of six years and has one vote in the Senate. At first, state legislatures elected Senators, but the 17th Amendment changed the way Senators are chosen. Senators are now elected directly by the people.

2. Immediately after they shall be assembled in consequence of the first election, they shall be divided as equally as may be into three classes. The seats of the Senators of the first class shall be vacated at the expiration of the second year, of the second class at the expiration of the fourth year, and of the third class at the expiration of the sixth year, so that one third may be chosen every second year; and if vacancies happen by resignation, or otherwise, during the recess of the legislature of any state, the executive thereof may make temporary appointments until the next meeting of the legislature, which shall then fill such vacancies.

2. One third of the Senate seats are up for election every two years. The 17th Amendment changed the way empty seats are filled.

3. No person shall be a Senator who shall not have attained to the age of thirty years, and been nine years a citizen of the United States, and who shall not, when elected, be an inhabitant of that state for which he shall be chosen.

3. To be a Senator, a person must be at least 30 years old, a citizen of the United States for at least nine years, and live in the state he or she represents.

4. The Vice President of the United States shall be president of the Senate, but shall have no vote, unless they be equally divided.

4. The Vice President of the United States is the officer in charge of the Senate but votes only to break a tie.

5. The Senate shall choose their other officers, and also a president pro tempore, in the absence of the Vice President, or when he shall exercise the office of the President of the United States.

6. The Senate shall have the sole power to try all impeachments. When sitting for that purpose, they shall be on oath or affirmation. When the President of the United States is tried, the Chief Justice shall preside; and no person shall be convicted without the concurrence of two thirds of the members present.

7. Judgment in cases of impeachment shall not extend further than to removal from office, and disqualification to hold and enjoy any office of honor, trust or profit under the United States; but the party convicted shall nevertheless be liable and subject to indictment, trial, judgment and punishment, according to law.

Section 4. Elections and Meetings of Congress

1. The times, places and manner of holding elections for Senators and Representatives shall be prescribed in each state by the legislature thereof; but the Congress may at any time by law make or alter such regulations, ~~except as to the places of choosing Senators.~~

2. The Congress shall assemble at least once in every year ~~and such meeting shall be on the first Monday in December, unless they shall by law appoint a different day.~~

Section 5. Rules of Procedure for Congress

1. Each house shall be the judge of the elections, returns and qualifications of its own members, and a majority of each shall constitute a quorum to do business; but a smaller number may adjourn from day to day, and may be authorized to compel the attendance of absent members, in such manner, and under such penalties as each house may provide.

2. Each house may determine the rules of its proceedings, punish its members for disorderly behavior, and with the concurrence of two thirds, expel a member.

3. Each house shall keep a journal of its proceedings, and from time to time publish the same, excepting such parts as may in their judgment require secrecy; and the yeas and nays of the members of either house on any question shall, at the desire of one fifth of those present, be entered on the journal.

4. Neither house, during the session of Congress, shall, without the consent of the other, adjourn for more than

---

5. Senators choose their own leaders. When the Vice President is absent, the Senate leader is called the President *pro tempore* (prō tem′pə rē), or temporary President.

6. The Senate holds all impeachment trials. When the President of the United States is impeached, the Chief Justice of the Supreme Court is the judge for the trial. Conviction, or judgment of guilt, is decided by a two-thirds vote.

7. Impeached officials convicted by the Senate can be removed from office and barred from serving again in government. Regular courts of law may bring other actions.

1. State lawmakers set rules for Congressional elections. Congress can change some of these rules.

2. Congress meets at least once a year, beginning in December. The 20th Amendment changed this date to January 3.

1. The Senate and House of Representatives decide if their members were elected fairly and are qualified to take their seats. At least half the members of each house of Congress must be present for Congress to do most business. Absent members can be required to attend sessions of Congress.

2. Each house of Congress may set its own rules and punish members for breaking them. A two-thirds vote is needed to expel, or force out, a member.

3. Each house of Congress keeps and publishes a record of its activities. Secret matters may be left out of the published record. If one fifth of the members demand it, a vote on any matter will be published.

4. During a session of Congress, neither house can stop meeting for

three days, nor to any other place than that in which the two houses shall be sitting.

Section 6. Privileges and Restrictions of Members of Congress

1. The Senators and Representatives shall receive a compensation for their services, to be ascertained by law, and paid out of the Treasury of the United States. They shall in all cases, except treason, felony and breach of the peace, be privileged from arrest during their attendance at the session of their respective houses, and in going to and returning from the same; and for any speech or debate in either house, they shall not be questioned in any other place.

2. No Senator or Representative shall, during the time for which he was elected, be appointed to any civil office under the authority of the United States, which shall have been created, or the emoluments whereof shall have been increased during such time; and no person holding any office under the United States, shall be a member of either house during his continuance in office.

Section 7. How Laws Are Made

1. All bills for raising revenue shall originate in the House of Representatives; but the Senate may propose or concur with amendments as on other bills.

2. Every bill which shall have passed the House of Representatives and the Senate, shall, before it become a law, be presented to the President of the United States. If he approve he shall sign it, but if not he shall return it, with his objections to that house in which it shall have originated, who shall enter the objections at large on their journal, and proceed to reconsider it. If after such reconsideration two thirds of that house shall agree to pass the bill, it shall be sent, together with the objections, to the other house, by which it shall likewise be reconsidered, and if approved by two thirds of that house, it shall become a law. But in all such cases the votes of both houses shall be determined by yeas and nays, and the names of the persons voting for and against the bill shall be entered on the journal of each house respectively. If any bill shall not be returned by the President within ten days (Sundays excepted) after it shall have been presented to him, the same shall be a law, in like manner as if he had signed it, unless the Congress by their adjournment prevent its return, in which case it shall not be a law.

3. Every order, resolution, or vote to which the concurrence of the Senate and House of Representatives may be necessary (except on a question of adjournment) shall be presented to the President of the United States; and before the same shall take effect, shall be approved by him, or being disapproved

more than three days or decide to meet somewhere else unless the other house agrees.

1. Each member of Congress receives a salary from the United States government. Except for very serious crimes, no member can be arrested in the place where Congress is meeting while in session. Members cannot be arrested for anything they say in Congress.

2. Senators and Representatives may not hold any other job in the federal government while they serve in Congress.

1. All money and tax bills must begin in the House of Representatives. The Senate can later pass or change these bills.

2. After a bill, or suggested law, passes both the House of Representatives and the Senate, it goes to the President. If the President signs the bill, it becomes a law. If the President vetoes, or rejects, the bill, it goes back to Congress. A President's veto can be overridden, or upset, if Congress votes again and two thirds of the members of each house vote in favor of the bill. The bill then becomes a law. If the President neither signs nor vetoes a bill within 10 days (not counting Sundays) of first receiving it, the bill becomes a law. If Congress stops meeting *before* 10 days have passed, however, the bill does *not* become a law. This last type of action is called a "pocket veto."

3. Every act passed by Congress must be presented to the President either to be signed or vetoed. The only exception is when Congress votes to adjourn, or stop meeting.

by him, shall be repassed by two thirds of the Senate and House of Representatives, according to the rules and limitations prescribed in the case of a bill.

Section 8. Powers Granted to Congress

1. The Congress shall have power to lay and collect taxes, duties, imposts and excises, to pay the debts and provide for the common defense and general welfare of the United States; but all duties, imposts and excises shall be uniform throughout the United States;

2. To borrow money on the credit of the United States;

3. To regulate commerce with foreign nations, and among the several states, and with the Indian tribes;

4. To establish a uniform rule of naturalization, and uniform laws on the subject of bankruptcies throughout the United States;

5. To coin money, regulate the value thereof, and of foreign coin, and fix the standard of weights and measures;

6. To provide for the punishment of counterfeiting the securities and current coin of the United States;

7. To establish post offices and post roads;

8. To promote the progress of science and useful arts, by securing for limited times to authors and inventors the exclusive right to their respective writings and discoveries;

9. To constitute tribunals inferior to the Supreme Court;

10. To define and punish piracies and felonies committed on the high seas and offenses against the law of nations;

11. To declare war, ~~grant letters of marque and reprisal~~, and make rules concerning captures on land and water;

12. To raise and support armies, but no appropriation of money to that use shall be for a longer term than two years;

13. To provide and maintain a navy;

14. To make rules for the government and regulation of the land and naval forces;

15. To provide for calling forth the militia to execute the laws of the Union, suppress insurrections and repel invasions;

Congress has the power to:

1. raise and collect taxes to both pay debts and to protect and serve the nation, but taxes must be the same everywhere in the United States;

2. borrow money;

3. control trade with foreign nations, between states, and with Native Americans;

4. decide how people from foreign countries can become citizens of the United States and to make laws dealing with people and businesses unable to pay their debts;

5. print money, set its value, and set the standards of weights and measures used throughout the nation;

6. punish people who make counterfeit, or fake, money and bonds;

7. set up post offices and roads for mail delivery;

8. protect the rights and creations of scientists, artists, authors, and inventors;

9. create federal, or national, courts lower than the Supreme Court;

10. punish crimes committed at sea;

11. declare war;

12. establish and support an army, but no amount of money set aside for this purpose can be for a term longer than two years;

13. establish and support a navy;

14. make rules for the armed forces;

15. call the militia (today called the National Guard) to enforce federal laws, put down rebellions, and fight invasions;

16. To provide for organizing, arming, and disciplining, the militia, and for governing such part of them as may be employed in the service of the United States, reserving to the states respectively, the appointment of the officers, and the authority of training the militia according to the discipline prescribed by Congress;

17. To exercise exclusive legislation in all cases whatsoever, over such district (not exceeding ten miles square) as may, by cession of particular states, and the acceptance of Congress, become the seat of the government of the United States, and to exercise like authority over all places purchased by the consent of the legislature of the state in which the same shall be, for the erection of forts, magazines, arsenals, dockyards, and other needful buildings;—and

18. To make all laws which shall be necessary and proper for carrying into execution the foregoing powers, and all other powers vested by this Constitution in the government of the United States, or in any department or officer thereof.

Section 9. Powers Denied to Congress

1. ~~The migration or importation of such persons as any of the states now existing shall think proper to admit, shall not be prohibited by the Congress prior to the year one thousand eight hundred and eight, but a tax or duty may be imposed on such importation, not exceeding ten dollars for each person.~~

2. The privilege of the writ of habeas corpus shall not be suspended, unless when in cases of rebellion or invasion the public safety may require it.

3. No bill of attainder or ex post facto law shall be passed.

4. No capitation, or other direct, tax shall be laid, unless in proportion to the census or enumeration herein before directed to be taken.

5. No tax or duty shall be laid on articles exported from any state.

6. No preference shall be given any regulation of commerce or revenue to the ports of one state over those of another; nor shall vessels bound to, or from, one state, be obliged to enter, clear, or pay duties in another.

7. No money shall be drawn from the Treasury, but in consequence of appropriations made by law; and a regular statement and account of the receipts and expenditures of all public money shall be published from time to time.

16. organize, train, and discipline the National Guard. States have the power to name officers and train soldiers in the National Guard under rules set by Congress;

17. govern the capital and military sites of the United States; and

18. make all laws necessary to carry out the powers of Congress. This is called the "elastic clause" because it stretches the powers of Congress.

Congress does *not* have the power to:

1. stop enslaved people from being brought into the United States before 1808. In 1808, the first year allowed, Congress passed a law banning the slave trade;

2. arrest and jail people without charging them with a crime. The only exception is during a rebellion or emergency;

3. punish a person without a trial in a court of law; nor punish a person for doing something wrong that was not against the law when the person did it;

4. pass a direct tax (such as an income tax) unless it is in proportion to the population. The 16th Amendment allowed an income tax;

5. tax goods sent out of a state;

6. give ports of one state an advantage over ports of another state; nor can one state tax the ships of another state that enter its borders;

7. spend money without both passing a law and keeping a record of all its accounts;

8. No title of nobility shall be granted by the United States; and no person holding any office of profit or trust under them, shall, without the consent of the Congress, accept of any present, emolument, office, or title, of any kind whatever, from any king, prince, or foreign state.

Section 10. Powers Denied to the States

1. No state shall enter into any treaty, alliance, or confederation; grant letters of marque and reprisal; coin money; emit bills of credit; make anything but gold and silver coin a tender in payment of debts; pass any bill of attainder, ex post facto law, or law impairing the obligation of contracts, or grant any title of nobility.

2. No state shall, without the consent of the Congress, lay any imposts or duties on imports or exports, except what may be absolutely necessary for executing its inspection laws; and the net produce of all duties and imposts, laid by any state on imports or exports, shall be for the use of the Treasury of the United States; and all such laws shall be subject to the revision and control of the Congress.

3. No state shall, without the consent of Congress, lay any duty of tonnage, keep troops, or ships of war in time of peace, enter into any agreement or compact with another state, or with a foreign power, or engage in war, unless actually invaded, or in such imminent danger as will not admit of delay.

Article 2. The Executive Branch

Section 1. Office of President and Vice President

1. The executive power shall be vested in a President of the United States of America. He shall hold his office during the term of four years, and, together with the Vice President, chosen for the same term, be elected, as follows:

2. Each state shall appoint, in such manner as the legislature thereof may direct, a number of electors, equal to the whole number of Senators and Representatives to which the state may be entitled in the Congress; but no Senator or Representative, or person holding an office or trust or profit under the United States, shall be appointed an elector.

3. ~~The electors shall meet in their respective states, and vote by ballot for two persons, of whom one at least shall not be an inhabitant of the same state with themselves. And they shall make a list of all the persons voted for, and of the number of votes for each; which list they shall sign and certify, and transmit sealed to the seat of the government of the United States, directed to the president of the Senate. The president of the Senate shall, in the presence of the~~

8. grant any title of nobility (such as king or queen); nor may any worker in the federal government accept any gift or title from a foreign government.

State governments do *not* have the power to:

1. make treaties, print money, or do anything forbidden to the federal government outlined in Section 9 of the Constitution, above;

2. tax goods sent into and out of a state unless Congress agrees;

3. keep armed forces, go to war, or make agreements with others states or foreign countries unless Congress agrees.

1. The President has the power to execute, or carry out, the laws of the United States. The President and Vice President together serve a term of four years.

2. The President is chosen by electors from each state. Today these electors are chosen by the voters and called the *Electoral College*. The number of electoral votes for each state is determined by adding up the number of the state's Senators and Representatives.

3. This part of the Constitution describes an early method of electing the President and Vice President. The 12th Amendment changed this method. Originally, the person who received the most electoral votes became President and the person who received the next highest number became Vice President.

Senate and House of Representatives, open all the certificates, and the votes shall then be counted. The person having the greatest number of votes shall be the President, if such number be a majority of the whole number of electors appointed; and if there be more than one who have such majority, and have an equal number of votes, then the House of Representatives shall immediately choose by ballot one of them for President; and if no person have a majority, then from the five highest on the list the said House shall in like manner choose the President. But in choosing the President, the votes shall be taken by states, the representation from each state having one vote; a quorum for this purpose shall consist of a member or members from two thirds of the states, and a majority of all the states shall be necessary to a choice. In every case, after the choice of the President, the person having the greatest number of votes of the electors shall be the Vice President. But if there should remain two or more who have equal votes, the Senate shall choose from them by ballot the Vice President.

4. The Congress may determine the time of choosing the electors, and the day on which they shall give their votes; which day shall be the same throughout the United States.

4. Congress decides when Presidential electors are chosen and when they vote. The electors vote on the same day throughout the United States. Today people vote for the electors on the Tuesday after the first Monday of November. Presidential elections take place every four years.

5. No person except a natural born citizen, or a citizen of the United States, at the time of the adoption of this Constitution, shall be eligible to the office of President; neither shall any person be eligible to that office who shall not have attained to the age of thirty-five years, and been fourteen years a resident within the United States.

5. To be President, a person must be a citizen born in the United States, at least 35 years old, and have lived in the United States for at least 14 years.

6. In case of the removal of the President from office, or of his death, resignation, or inability to discharge the powers and duties of the said office, the same shall devolve on the Vice President, and the Congress may by law provide for the case of removal, death, resignation, or inability, both of the President and Vice President, declaring what officer shall then act as President, and such officer shall act accordingly, until the disability be removed, or a President shall be elected.

6. If the President leaves office for any reason or can no longer serve as President, the Vice President becomes President. If there is no Vice President, Congress may decide who becomes President. The 25th Amendment changed the method of filling these vacancies, or empty offices.

7. The President shall, at stated times receive for his services, a compensation, which shall neither be increased nor diminished during the period for which he shall have been elected, and he shall not receive within that period any other emolument from the United States, or any of them.

7. The President receives a set salary that can neither be raised nor lowered during the President's term of office. The President can receive no other gift or salary from the United States or any of the states while in office.

8. Before he enter on the execution of his office, he shall take the following oath or affirmation:— "I do solemnly swear (or affirm) that I will faithfully execute the office

8. Before taking office, the person elected President takes an oath. In this oath, the person promises to carry out

of President of the United States, and will to the best of my ability, preserve, protect and defend the Constitution of the United States."

the laws of the United States and defend the Constitution.

Section 2. Powers Granted to the President

1. The President shall be Commander in Chief of the Army and Navy of the United States, and of the militia of the several states, when called into the actual service of the United States; he may require the opinion, in writing, of the principal officer in each of the executive departments, upon any subject relating to the duties of their respective offices, and he shall have power to grant reprieves and pardons for offenses against the United States, except in cases of impeachment.

1. The President is in charge of the armed forces and state militias (today the National Guard) of the United States. The President can demand advice and opinions, in writing, of the people in charge of each executive department. These advisers are called the President's Cabinet. The President also has the power to pardon, or free, people convicted of federal crimes, except in cases of impeachment.

2. He shall have power, by and with the advice and consent of the Senate, to make treaties, provided two thirds of the Senators present concur; and he shall nominate, and by and with the advice and consent of the Senate, shall appoint ambassadors, other public ministers and consuls, judges of the Supreme Court, and all other officers of the United States, whose appointments are not herein otherwise provided for, and which shall be established by law; but the Congress may by law vest the appointment of such inferior officers, as they think proper, in the President alone, in the courts of law, or in the heads of departments.

2. The President has the power to make treaties, but they must be approved by two thirds of the Senate. The President also has the power to name ambassadors, important government officials, and judges of the Supreme Court and other federal courts, with the approval of the Senate.

3. The President shall have power to fill up all vacancies that may happen during the recess of the Senate, by granting commissions which shall expire at the end of their next session.

3. The President has the power to fill empty offices for a short time when the Senate is not meeting.

Section 3. Duties of the President

He shall from time to time give to the Congress information of the state of the Union, and recommend to their consideration such measures as he shall judge necessary and expedient; he may, on extraordinary occasions, convene both houses, or either of them, and in case of disagreement between them, with respect to the time of adjournment, he may adjourn them to such time as he shall think proper; he shall receive ambassadors and other public ministers; he shall take care that the laws be faithfully executed, and shall commission all the officers of the United States.

The President must inform Congress from time to time on the condition of the nation. Today, this speech is called the State of the Union Message and is given once a year, usually in late January. In this message, the President recommends laws to improve the nation. The President can also, in time of emergency, call Congress to meet. If, in other situations, Congress cannot decide whether or not to adjourn, the President can make this decision. The President receives foreign officials, makes sure the nation's laws are carried out, and signs orders naming officers in the armed forces.

Section 4. Removal from Office

The President, Vice President and all civil officers of the United States, shall be removed from office on impeachment for, and conviction of, treason, bribery, or other high crimes and misdemeanors.

The President, Vice President, and other non-military officers of the United States may be impeached, or accused of committing crimes, and removed from office if found guilty.

Article 3. The Judicial Branch

Section 1. Federal Courts

The judicial power of the United States shall be vested in one Supreme Court, and in such inferior courts as the Congress may from time to time ordain and establish. The judges, both of the Supreme and inferior courts, shall hold their offices during good behavior, and shall, at stated times, receive for their services, a compensation, which shall not be diminished during their continuance in office.

The judicial power, or the power to make decisions in courts of law, is held by the Supreme Court and other lower federal, or national, courts that Congress may set up. Supreme Court and other federal judges hold office for life if they act properly. Judges receive a set salary that cannot be lowered.

Section 2. Powers of Federal Courts

1. The judicial power shall extend to all cases, in law and equity, arising under this Constitution, the laws of the United States, and treaties made, or which shall be made, under their authority; to all cases affecting ambassadors, other public ministers and consuls; to all cases of admiralty and maritime jurisdiction; to controversies to which the United States shall be a party; to controversies between two or more states; between a state and citizens of another state; between citizens of different states, between citizens of the same state claiming lands under grants of different states, and between a state, or the citizens thereof, and foreign states, citizens or subjects.

1. Federal courts have legal authority over:
a) all laws made under the Constitution;
b) treaties made with foreign governments;
c) cases involving matters occurring at sea;
d) cases involving the federal government;
e) cases involving different states or citizens of different states; and
f) cases involving foreign citizens or governments.
The 11th Amendment partly limits which cases federal courts can hear.

2. In all cases affecting ambassadors, other public ministers and consuls, and those in which a state shall be party, the Supreme Court shall have original jurisdiction. In all the other cases before mentioned, the Supreme Court shall have appellate jurisdiction, both as to law and fact, with such exceptions, and under such regulations as the Congress shall make.

2. In cases involving either states or ambassadors and government officials, the Supreme Court is the first and only court that makes a judgment. All other cases begin in lower courts but may later be appealed to, or reviewed by, the Supreme Court.

3. The trial of all crimes, except in cases of impeachment, shall be by jury; and such trial shall be held in the state where the said crimes shall have been committed; but when not committed within any state, the trial shall be at such place or places as the Congress may by law have directed.

3. All criminal cases, except those of impeachment, are judged by trial and jury in the state where the supposed crime took place. If a crime occurs outside of any state, Congress decides where the trial takes place.

Section 3. The Crime of Treason

1. Treason against the United States shall consist only in levying war against them, or in adhering to their enemies, giving them aid and comfort. No person shall be convicted of treason unless on the testimony of two witnesses to the same overt act, or on confession in open court.

1. Treason is the crime of making war against the United States or helping its enemies. To be found guilty of treason, a person must confess to the crime or two witnesses must swear to having seen the crime committed.

2. The Congress shall have power to declare the punishment of treason, but no attainder of treason shall work corruption of blood, or forfeiture except during the life of the person attainted.

2. Congress decides the punishment for treason. Relatives of people convicted of treason cannot also be punished for the crime.

Article 4. Relations Among the States

Section 1. Recognition by Each State of Acts of Other States

Full faith and credit shall be given in each state to the public acts, records, and judicial proceedings of every other state. And the Congress may by general laws prescribe the manner in which such acts, records and proceedings shall be proved, and the effect thereof.

Each state must respect the laws, records, and court decisions of every other state in the United States. Congress may pass laws to help carry out these matters.

Section 2. Rights of Citizens in Other States

1. The citizens of each state shall be entitled to all privileges and immunities of citizens in the several states.

1. Citizens are guaranteed all their basic rights when visiting other states.

2. A person charged in any state with treason, felony, or other crime, who shall flee from justice, and be found in another state, shall on demand of the executive authority of the state from which he fled, be delivered up, to be removed to the state having jurisdiction of the crime.

2. A person charged with a crime, who flees to another state, must be returned to the state where the crime took place if the governor of the state demands.

3. ~~No person held to service or labor in one state, under the laws thereof, escaping into another, shall, in consequence of any law or regulation therein, be discharged from such service or labor, but shall be delivered up on claim of the party to whom such service or labor may be due.~~

3. A person enslaved in one state, who escapes to another state, is still considered enslaved and must be returned to the person's owner. The 13th Amendment, which outlawed slavery, nullified, or overturned, this section of the Constitution.

Section 3. Treatment of New States and Territories

1. New states may be admitted by the Congress into this Union; but no new state shall be formed or erected within the jurisdiction of any other state; nor any state be formed by the junction of two or more states, or parts of states, without the consent of the legislatures of the states concerned as well as of the Congress.

1. Congress may let new states become part of the United States. No new state can be formed from another state or by joining parts of other states, unless Congress and the legislatures of the states involved approve.

2. The Congress shall have power to dispose of and make all needful rules and regulations respecting the territory or other property belonging to the United States; and nothing in this Constitution shall be so construed as to prejudice any claims of the United States, or of any particular state.

2. Congress has the power to make all laws and rules over territories and government properties of the United States.

Section 4. Guarantees to the States

The United States shall guarantee to every state in this Union a republican form of government, and shall protect each of them against invasion; and on application of the legislature, or of the executive (when the legislature cannot be convened) against domestic violence.

The federal government guarantees that the people of each state have the right to elect their leaders. The federal government also promises to protect each state from invasion, rebellion, and violent disorders.

Article 5. Amending the Constitution

The Congress, whenever two thirds of both houses shall deem it necessary, shall propose amendments to this

There are two ways to make amendments, or changes, to the

Constitution, or, on the application of the legislatures of two thirds of the several states, shall call a convention for proposing amendments, which, in either case, shall be valid to all intents and purposes, as part of this Constitution, when ratified by the legislatures of three fourths of the several states, or by conventions in three fourths thereof, as the one or the other mode of ratification may be proposed by the Congress; provided that ~~no amendment which may be made prior to the year one thousand eight hundred and eight shall in any manner affect the first and fourth clauses in the Ninth Section of the First Article; and that~~ no state, without its consent, shall be deprived of its equal suffrage in the Senate.

Constitution: two thirds of each branch of Congress can suggest an amendment; or, two thirds of the state legislatures can call a convention to suggest an amendment. Once the amendment has been suggested, three fourths of the state legislatures or three fourths of special state conventions must approve the amendment for it to become part of the Constitution. No state can be denied its equal vote in the Senate without its approval. No amendment could be made before 1808 that affected either the slave trade or certain direct taxes.

Article 6. Debts, Federal Supremacy, Oaths of Office

Section 1. Prior Debts of the United States

1. All debts contracted and engagements entered into, before the adoption of this Constitution, shall be as valid against the United States under this Constitution, as under the Confederation.

The United States government promises to pay back all debts and honor all agreements made by the government under the Articles of Confederation.

Section 2. The Supreme Law of the Land

This Constitution, and the laws of the United States which shall be made in pursuance thereof; and all treaties made, or which shall be made, under the authority of the United States, shall be the supreme law of the land; and the judges in every state shall be bound thereby, anything in the constitution or laws of any state to the contrary notwithstanding.

The Constitution and all the laws and treaties made under it are the supreme, or highest, law in the United States. If state or local laws disagree with federal law, the federal law must be obeyed. All judges must follow this rule.

Section 3. Oaths of Office

The Senators and Representatives before mentioned, and the members of the several state legislatures, and all executive and judicial officers, both of the United States and of the several states, shall be bound by oath or affirmation, to support this Constitution; but no religious test shall ever be required as a qualification to any office or public trust under the United States.

All officials of the federal and state governments must promise to support the Constitution. A person's religion may never be used to qualify or disqualify a person from holding federal office.

Article 7. Ratification of the Constitution

The ratification of the conventions of nine states, shall be sufficient for the establishment of this Constitution between the states so ratifying the same.

The Constitution will become law when special conventions in 9 (of the 13 original) states approve it.

Done in convention by the unanimous consent of the States present the Seventeenth day of September in the year of our Lord one thousand seven hundred and eighty seven, and of the Independence of the United States of America the Twelfth.

This Constitution is completed by the agreement of everyone at this convention on September 17, 1787, in the 12th year of the independence of the United States of America.

In witness whereof we have hereunto subscribed our names.

The people present have signed their names below.

George Washington, President and deputy from Virginia

DELAWARE
George Read
Gunning Bedford, Jr.
John Dickinson
Richard Bassett
Jacob Broom

MARYLAND
James McHenry
Daniel of St. Thomas Jenifer
Daniel Carroll

VIRGINIA
John Blair
James Madison, Jr.

NORTH CAROLINA
William Blount
Richard Dobbs Spaight
Hugh Williamson

SOUTH CAROLINA
John Rutledge
Charles Cotesworth Pinckney
Charles Pinckney
Pierce Butler

GEORGIA
William Few
Abraham Baldwin

NEW HAMPSHIRE
John Langdon
Nicholas Gilman

MASSACHUSETTS
Nathaniel Gorham
Rufus King

CONNECTICUT
William Samuel Johnson
Roger Sherman

NEW YORK
Alexander Hamilton

NEW JERSEY
William Livingston
David Brearley
William Paterson
Jonathan Dayton

PENNSYLVANIA
Benjamin Franklin
Thomas Mifflin
Robert Morris
George Clymer
Thomas FitzSimons
Jared Ingersoll
James Wilson
Gouverneur Morris

Attest: William Jackson, Secretary.

Amendments to the Constitution
Amendment 1. Freedom of Religion, Speech, Press, Assembly, and Petition (1791)

Congress shall make no law respecting an establishment of religion, or prohibiting the free exercise thereof; or abridging the freedom of speech, or of the press; or the right of the people peaceably to assemble, and to petition the government for a redress of grievances.

The first ten amendments to the Constitution ensure basic freedoms and are known as the Bill of Rights. Under the First Amendment, Congress cannot make laws:

1) setting up an official religion;
2) preventing people from practicing their religion;
3) stopping people or the press from saying what they want;
4) preventing people from gathering peacefully and asking the government to listen to their complaints and to correct problems.

Amendment 2. Right to Keep Weapons (1791)

A well-regulated militia, being necessary to the security of a free state, the right of the people to keep and bear arms shall not be infringed.

People have the right to keep weapons and be part of the state militia (today the National Guard).

Amendment 3. Protection Against Quartering Soldiers (1791)

No soldier shall, in time of peace, be quartered in any house, without the consent of the owner, nor in time of war, but in a manner to be prescribed by law.

During peacetime, people cannot be forced to quarter, or house and feed, soldiers in their homes. During time of war, Congress may set other rules.

Amendment 4. Freedom from Unreasonable Search and Seizure (1791)

The right of the people to be secure in their persons, houses, papers, and effects, against unreasonable searches and seizures, shall not be violated, and no warrants shall issue, but upon probable cause, supported by oath or affirmation, and particularly describing the place to be searched, and the persons or things to be seized.

People are protected against unreasonable arrests and searches of their homes and property. To search a person's home or property, the government must get a search warrant, or special approval, describing exactly what place is to be searched and what items are expected to be found.

Amendment 5. Rights of Persons Accused of a Crime (1791)

No person shall be held to answer for a capital, or otherwise infamous, crime, unless on a presentment or indictment of a grand jury, except in cases arising in the land or naval forces, or in the militia, when in actual service in time of war or public danger; nor shall any person be subject for the same offense to be twice put in jeopardy of life or limb; nor shall be compelled in any criminal case to be a witness against himself, nor be deprived of life, liberty, or property, without due process of law; nor shall private property be taken for public use, without just compensation.

A person cannot be charged with a serious crime unless a grand jury, or a group of citizens appointed to study criminal evidence, decides that a good reason exists to put the person on trial. (The only exceptions are cases involving people in the armed forces.) A person judged innocent by a court of law cannot be put on trial again for the same crime. People on trial cannot be forced to testify, or speak in court, against themselves. A person cannot have life, liberty, or property taken away unless fairly decided by a court of law. If the government takes away property for public use, a fair price must be paid the owner.

Amendment 6. Right to a Jury Trial in Criminal Cases (1791)

In all criminal prosecutions, the accused shall enjoy the right to a speedy and public trial, by an impartial jury of the state and district wherein the crime shall have been committed, which district shall have been previously ascertained by law, and to be informed of the nature and cause of the accusation; to be confronted with the witnesses against him; to have compulsory process for obtaining witnesses in his favor, and to have the assistance of counsel for his defense.

In all criminal cases, a person accused of a crime has the right to a fast, public trial by a fair jury in the place where the crime took place. All persons accused of a crime have the right to:
1) know the charges against them;
2) hear the evidence and witnesses against them;
3) call witnesses in their defense;
4) have a lawyer.

Amendment 7. Right to Jury Trial in Civil Cases (1791)

In suits at common law, where the value in controversy shall exceed twenty dollars, the right of trial by jury shall be preserved, and no fact tried by a jury shall be otherwise re-examined in any court of the United States than according to the rules of the common law.

A person has the right to a trial by jury in civil, or noncriminal, cases involving more than $20.

Amendment 8. Protection from Unfair Fines and Punishment (1791)

Excessive bail shall not be required, nor excessive fines imposed, nor cruel and unusual punishments inflicted.

The government cannot require very high bail, or deposit of money, from a person accused of a crime. People convicted of crimes cannot be fined an unfairly high amount. Nor can they be punished in a cruel or unusual way.

Amendment 9. Other Rights of the People (1791)

The enumeration in the Constitution, of certain rights, shall not be construed to deny or disparage others retained by the people.

The rights of the people are not limited to those stated in the Constitution.

Amendment 10. Powers of the States and the People (1791)

The powers not delegated to the United States by the Constitution, nor prohibited by it to the states, are reserved to the states respectively, or to the people.

Powers not granted to the United States government and not forbidden to the states are left to the states or to the people.

Amendment 11. Limiting Law Cases Against States (1798)

The judicial power of the United States shall not be construed to extend to any suit in law or equity, commenced or prosecuted against one of the United States, by citizens of another state, or by citizens or subjects of any foreign state.

A state government cannot be sued in a federal court by people of another state or by people from a foreign country.

Amendment 12. Election of President and Vice President (1804)

The electors shall meet in their respective states, and vote by ballot for President and Vice President, one of whom, at least, shall not be an inhabitant of the same state with themselves; they shall name in their ballots the person voted for as President, and in distinct ballots the person voted for as Vice President, and they shall make distinct lists of all persons voted for as President, and of all persons voted for as Vice President, and of the number of votes for each, which lists they shall sign and certify, and transmit, sealed, to the seat of government of the United States, directed to the President of the Senate; the President of the Senate shall, in the presence of the Senate and House of Representatives, open all the certificates and the votes shall then be counted; the person having the greatest number of votes for President shall be the President, if such number be a majority of the whole number of electors appointed; and if no person have such majority, then from the persons having the highest numbers not exceeding three on the list of those voted for as President, the House of Representatives shall choose immediately, by ballot, the President. But in choosing the President, the votes shall be taken by states, the representation from each state having one vote; a quorum for this purpose shall consist of a member or members from two thirds of the states, and a majority of all the states shall be necessary to a choice. And if the House of Representatives shall not choose a President whenever the right of choice shall devolve upon them, before the fourth day of March next following, then the Vice President

This amendment changed the method of choosing a President and Vice President. This method is called the Electoral College. The main change caused by this amendment is that candidates for President and Vice President now run for office together, and each elector casts only one vote. Before, candidates for President and Vice President ran for office separately, and each elector cast two votes. Under the Electoral College, people called electors meet in their home states and vote for President and Vice President. Electors choose one person for President and a different person for Vice President. (One of the people voted for must be from a different state than the elector.) These electoral votes are then sent to the United States Senate where all the electoral votes for President are counted. The person who receives more than half the electoral votes for President is elected President. The person who receives more than half the electoral votes for Vice President is elected Vice President. If no person receives more than half the electoral votes for President, the House of Representatives chooses the President. A list of the top three vote-getters is sent to the House of Representatives. From this list, the Representatives vote for President with each state entitled to one vote. The person who receives more than half the votes of the states in the

~~shall act as President, as in the case of the death or other constitutional disability of the President.~~ The person having the greatest number of votes as Vice President, shall be the Vice President, if such number be a majority of the whole number of electors appointed, and if no person have a majority, then from the two highest numbers on the list, the Senate shall choose the Vice President; a quorum for the purpose shall consist of two thirds of the whole number of Senators, and a majority of the whole number shall be necessary to a choice. But no person constitutionally ineligible to the office of President shall be eligible to that of Vice President of the United States.

House of Representatives is elected President. If no person receives more than half the vote, the Representatives vote again. If the Representatives fail to elect a President by March 4 (later changed to January 20), the Vice President serves as President. If no person receives at least half the electoral votes for Vice President, no one becomes Vice President and a list of the top two vote-getters is sent to the Senate. From this list, the Senators then vote for Vice President, with each Senator entitled to one vote. The person who receives more than half the votes in the Senate becomes Vice President. Qualifications for the office of Vice President are the same as those of President.

Amendment 13. Slavery Outlawed (1865)

Section 1. Abolition of Slavery

Neither slavery nor involuntary servitude, except as a punishment for crime whereof the party shall have been duly convicted, shall exist within the United States, or any place subject to their jurisdiction.

Slavery is outlawed in the United States.

Section 2. Enforcement

Congress shall have power to enforce this article by appropriate legislation.

Congress can pass any laws necessary to carry out this amendment.

Amendment 14. Rights of Citizens (1868)

Section 1. Citizenship

All persons born or naturalized in the United States and subject to the jurisdiction thereof, are citizens of the United States and of the state wherein they reside. No state shall make or enforce any law which shall abridge the privileges or immunities of citizens of the United States; nor shall any state deprive any person of life, liberty, or property, without due process of law; nor deny to any person within its jurisdiction the equal protection of the laws.

All people born in or made citizens by the United States are citizens of both the United States and the state in which they live. No state can deny any citizen the basic rights outlined in the 5th Amendment. All states must treat people equally under the law. This amendment made formerly enslaved people citizens of both the United States and the states in which they lived.

Section 2. Representation in Congress

Representatives shall be apportioned among the several states according to their respective numbers, counting the whole number of persons in each state, ~~excluding Indians not taxed.~~ But when the right to vote at any election for the choice of electors for President and Vice President of the United States, Representatives in Congress, the executive and judicial officers of a state, or the members of the legislature thereof, is denied to any of the ~~male~~ inhabitants of such state, being ~~twenty-one years of age and~~

The number of a state's Representatives in Congress can be lowered if the state prevents qualified citizens from voting. This section aimed to force states in the South to allow African Americans to vote.

69

citizens of the United States, or in any way abridged, except for participation in rebellion, or other crime, the basis of representation therein shall be reduced in the proportion which the number of such ~~male~~ citizens shall bear to the whole number of ~~male~~ citizens ~~twenty-one years of age~~ in such state.

Section 3. Penalties for Confederate Leaders

No person shall be a Senator or Representative in Congress, or elector of President and Vice President, or hold any office, civil or military, under the United States, or under any state, who, having previously taken an oath, as a member of Congress, or as an officer of the United States, or as a member of any state legislature, or as an executive or judicial officer of any state, to support the Constitution of the United States, shall have engaged in insurrection or rebellion against the same, or given aid or comfort to the enemies thereof. But Congress may, by vote of two thirds of each house, remove such disability.

Any official of the federal or state governments who took part in the Civil War against the United States cannot again hold any federal or state office. But Congress can remove this restriction by a two-thirds vote.

Section 4. Responsibility for Public Debt

The validity of the public debt of the United States, authorized by law, including debts incurred for payment of pensions and bounties for services in suppressing insurrection or rebellion, shall not be questioned. But neither the United States nor any state shall assume or pay any debt or obligation incurred in aid of insurrection or rebellion against the United States ~~or any claim for the loss or emancipation of any slave;~~ but all such debts, obligations, and claims shall be held illegal and void.

All money borrowed by the United States government to fight the Civil War is to be paid back. No debts owed to the Confederate states or to the Confederate government to pay for the Civil War are to be paid back by the federal or state governments. No money would be paid to anyone for the loss of people they once held in slavery.

Section 5. Enforcement

The Congress shall have power to enforce, by appropriate legislation, the provisions of this article.

Congress can pass any laws necessary to carry out this amendment.

Amendment 15. Voting Rights (1870)

Section 1. Black Suffrage

The right of citizens of the United States to vote shall not be denied or abridged by the United States or any state on account of race, color, or previous condition of servitude.

No federal or state government can prevent people from voting because of their race, color, or because they were once enslaved. This amendment aimed to give black men the right to vote.

Section 2. Enforcement

The Congress shall have power to enforce this article by appropriate legislation.

Congress can pass any laws necessary to carry out this amendment.

Amendment 16. Income Tax (1913)

The Congress shall have the power to lay and collect taxes on incomes, from whatever source derived, without apportionment among the several states, and without regard to any census or enumeration.

Congress has the power to collect an income tax regardless of the population of any state.

Amendment 17. Direct Election of Senators (1913)

Section 1. Method of Election

The Senate of the United States shall be composed of two Senators from each state, elected by the people thereof, for six years; and each Senator shall have one vote. The electors in each state shall have the qualifications requisite for electors of the most numerous branch of the state legislatures.

Senators are to be elected by the voters of each state. This amendment changed the method by which state legislatures elected Senators as outlined in Article 1, Section 3, Clause 1 of the Constitution.

Section 2. Vacancies

When vacancies happen in the representation of any state in the Senate, the executive authority of such state shall issue writs of election to fill such vacancies: *provided* that the legislature of any state may empower the executive thereof to make temporary appointments until the people fill the vacancies by election as the legislature may direct.

Special elections can be held to fill empty seats in the Senate. State legislatures may permit the governor to name a person to fill an empty seat for a short time until the next election.

Section 3. Those Elected under Previous Rules

~~This amendment shall not be so construed as to affect the election or term of any Senator chosen before it becomes valid as part of the Constitution.~~

This amendment does not affect the election or term of office of any Senator in office before the amendment becomes part of the Constitution.

Amendment 18. Prohibition of Alcoholic Drinks (1919)

~~After one year from the ratification of this article the manufacture, sale, or transportation of intoxicating liquors within, the importation thereof into, or the exportation thereof from, the United States and all territory subject to the jurisdiction thereof for beverage purposes is hereby prohibited.~~

Making, selling, or transporting alcoholic, or intoxicating, drinks in the United States is illegal. This amendment was called the Prohibition Amendment because it prohibited, or banned, the use of alcohol.

Section 2. Enforcement

~~The Congress and the several states shall have concurrent power to enforce this article by appropriate legislation.~~

Both Congress and the states can pass any laws necessary to carry out this amendment.

Section 3. Time Limit on Ratification

~~This article shall be inoperative unless it shall have been ratified as an amendment to the Constitution by the legislatures of the several states, as provided in the Constitution, within seven years from the date of the submission hereof to the states by the Congress.~~

This amendment is to become part of the Constitution only if it is approved within seven years. It was repealed, or canceled, by the 21st Amendment.

Amendment 19. Women's Right to Vote (1920)

Section 1. Women Made Voters

The right of citizens of the United States to vote shall not be denied or abridged by the United States or by any state on account of sex.

No federal or state government can prevent people from voting because of their sex. This amendment grants women the right to vote.

71

Section 2. Enforcement

Congress shall have power to enforce this article by appropriate legislation.

Congress can pass any laws necessary to carry out this amendment.

Amendment 20. Terms of Office (1933)

Section 1. Start of Terms of Office

The terms of the President and Vice President shall end at noon on the 20th day of January, and the terms of Senators and Representatives at noon on the 3rd day of January, of the years in which such terms would have ended if this article had not been ratified; and the terms of their successors shall then begin.

The terms of office for the President and Vice President begin on January 20. This date is called Inauguration Day. The terms of office for members of Congress begin on January 3. Originally their terms began on March 4.

Section 2. Meeting Time of Congress

The Congress shall assemble at least once in every year, and such meeting shall begin at noon on the 3rd day of January, unless they shall by law appoint a different day.

Congress must meet at least once a year beginning at noon on January 3. However, Congress may pick a different day to first meet.

Section 3. Providing for a Successor of the President-Elect

If at the time fixed for the beginning of the term of the President, the President-elect shall have died, the Vice President-elect shall become President. If a President shall not have been chosen before the time fixed for the beginning of his term, or if the President-elect shall have failed to qualify, then the Vice President-elect shall act as President until a President shall have qualified; and the Congress may by law provide for the case wherein neither a President-elect nor a Vice President-elect shall have qualified, declaring who shall then act as President, or the manner in which one who is to act shall be selected, and such person shall act accordingly until a President or Vice President shall have qualified.

If the person elected President dies before taking office, the Vice President becomes President. If no person is elected President before the term of office begins, or if the person elected President is not qualified to serve, then the Vice President acts as President until a qualified President is chosen. If both the person elected President and the person elected Vice President are disqualified from holding office, Congress selects the President.

Section 4. Elections Decided by Congress

The Congress may by law provide for the case of the death of any of the persons from whom the House of Representatives may choose a President whenever the right of choice shall have devolved upon them, and for the case of the death of any of the persons from whom the Senate may choose a Vice President whenever the right of choice shall have devolved upon them.

If, during the time Congress is selecting the President and Vice President, one of these two people dies, Congress may pass a law determining how to choose the President and Vice President.

Section 5. Effective Date

~~Sections 1 and 2 shall take effect on the 15th day of October following the ratification of this article.~~

Sections 1 and 2 of this amendment take effect on the 15th day of October after this amendment becomes part of the Constitution.

Section 6. Time Limit on Ratification

~~This article shall be inoperative unless it shall have been ratified as an amendment to the Constitution by the~~

This amendment is to become part of the Constitution only if it is approved by

~~legislatures of three fourths of the several states within seven years from the date of its submission.~~

three fourths of the state legislatures within seven years.

Amendment 21. Repeal of Prohibition (1933)

Section 1. Prohibition Ends

The Eighteenth article of amendment to the Constitution of the United States is hereby repealed.

The 18th Amendment is repealed, or no longer in effect.

Section 2. Protection of State and Local Prohibition Laws

The transportation or importation into any state, territory, or possession of the United States for delivery or use therein of intoxicating liquors, in violation of the laws thereof, is hereby prohibited.

Any state or territory of the United States may pass prohibition laws.

Section 3. Time Limit on Ratification

~~This article shall be inoperative unless it shall have been ratified as an amendment to the Constitution by conventions in the several states, as provided in the Constitution, within seven years from the date of the submission hereof to the states by the Congress.~~

This amendment is to become part of the Constitution only if state conventions approve it within seven years.

Amendment 22. President Limited to Two Terms (1951)

Section 1. Limit on Number of Terms

No person shall be elected to the office of the President more than twice, and no person who has held the office of President, or acted as President, for more than two years of a term to which some other person was elected President shall be elected to the office of the President more than once. ~~But this Article shall not apply to any person holding the office of President when this Article was proposed by the Congress, and shall not prevent any person who may be holding the office of President, or acting as President, during the term within which this Article becomes operative from holding the office of President or acting as President during the remainder or such term.~~

No person can be elected more than two times to the office of President. No person can be elected more than once to the office of President who has served more than two years of another President's term. This amendment does not affect any President who is in office when this amendment becomes part of the Constitution.

Section 2. Time Limit on Ratification

~~This Article shall be inoperative unless it shall have been ratified as an amendment to the Constitution by the legislatures of three fourths of the several states within seven years from the date of its submission to the states by the Congress.~~

This amendment is to become part of the Constitution only if three fourths of the state legislatures approve it within seven years.

Amendment 23. Presidential Elections for the District of Columbia (1961)

Section 1. Presidential Electors in the District of Columbia

The District constituting the seat of Government of the United States shall appoint in such manner as the Congress may direct: A number of electors of President and Vice President equal to the whole number of Senators and Representatives in Congress to which the District would be entitled if it were a State, but in no event more than the least populous State; they shall be in addition to those appointed by the States, but they shall be considered, for the purposes of the election of President and Vice President, to be electors appointed by a State; and they shall meet in the District and perform such duties as provided by the twelfth article of amendment.

People living in Washington, D.C. (the District of Columbia), have the right to vote in Presidential elections. The number of electoral votes of Washington, D.C., can never be more than the number of electoral votes of the state with the fewest number of people.

Section 2. Enforcement

The Congress shall have power to enforce this article by appropriate legislation.

Congress can pass any laws necessary to carry out this amendment.

Amendment 24. Poll Tax Ended (1964)

Section 1. Poll Taxes Not Allowed in Federal Elections

The right of citizens of the United States to vote in any primary or other election for President or Vice President, for electors for President or Vice President, or for Senator or Representative in Congress, shall not be denied or abridged by the United States or any state by reason of failure to pay any poll tax or other tax.

No person can be prevented from voting in a federal election for failing to pay a poll tax or any other kind of tax.

Section 2. Enforcement

The Congress shall have the power to enforce this article by appropriate legislation.

Congress can pass any laws necessary to carry out this amendment.

Amendment 25. Presidential Succession (1967)

Section 1. Filling the Vacant Office of President

In case of the removal of the President from office or of his death or resignation, the Vice President shall become President.

If the President dies, resigns, or is removed from office, the Vice President becomes President.

Section 2. Filling the Vacant Office of Vice President

Whenever there is a vacancy in the office of the Vice President, the President shall nominate a Vice President who shall take the office upon confirmation by a majority vote of both houses of Congress.

If the office of Vice President becomes empty, the President names a new Vice President, with the approval of both houses of Congress.

Section 3. Disability of the President

Whenever the President transmits to the President pro tempore of the Senate and the Speaker of the House of Representatives his written declaration that he is unable to discharge the powers and duties of his office, and until he transmits to them a written declaration to the contrary, such

If the President is unable to carry out the powers and duties of office, the President may inform the leaders of Congress. The Vice President then serves as Acting President. The President may return to office only when he or she

powers and duties shall be discharged by the Vice President as Acting President.

Section 4. When Congress Designates an Acting President

Whenever the Vice President and a majority of either the principal officers of the executive departments or of such other body as Congress may by law provide, transmit to the President pro tempore of the Senate and the Speaker of the House of Representatives their written declaration that the President is unable to discharge the powers and duties of his office, the Vice President shall immediately assume the powers and duties of the office as Acting President. Thereafter, when the President transmits to the President pro tempore of the Senate and the Speaker of the House of Representatives his written declaration that no inability exists, he shall resume the powers and duties of his office unless the Vice President and a majority of either the principal officers of the executive departments or of such other body as Congress may by law provide, transmit within four days to the President pro tempore of the Senate and the Speaker of the House of Representatives their written declaration that the President is unable to discharge the powers and duties of his office. Thereupon Congress shall decide the issue, assembling within 48 hours for that purpose if not in session. If the Congress, within 21 days after receipt of the latter written declaration, or, if Congress is not in session, within 21 days after Congress is required to assemble, determines by two thirds vote of both houses that the President is unable to discharge the powers and duties of his office, the Vice President shall continue to discharge the same as Acting President; otherwise, the President shall assume the powers and duties of his office.

Amendment 26.   Vote for Eighteen-Year-Olds (1971)

Section 1. Voting Age

The right of citizens of the United States, who are 18 years of age or older, to vote shall not be denied or abridged by the United States or any state on account of age.

Section 2. Enforcement

The Congress shall have the power to enforce this article by appropriate legislation.

Amendment 27.   Limits on Salary Changes (1992)

No law, varying the compensation for the services of the Senators and Representatives, shall take effect, until an election of Representatives shall have intervened.

informs the leaders of Congress that he or she can again carry out the powers and duties of office.

If the Vice President and at least half the Cabinet, or President's top advisers (or a special committee), inform the leaders of Congress that the President cannot carry out the powers and duties of office, the Vice President immediately becomes Acting President. If the President informs the leaders of Congress that he or she is able to serve as President, he or she again becomes President. But if, within four days, the Vice President and at least half the Cabinet (or a special committee) inform the leaders of Congress that the President still cannot carry out the powers and duties of office, the President does not return to office. Instead, Congress must meet within 48 hours. In the next 21 days, Congress must decide if the President is able to carry out the powers and duties of office. If two thirds of both houses of Congress vote that the President is unable to serve, the President is removed from office and the Vice President becomes Acting President. If two thirds do not vote this way, the President stays in office.

No federal or state government can prevent people 18 years of age or older from voting because of their age. This amendment grants people who are at least 18 years old the right to vote.

Congress can pass any laws necessary to carry out this amendment.

No law changing the salaries of members of Congress can take effect until after the next election of the House of Representatives.

Escape from Washington

by Dolley Madison, 1814

On August 23, 1814, the two-year-old War of 1812 moved onto the very doorstep of the White House, which was then known as the President's House. Residents of the city began fleeing as British troops marched toward the capital. While President James Madison (1751-1836) rode out to support the American troops waiting to fight the British, his wife Dolley Madison (1768-1849) remained in the President's House. She refused to leave until she received further instructions from her husband. During these long, tense hours spent waiting, Dolley Madison wrote the following letter to her sister, describing the danger and confusion around her. What does Dolley Madison consider her main duties in this time of danger?

Dear Sister,

Tuesday, August 23, 1814

My husband left me yesterday morning to join **General Winder**. He inquired anxiously whether I had courage or firmness to remain in the President's house until his return . . . and on my assurance that I had no fear but for him, and the success of our army, he left, **beseeching** me to take care of myself, and of the Cabinet papers, public and private. I have since received two **despatches** from him, written with a pencil. The last is alarming, because he desires I should be ready at a moment's warning to enter my carriage, and leave the city; that the enemy seemed stronger than had at first been reported, and it might happen that they would reach the city with the intention of destroying it. I am accordingly ready; I have pressed as many Cabinet papers into trunks as to fill one carriage; our private property must be **sacrificed**, as it is impossible to **procure** wagons for its transportation. I am determined not to go myself until I see Mr. Madison safe, so that he can accompany me, as I hear of much hostility towards him. **Disaffection** stalks around us. My friends and acquaintances are all gone. . . .

Wednesday Morning, August 24, 1814, twelve o'clock

Since sunrise I have been turning my spy-glass in every direction, and watching with unwearied anxiety, hoping to discover the approach of my dear husband and his friends; but, alas! I can **descry** only groups of military, wandering in all

General Winder: commander of troops outside Washington, D.C.

beseeching: begging

despatches: reports

sacrificed: given up

procure: get

disaffection: disloyalty

descry: spot

directions, as if there was a lack of **arms**, or of spirit to fight for their own fireside.

Three o'clock

Will you believe it, my sister? we have had a battle, or skirmish, near **Bladensburg**, and here I am still, within sound of the cannon! Mr. Madison comes not. May God protect us! Two messengers, covered with dust, come to bid me fly; but here I mean to wait for him. . . . At this late hour a wagon has been procured, and I have had it filled with **plate** and the most valuable **portable** articles, belonging to the house. Whether it will reach its destination . . . or fall into the hands of British soldiery, events must determine. Our kind friend, Mr. Carroll, has come to hasten my departure, and [is] in a very bad **humor** with me, because I insist on waiting until the large picture of General Washington is **secured**, and it requires to be unscrewed from the wall. This process was found too **tedious** for these **perilous** moments; I have ordered the frame to be broken, and the canvas taken out. It is done! and the precious portrait [is now] placed . . . for safe keeping. And now, dear sister, I must leave this house, or the retreating army will make me a prisoner in it by filling up the road I am directed to take. When I shall again write to you, or where I shall be tomorrow, I cannot tell!

arms: weapons

Bladensburg: Maryland town bordering Washington, D.C.

plate: costly dishes and silverware
portable: movable

humor: mood
secured: safe

tedious: long and difficult
perilous: dangerous

A few hours after Dolley Madison left Washington, D.C., on August 24, 1814, British soldiers marched in and set fire to the President's House and the rest of the city. Light from the enormous blaze could be seen 40 miles (64 km) away. Dolley Madison, dressed in the disguise of a poor country woman, escaped safely through the burning city to nearby Virginia. Several days later she returned to Washington and found much of the capital in ruins. Because the President's House had burned down, Dolley Madison and her husband had to live in a different house for the next two and a half years. When the President's House was rebuilt several years later, its outside walls were painted white. This is probably why it became known as the White House.

Source: *Memoirs and Letters of Dolley Madison, Wife of James Madison, President of the United States.* Boston: Houghton, Mifflin and Company, 1887.

Letter from a Cherokee Girl

by Jane Bushyhead, 1838

In 1830 Congress passed the Indian Removal Act. This law ordered the removal of Native Americans from the southeastern United States where they had lived for hundreds of years. The Cherokee, the Seminole, and other Indian groups fought this removal. But in 1838, the United States army began preparing to remove Native Americans by force to what is today Oklahoma. Jane Bushyhead was a Cherokee girl living in Red Clay, the traditional capital of the Cherokee Nation in Tennessee. Her father, Reverend Jesse Bushyhead, had been in Florida to help the Seminole and was now in Washington, D.C., fighting for the Cherokee. Jane wrote the following letter to her friend Martha Thompson, a white classmate at Kingston Academy in Marysville, Tennessee, in 1838. How does Jane feel about being forced to move?

Red Clay, Cherokee Nation
March 10, 1838

Beloved Martha,

I have delayed writing to you so long I expect you have **relinquished** all thought of receiving anything from me. But my Dear Martha I have not forgotten my promise. I have often wished to enjoy your company once more but it is very uncertain whether I shall ever again have that pleasure. If we Cherokees are to be driven to the west by the cruel hand of oppression to seek a home in the west it will be impossible [to see you again]. My father is now in **Washington City**. He was one of the delegates who went to Florida last October. We do not know when he will return. Not long [ago] **Mr. Stephen Foreman** received a letter from father. He was absent when the letter came home and before he arrived the troops had been there and taken it to... **General [Nathaniel] Smith** and he handed it round for all to read. It is thus all our rights are invaded....

It will not be long before our next vacation. Then we expect to go home. Perhaps it may be the last time we shall have the privilege of attending school in this nation. But we are not certain.

If we should [be removed to Oklahoma] I should still hope to continue our correspondence. Please ... present my best respects to your father & family ... write ... me in love to you.

Your Sincere friend,

Jane Bushyhead

relinquished: given up

Washington City: Washington, D.C.

Mr. Stephen Foreman: a friend of the Bushyheads

General Nathaniel Smith: director of Cherokee removal for the United States government

Soon after Jane Bushyhead wrote this letter, the United States forced her, her family, and 15,000 other Cherokee to leave their homeland. For a description of their forced journey west, read the next document on pages 79-80.

Source: *Journal of Cherokee Studies*, Volume 3, Summer 1978.

The Removal of the Cherokee

by John G. Burnett, 1890

During the 1830s many Cherokee and other Native Americans fought the Indian Removal Act, which ordered them to leave their homes in the southeastern United States. The Cherokee, who had their own constitution and government, took their case to the Supreme Court. The Court supported their right to the land, but President Andrew Jackson and his successor, Martin Van Buren, refused to follow the Court's decision. In 1838 the United States army began to remove more than 15,000 Cherokee—including Jane Bushyhead, whom you read about on page 78—from their homeland by force. One of the soldiers in the army was John G. Burnett, a 27-year-old native of Tennessee who had grown up among the Cherokee. Over 50 years later, in 1890, Burnett wrote down his memories of this forced 800-mile (1287-km) march of the Cherokee, which came to be known as the "Trail of Tears." As you read this excerpt, think about the cruelties of this march and why Burnett might have written down what happened.

In the year of 1828, a little Indian boy living on Ward creek had sold a Gold nugget to a white trader, and that nugget sealed the doom of the Cherokees. In a short time the country was over run with armed **brigands** claiming to be Government Agents, who paid no attention to the rights of the Indians who were the legal possessors of the country. Crimes were committed that were a disgrace to civilization. Men were shot in cold blood, lands were **confiscated.** Homes were burned and the inhabitants driven out by these Gold hungry brigands. . . .

brigands: bandits

confiscated: taken away

Chief John Ross sent . . . an **envoy** to plead with President Jackson for protection for his people, but Jackson's manner was cold and indifferent. . . . "Sir [Jackson said] your audience is ended, there is nothing I can do for you." The doom of the Cherokee was sealed, Washington, D.C. had decreed that they must be driven West, and their lands given to the white man, and in May 1838 an Army of four thousand regulars, and three thousand volunteer soldiers . . . marched into the Indian country and wrote the blackest chapter on the pages of American History. . . .

Chief John Ross: leader of the Cherokee
envoy: representative

The removal of the Cherokee Indians from their life long homes in the year of 1838 found me . . . a Private soldier in the American Army. Being acquainted with many of the Indians and able to **fluently** speak their language, I was sent as interpreter into the **Smoky Mountain Country** in May, 1838, and witnessed the execution of the most brutal order in the History of American Warfare. I saw the helpless Cherokees arrested and dragged from their homes, and

fluently: easily
Smoky Mountain Country: mountain region of Georgia, North Carolina, and Tennessee

79

driven at the **bayonet** point into the **stockades**. And in the chill of a drizzling rain on an October morning I saw them loaded like cattle or sheep into six hundred and forty-five wagons and started toward the west.

One can never forget the sadness and **solemnity** of that [October] morning [in 1838]. Chief John Ross led in prayer and when the bugle sounded and the wagons started rolling many of the children rose to their feet and waved their little hands good-by to their mountain homes, knowing they were leaving them forever. Many of these helpless people did not have blankets and many of them had been driven from home barefooted.

On the morning of November the 17th we encountered a terrific sleet and snow storm with freezing temperatures and from that day until we reached the end of the fateful journey on March the 26th 1839, the sufferings of the Cherokees were awful. The trail of the **exiles** was a trail of death. They had to sleep in the wagons and on the ground without fire. And I have known as many as twenty-two of them to die in one night of pneumonia due to ill treatment, cold, and exposure. Among this number was the . . . wife of Chief John Ross. This noble hearted woman died a **martyr** to childhood, giving her only blanket for the protection of a sick child. She rode thinly clad through a blinding sleet and snow storm, developed pneumonia and died in the still hours of a bleak winter night, with her head resting on Lieutenant Gregg's saddle blanket. . . .

I was on guard duty the night Mrs. Ross died. When **relieved** at midnight I did not **retire**, but remained around the wagon out of sympathy for Chief Ross, and at daylight was **detailed** by Captain McClellan to assist in the burial. . . . Her uncoffined body was buried in a shallow grave by the roadside far from her native mountain home, and the sorrowing **Cavalcade** moved on. . . .

The long painful journey to the west ended March 26th, 1839, with four-thousand silent graves reaching from the foothills of the Smoky Mountains to what is known as Indian territory in the West. And **covetousness** on the part of the white race was the cause of all that the Cherokees had to suffer. . . .

School children of today do not know that we are living on lands that were taken . . . at the bayonet point to satisfy the white man's greed for gold. . . . Let the Historian of a future day tell the sad story with its sighs, its tears and dying groans.

Not all the Cherokee made this tragic trip. A few hundred managed to hide in the mountains of North Carolina and escape removal from their land. Today their descendants are known as the Eastern Cherokee. Those who survived the Trail of Tears settled in present-day Oklahoma. There the Cherokee and other Native Americans set up new homes and governments based on written constitutions. White settlers, however, soon began taking these lands just as they had in the Southeast. In the late 1800s many of the same Cherokee and Native Americans would be forced out of Oklahoma.

Source: *Journal of Cherokee Studies*, Vol. 3, Summer 1978.

Margin glossary:

bayonet: steel blade on the tip of a rifle

stockades: military prisons

solemnity: seriousness

exiles: people forced from their country

martyr: person who suffers death for a cause

relieved: freed from duty

retire: go to bed

detailed: ordered

cavalcade: group of wagons

covetousness: greed, wanting another's possessions

ERIE CANAL

Traditional Song, 1800s

When the Erie Canal opened in 1825, it became one of the busiest transportation routes in the United States. The canal carried travelers and goods between Albany and Buffalo in New York State. As they labored, canal workers made up songs describing their lives, their jobs, and even the mules that towed the boats under very low bridges by walking on paths alongside the canal. What does the following song tell you about working on the Erie Canal?

I got a mule, her name is Sal, Fif-teen miles on the E-rie Ca-nal!__ She's a good old work-er and a good old pal, Fif-teen miles on the E-rie Ca-nal!__ We've hauled some barg-es in our day, Filled with lum-ber, coal and hay, And we know ev-'ry inch of the way From Al-ba-ny__ to__ Buf-fa-lo. Low bridge, ev-'ry-bod-y down, Low bridge, 'cause we're com-ing to a town; And you'll al-ways know your neigh-bor, You'll al-ways know your pal, If you ev-er nav-i-gat-ed on the E-rie Ca-nal.__

Source: *Music and You*. New York: Macmillan Publishing Company, 1988.

The Factory Bell

by an Unknown Factory Girl, 1844

The first large group of factory workers in the United States was made up of New England girls and women ranging in age from about 11 to 25. In the early and middle 1800s many left their small farms in the country for jobs in the mill towns. On the farm, the rising and setting of the sun and the changing of the seasons had determined which tasks people did each day. In the factory, however, all this changed. In mill towns across New England, daily life was suddenly shaped by clocks and bells that told workers when to wake, when to eat, when to work, and when to sleep. Look at the timetable of the Lowell Mills in Massachusetts printed on the next page. How might it have felt to live by such a strict schedule? To get an idea, read the poem below by an unknown factory girl. This poem first appeared on May 25, 1844, in the Factory Girl's Garland, *a mill workers' newspaper in Exeter, New Hampshire. Why do you think the poet wrote a poem about bells?*

Loud the morning bell is ringing,
   Up, up sleepers, haste away;
Yonder sits the redbreast singing,
   But to **list** we must not stay.

Not for us is morning breaking,
   Though we with **Aurora** rise;
Nor for us is Nature waking,
   All her smiles through earth and skies.

Sisters, haste, the bell is **tolling**,
   Soon will close the dreadful gate;
Then, alas! we must go strolling,
   Through the **counting-room**, too late.

Now the sun is upward climbing,
   And the breakfast hour has come;
Ding, dong, ding, the bell is chiming,
   Hasten, sisters, hasten home.

Quickly now we take our **ration**,
   For the bell will babble soon;
Each must hurry to her station,
   There to toil till weary noon.

Mid-day sun in heaven is shining,
   Merrily now the clear bell rings,
And the grateful hour of dining,
   To us weary sisters brings.

Now we give a welcome greeting,
   To these **viands** cooked so well;
Horrors! oh! not half done eating—
   Rattle, rattle goes the bell!

Sol behind the hills descended,
   Upward throws his ruby light;
Ding dong ding,—our toil is ended,
   Joyous bell, good night, good night.

list: listen
Aurora: dawn
tolling: ringing
counting-room: business room in the factory
ration: food
viands: meals
Sol: sun

TIME TABLE OF THE LOWELL MILLS,

Arranged to make the working time throughout the year average 11 hours per day.

TO TAKE EFFECT SEPTEMBER 21st., 1853.

The Standard time being that of the meridian of Lowell, as shown by the Regulator Clock of AMOS SANBORN, Post Office Corner, Central Street.

From March 20th to September 19th, inclusive.

COMMENCE WORK, at 6.30 A. M. LEAVE OFF WORK, at 6.30 P. M., except on Saturday Evenings.
BREAKFAST at 6 A. M. DINNER, at 12 M. Commence Work, after dinner, 12.45 P. M.

From September 20th to March 19th, inclusive.

COMMENCE WORK at 7.00 A. M. LEAVE OFF WORK, at 7.00 P. M., except on Saturday Evenings.
BREAKFAST at 6.30 A. M. DINNER, at 12.30 P.M. Commence Work, after dinner, 1.15 P. M.

BELLS.

From March 20th to September 19th, inclusive.

Morning Bells.	*Dinner Bells.*	*Evening Bells.*
First bell,..........4.30 A. M.	Ring out,.............12.00 M.	Ring out,............6.30 P. M.
Second, 5.30 A. M. ; Third, 6.20.	Ring in,...........12.35 P. M.	Except on Saturday Evenings.

From September 20th to March 19th, inclusive.

Morning Bells.	*Dinner Bells.*	*Evening Bells.*
First bell,..........5.00 A. M.	Ring out,..........12.30 P. M.	Ring out at...........7.00 P. M.
Second, 6.00 A. M. ; Third, 6.50.	Ring in,............1.05 P. M.	Except on Saturday Evenings.

SATURDAY EVENING BELLS.

During APRIL, MAY, JUNE, JULY, and AUGUST, Ring Out, at 6.00 P. M.
The remaining Saturday Evenings in the year, ring out as follows :

SEPTEMBER.	NOVEMBER.	JANUARY.
First Saturday, ring out 6.00 P. M.	Third Saturday ring out 4.00 P. M.	Third Saturday, ring out 4.25 P. M.
Second " " 5.45 "	Fourth " " 3.55 "	Fourth " " 4.35 "
Third " " 5.30 "		
Fourth " " 5.20 "	**DECEMBER.**	**FEBRUARY.**
	First Saturday, ring out 3.50 P. M.	First Saturday, ring out 4.45 P. M.
OCTOBER.	Second " " 3.55 "	Second " " 4.55 "
First Saturday, ring out 5.05 P. M.	Third " " 3.55 "	Third " " 5.00 "
Second " " 4.55 "	Fourth " " 4.00 "	Fourth " " 5.10 "
Third " " 4.45 "	Fifth " " 4.00 "	
Fourth " " 4.35 "		**MARCH.**
Fifth " " 4.25 "		First Saturday, ring out 5.25 P. M.
NOVEMBER.	**JANUARY.**	Second " " 5.30 "
First Saturday, ring out 4.15 P. M.	First Saturday, ring out 4.10 P. M.	Third " " 5.35 "
Second ". " 4.05 "	Second " " 4.15 "	Fourth " " 5.45 "

YARD GATES will be opened at the first stroke of the bells for entering or leaving the Mills.

SPEED GATES commence hoisting three minutes before commencing work.

During the 1800s factory towns like Lowell, Massachusetts, and Exeter, New Hampshire, began growing throughout the United States. More and more Americans began to live according to clocks, rather than the sun, as they took jobs in new factories and cities. Today it is hard for most Americans to think of living without clocks. How much does your own life revolve around clocks and bells? Imagine living without them. How would your life be different?

Source: *Factory Girl's Garland*, May 25, 1844, reprinted in Philip S. Foner, ed., *The Factory Girls*. Urbana, IL: University of Illinois Press, 1977.

Mexican Emancipation Proclamation

Vicente Guerrero, 1829

During the 1820s, United States citizens began settling in Texas—which was then part of Mexico—with enslaved African Americans. Mexico passed several laws limiting slavery but settlers ignored them. Then on September 15, 1829, Mexican President Vicente Guerrero (vē sän' tä ger e' rō, 1783-1831) issued an emancipation proclamation, or official order that ended slavery. Read the document in its original Spanish or in the English translation. In what ways does this proclamation remind you of the Declaration of Independence and the Petition for Freedom on pages 40-46? In what ways does it not?

El presidente de los Estados Unidos Mexicanos á los habitantes de la república, sabed:

Que deseando señalar en el año de 1829 el aniversario de la independencia con un acto de justicia y de beneficencia nacional . . . y que reintegre á una parte desgraciada de sus habitantes en los derechos sagrados que les dió naturaleza y protege la nación por leyes sabias y justas, . . . he venido en decretar:

1. Queda abolida la esclavitud en la república.

2. Son por consiguiente libres los que hasta hoy se habían considerado como esclavos.

3. Cuando las circunstancias del erario lo permitan se indemnizará á los propietarios de esclavos en los términos que dispusieren las leyes.

Y para que todo lo contenido en este decreto tenga su más cabal cumplimiento, mando se imprima, publique y circule á quienes corresponda.

Dado en el palacio federal de México á 15 de septiembre de 1829.

The President of the United States of Mexico to the inhabitants of the republic, know ye:

That desiring to celebrate in the year of 1829 the anniversary of our independence with an act of justice and national goodwill, . . . which might restore an unfortunate part of its inhabitants in the sacred rights which nature gave them, . . . I have thought it proper to order:

1st. Slavery is abolished [ended] in the republic.

2nd. Therefore, those who have been until now considered slaves are free.

3rd. When the circumstances of the treasury may permit, the owners of the slaves will be repaid in the manner that the laws may provide.

And in order that every part of this order may be fully obeyed, let it be printed, published, and circulated.

Given at the Federal Palace of Mexico, the 15th of September, 1829.

In issuing this Emancipation Proclamation in 1829, Mexico tried to end slavery before both Britain and the United States. The new settlers in Texas, however, refused to obey the proclamation, and they began to take steps to separate themselves from Mexico.

Source: *Memorias para la Historia de México Independente, 1822–1846*, Tomo II. México: Imprenta del Gobierna Federal en el Ex-Arzodispado, 1892.

Diary of an Overland Journey to California

by Sallie Hester, 1849

During the middle 1800s up to half a million people made the rugged overland journey to California and Oregon. Among them were 12-year-old Sallie Hester and her family from Indiana. Like many pioneers, Sallie kept a diary of her seven-month, westward journey across the continent in 1849. As you read excerpts of Sallie's diary, think of the adventures she experienced and the hardships she faced. What type of skills and personal qualities would it have taken to survive this journey?

Bloomington, Indiana, March 20, 1849. Our family, consisting of father, mother, two brothers and one sister, left this morning for that far and much talked of country, California. Our **train** numbered fifty wagons. The last hours were spent in bidding goodby to old friends. My mother is heartbroken over this separation of relatives and friends. . . . The last goodby has been said, the last glimpse of our old home on the hill, and wave of hand at the old **Academy** with a goodby to kind teachers and schoolmates, and we are off.

train: traveling group

academy: school

New Albany, March 24. This is my first experience of a big city. We have been several days reaching it on account of the terrible conditions of the roads. Our carriage **upset** at one place. All were thrown out but no one was hurt. My mother thought it a bad **omen** and wanted to give up the trip.

upset: overturned
omen: sign

March 26. Took the steamboat *Meteor* this evening for **St. Joe.** Now sailing on the broad Ohio [River], toward the far west.

St. Joe: St. Joseph, Missouri

St. Joe, April 27. Here we are at last, safe and sound, laying in supplies and waiting our turn to be ferried across the river. As far as the eye can reach, so great is the **emigration**, you see nothing but wagons. This town presents a striking appearance — a vast army on wheels — crowds of men, women, and lots of children, and last but not least the cattle and horses upon which our lives will depend.

emigration: number of people moving

May 21. Camped on the beautiful [**Big**] **Blue River**, 215 miles [346 km] from St. Joe, with plenty of wood and water and good grazing for cattle. . . . We had two deaths in our train within the past week of **cholera** — young men going west to seek their fortunes. We buried them on the banks of the Blue River, far from home and friends.

Big Blue River: river in southeastern Nebraska

cholera: a deadly disease

We are now in the Pawnee Nation. . . . When we camp at night we form a **corral** with our wagons and pitch our tents on the outside, and inside of this corral we drive our cattle, with guards stationed on the outside of the tents.

corral: circle

We have a cooking stove made of sheet iron, a **portable** table, tin plates and cups, cheap knives and forks (best ones packed away) and camp stools. We sleep in our wagons on feather beds. The men who drive for us sleep in the tent. We live on bacon, ham, rice, dried fruits, molasses, packed butter, bread, coffee, tea and milk as we have our own cows. Occasionally the men kill an antelope and then we have a feast; and sometimes we have fish on Sunday.

portable: movable

June 3. Our tent is now pitched on the beautiful **Platte River**, 315 miles [507 km] from St. Joe. The cholera is raging. A great many deaths. Graves everywhere. We [my family] are all in good health. **Game** is scarce; a few antelope in sight. Roads bad.

Platte River: river in central Nebraska

game: animals hunted for food

adobe: bricks made of dried earth

Fort Laramie, Wyoming, June 19. This fort is of **adobe**, enclosed with a high wall. The entrance is a hole in the wall just large enough for a person to crawl through. The impression you have on entering is that you are in a small town. Men are engaged in all kinds of business from blacksmith up. We camped a mile from the fort, where we remained a few days to wash and **lighten up**.

lighten up: relax

struck: arrived at

June 21. Started over sixty miles [97 km] of the worst road in the world. Have again **struck** the Platte [River] and followed it until we came to the ferry. We had a great deal of trouble swimming our cattle across [and] taking our wagons to pieces. . . . A number of accidents happened here. A lady and four children were drowned through the carelessness of those in charge of the ferry.

July 2. Passed **Independence Rock**. This rock is covered with names. With great difficulty I found a place to cut mine. . . .

During the week we went over the South Pass and the **summit** of the Rocky Mountains.

Independence Rock: stone landmark in central Wyoming on which pioneers carved their names when they passed by

summit: peak

July 4. Had the pleasure of eating ice. . . . Had neither wood nor water for fifty-two miles [84 km]. Traveled in the night. At the

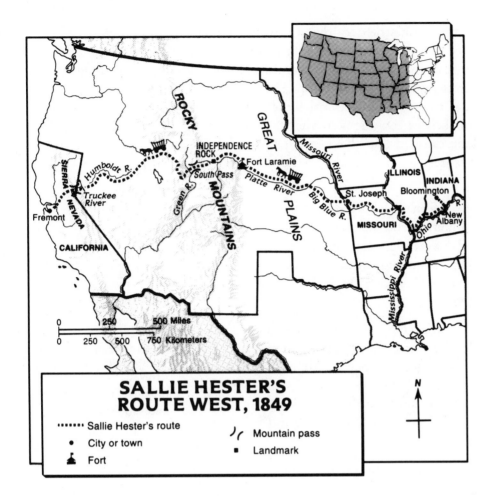

SALLIE HESTER'S ROUTE WEST, 1849

······· Sallie Hester's route
• City or town
⛫ Fort
)(Mountain pass
▪ Landmark

Green River we lay by two days to rest man and beast after our long and weary journey.

August 18. This week some of our company left us, all young men. They were jolly, merry fellows and gave life to our lonely evenings. We all miss them very much. Some had violins, others guitars, and some had fine voices. They were anxious to hurry on without the Sunday stops. Roads are rocky and trying to our wagons, and the dust is horrible. The men wear veils tied over their hats as a protection. When we reach camp at night they are covered with dust from head to heels.

Humboldt River, August 20. We are now 348 miles [560 km] from the [gold] mines. We expect to travel that distance in three weeks and a half. Water and grass scarce. Though the water is not fit to drink— **slough** water—we are obliged to use it for it's all we have.

September 7. Stopped and cut grass for the cattle and supplied ourselves with water for the desert. Had a **trying** time crossing it. Several of our cattle gave out and we left one. Our journey through the desert was from Monday, three o'clock in the afternoon, until Thursday morning at sunrise. The weary journey that last night, the mooing of the cattle for water, the cry, "Another ox down," the

Green River: river in southwestern Wyoming

Humboldt River: river in northern Nevada

slough: swamp

trying: hard

87

stopping of the train to **unyoke** the poor dying **brute**, to let him follow at will or stop by the wayside and die, and the weary, weary tramp of men and beasts, worn out with heat and **famished** for water, will never be erased from my memory. Just at dawn in the distance we had a glimpse of the **Truckee River**, and with it the feeling: Saved at last! Poor cattle; they kept on mooing even when they stood knee deep in water. The long, dreaded desert has been crossed and we are all safe and well. Grass green and beautiful, and the cattle are up to their eyes in it.

September 11. Made eighteen miles [29 km]. Crossed Truckee River ten times. Came near being drowned at one of the crossings. Got frightened and jumped out of the carriage into the water. The current was very swift and carried me some distance down the stream. In jumping I expected to reach the shore; instead I landed in the water, but was rescued in time all right.

September 14. It was night when we crossed the summit of the **Sierra Nevada**, and I shall never forget our descent to the place where we are now encamped— our **tedious** march with pine **knots** blazing in the darkness and the tall, majestic pines towering above our heads. The scene was grand and gloomy beyond description. We could not ride—roads too narrow and rocky. It was a footsore and weary crowd that reached this camp.

September 21. Reached Bear Valley by descending a tremendous hill. We let the wagons down with ropes. Left one of our wagons and the springs of our carriage. Cut down trees for our cattle to **browse** on.

Vernon, California, October 6. Well, after a five-months trip from St. Joe, Missouri, our party of fifty wagons, now only thirteen, has at last reached this **haven** of rest. Strangers in a strange land, what will our future be?

Fremont, October 10. This is a small town on the opposite side of the river from Vernon. My father has decided to remain here for the winter. We have had a small house put up of two rooms made of boards with **puncheon** floor.

April 27 [1850]. Have met a number of nice young men here. I am too young for **beaux**, but the young men don't seem to think so.

unyoke: free
brute: animal
famished: dying of thirst

Truckee River: river in northwestern Nevada

Sierra Nevada: mountain range in California and Nevada
tedious: tiring
knots: branches

browse: graze

Vernon: town near San Francisco

haven: peaceful place

puncheon: split log

beaux (bōz): boyfriends

Despite the attention that she received from young men upon her arrival in California in 1849, Sallie chose not to get married until 1871, when she was 34 years old. By that time, just 22 years after Sallie's seven-month journey from Indiana, people could travel across the entire country to California by train—a trip that took only six days!

Source: Josef and Dorothy Berger, *Small Voices.* New York: Paul S. Eriksson, Inc., 1966.

SWEET BETSY FROM PIKE

Traditional Song, 1800s

In 1849, soon after the discovery of gold in California, thousands of people rushed to the Sierra Nevada mountains, hoping to strike it rich. As many of these "Forty-Niners" bumped along in their covered wagons, they sang songs to help them pass the time. The song below was one of their favorites—and might have been sung by pioneer Sallie Hester, whose diary you read on pages 85-88. What parts of the song do you think held a special meaning for those traveling west?

Adapted by Merrill Staton

1. Oh, do you re-mem-ber sweet Bet-sy from Pike, Who crossed the wide prai-ries with her broth-er Ike? With two yoke of ox-en, a big yal-ler dog, A tall Shang-hai roos-ter, and one spot-ted hog.

Refrain Hoo-dle dang, fol-de-dye-do, hoo-dle dang, fol-de-day. Hoo-dle dang, fol-de dye-do, hoo-dle dang, fol-de-day.

2. They soon reached the desert where Betsy gave out,
   And down in the sand she lay rollin' about.
   When Ike saw sweet Betsy he said with surprise,
   "You'd better get up, you'll get sand in your eyes." *Refrain*

3. Said Ike, "Ole Pike County, I'll go back to you,"
   Said Betsy, "You'll go by yourself if you do,
   There's no time for pleasure and no time for rest,
   In spite of our troubles we'll keep headin' west." *Refrain*

4. They camped on the prairie for weeks upon weeks.
   They swam the wide rivers and crossed the tall peaks.
   And soon they were rollin' in nuggets of gold.
   You may not believe it but that's what we're told. *Refrain*

Source: *Music and You*. New York: Macmillan Publishing Company, 1988.

89

Digging for Gold

by Antonio Franco Coronel, 1877

In the 1840s California was part of Mexico and was home to more than 100,000 Mexicans and Indians. When the Mexican-American War ended in 1848, however, California became part of the United States. Soon after, the discovery of gold in the Sierra Nevada mountains sparked a great rush of newcomers to California from all over the world. Many Mexicans, who had been living in California for years, also raced off to find gold. One of them was Antonio Franco Coronel (1817-1894), a member of the Los Angeles City Council who had lived in California since 1834. Coronel packed up some supplies and headed north to the mining regions in 1849. In 1877, Coronel told an interviewer how he and other Mexican Americans found gold—and injustice—in the Sierra Nevadas. As you read a translation of his oral history, think about how Coronel might have felt about the way he was treated.

I arrived at the **Placer Seco** [about March 1849] and began to work at a regular digging.

In this place there was already a numerous population of Chileans, Peruvians, Californians, Mexicans, and many Americans, Germans, etc. The camps were almost separated according to nationalities. All, some more, some less, were profiting from the fruit of their work. Presently news was circulated that it had been **resolved** to **evict** all of those who were not American citizens from the **placers** because it was believed that the foreigners did not have the right to **exploit** the placers.

Placer Seco: Dry Diggings, a mining camp

resolved: decided
evict: throw out
placers: diggings
exploit: use; take advantage of

90

One Sunday, [notices] appeared in writing in Los Pinos and in several places, that anyone who was not an **American citizen** must abandon the place within twenty-four hours and that he who did not **comply** would be **obliged** to by force. This was supported by a gathering of armed men, ready to make that warning effective.

There was a considerable number of people of various nationalities who understood the order to leave—they decided to gather on a hill in order to be on the defensive in case of any attack. On the day in which the departure of the foreigners should take place, and for three or four more days, both **forces** remained prepared, but the thing did not go beyond cries, shots, and drunken men. Finally all fell calm and we returned to continue our work. Daily, though, the weakest were **dislodged** from their diggings by the strongest. . . .

I arrived at Sacramento with my mules, loaded them, and headed north to the place where I had left my tent in charge of my brother.

Some fourteen miles [23 km] distant from **Sutter's mill**, toward the north, I met my brother and the servants, and several others of the Spanish race, coming, fleeing on foot. They told me that a party of armed foreigners had run them out quickly, without permitting them to take either their animals or other things. I returned to the mill where there was a small population—there I had some **acquaintances**. My aim was to see if I could sell the cargo that I carried, in order to leave the placers. I sold the goods in different places, almost all the mules, etc., at prices so low that I lost two-thirds of the gold they had cost me. These people took advantage of the situation in which I found myself. . . .

On the following Monday, we **staked** out new diggings and proceeded to work them immediately. The work was harder because the gold was much deeper and there was more rock. . . . Almost everyone had to occupy the week working his diggings in order to reach the gold. But, during this time, a large number of armed men gathered daily [and began] **taking account** [of us]. . . . They had such complete knowledge of our business that on Saturday . . . armed

American citizen: despite pledges by the United States government, longtime Mexican residents of California were often not treated as citizens

comply: obey

obliged: required

forces: sides

dislodged: driven out

Sutter's mill: site where gold was first discovered

acquaintances: friends

staked: marked

taking account: watching

91

men began to slip in, making their camp immediately next to ours. Then I thought about the goal of those people and I charged everyone in our camp to be very **prudent** and **moderate** so that they not give the others a **pretext** to bother us.

prudent: careful
moderate: calm
pretext: excuse

Now all of us were piling up our dirt, which was rather rich and promised us better results than the first week. About ten in the morning all of these **merciless** people, numbering more than 100, invaded our diggings at a moment when all of us were inside of them. The invaders were so **courteous** that they asked who the leader of our party was. When I was pointed out to them, their leader and some eight more surrounded my digging. . . . All of these men raised their pistols [and] their Bowie knives; some had rifles, other[s] [had] pickaxes and shovels.

merciless: mean

courteous: polite

Their leader spoke to me . . . [and] led me to understand that this was theirs because before we took the place, one or two months before, he with his men took possession of this same [diggings] and that a boundary had been marked out from one side of the river to the other. He told me several things in English so that I did not understand him immediately, but all amounted to saying that this was his property. Excited, I answered him harshly, but fortunately he did not understand me. I was able to **reflect** for a moment that the gold was not worth risking my life in this way.

reflect: think and realize

The rest of the invaders took possession of the other diggings in the same way. My companions ran to our camp before me and armed themselves. I knew their hostile intentions. Already they had ordered that a number of horses be saddled. I arrived where they were and persuaded them to calm down. Indeed, whatever attempt they might make would be **fruitless**. For me the placers were finished.

fruitless: unsuccessful

We mounted our horses and left the place. The entire party **dispersed** and I left for Los Angeles without stopping in any place longer than was necessary.

dispersed: broke up

In the years following the gold rush, many Mexican Americans and Indians lost their lands in northern California. Southern California, however, continued to be controlled by Mexican Americans until the late 1800s. After being forced from the gold fields in 1849, Antonio Franco Coronel returned to his home in Los Angeles. He became the city's mayor in 1853 and later served as State Treasurer of California.

Source: Antonio Franco Coronel, "Cosas de California," dictated to Thomas Savage for the Bancroft Library, 1877, and published by permission of the Director, the Bancroft Library. Translated by David J. and Carol S. Weber. Reprinted in David J. Weber, *Foreigners in Their Native Land*. Albuquerque, NM: University of New Mexico Press, 1973.

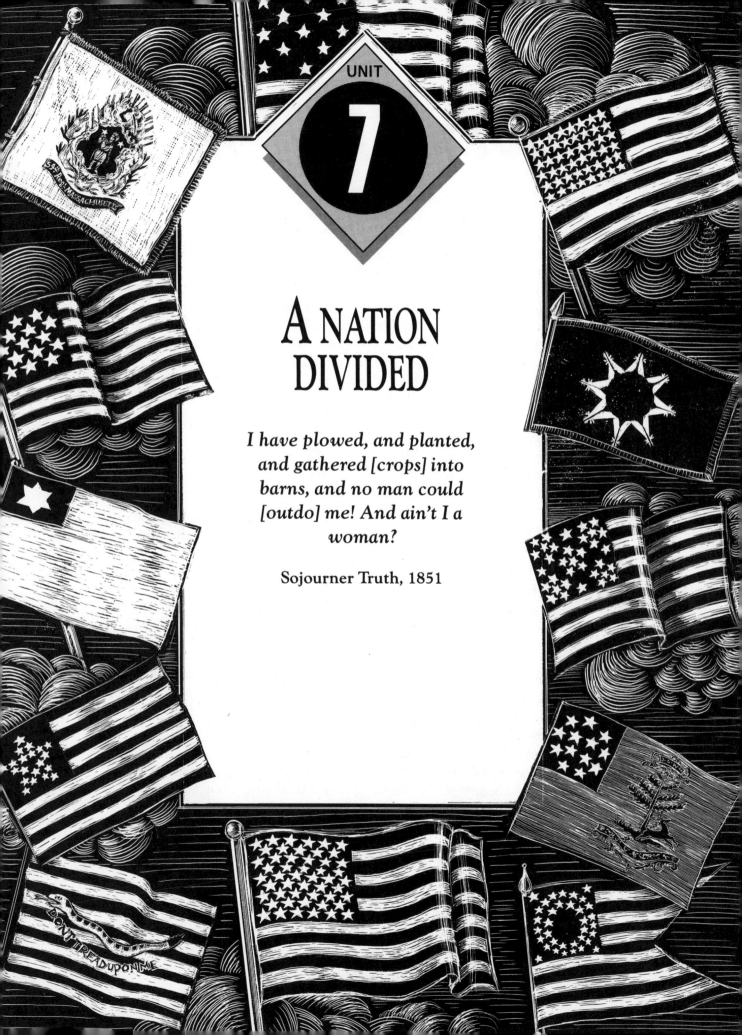

UNIT

7

A NATION DIVIDED

I have plowed, and planted, and gathered [crops] into barns, and no man could [outdo] me! And ain't I a woman?

Sojourner Truth, 1851

Slavery Defended

by George Fitzhugh, 1857

Was slavery right or wrong? Although today the answer seems clear to us, in the 1800s Americans disagreed strongly. Many people in the North felt slavery was evil. Many white Southerners, on the other hand, defended slavery and believed it was right. George Fitzhugh (1806-1881), a lawyer and slave owner from Port Royal, Virginia, was one of the fiercest defenders of slavery. In a book published in 1857, Fitzhugh claimed that slavery was good for black people, good for white people, and good for the country. As you read the excerpt below, notice how he compares the life of enslaved African Americans to the life of free white factory workers. In what ways does he suggest that blacks are not equal to whites? After reading what Fitzhugh wrote, compare his account with J. S. Buckingham's description of slavery on pages 95-96.

The negro slaves of the South are the happiest, and, in some sense, the freest people in the world. The children and the aged and **infirm** work not at all, and yet have all the comforts and **necessaries** of life provided for them. They enjoy liberty, because they are **oppressed** neither by care nor labor. The women do little hard work, and are protected from the **despotism** of their husbands by their **masters**. The negro men and stout boys work, on the average, in good weather, not more than nine hours a day. The balance of their time is spent in perfect **abandon**. Besides, they have their **Sabbaths** and holidays. White men, with so much of **license** and liberty, would die of **ennui**; but negroes **luxuriate in corporeal** and mental **repose**. With their faces upturned to the sun, they can sleep at any hour. . . . [This sleep] results from contentment with the present, and confident **assurance** of the future. We do not know whether free laborers [in the North] ever sleep. They are fools to do so; for, whilst they sleep, the **wily** and watchful **capitalist** is devising means to **ensnare** and **exploitate** them. The free laborer must work or starve. He is more of a slave than the negro, because he works longer and harder for less **allowance** than the slave, and has no holiday, because the cares of life with him begin when its labors end. He has no liberty, and not a single right. . . .

Free laborers have not a thousandth part of the rights and liberties of negro slaves. Indeed, they have not a single right or a single liberty, unless it be the right or liberty to die.

infirm: sick

necessaries: needed items

oppressed: burdened

despotism: cruel misuse of power

masters: owners

abandon: relaxation

Sabbaths: Sundays

license: freedom

ennui: boredom

luxuriate in: enjoy totally

corporeal: physical

repose: rest

assurance: certainty

wily: clever

capitalist: business or factory owner

ensnare: trap

exploitate: misuse

allowance: reward

Many Southerners agreed with Fitzhugh. They believed that slavery was fair and that enslaved African Americans lived easy lives. For a very different description of slavery, read the next document on pages 95-96.

Source: George Fitzhugh, *Cannibals All! or, Slaves Without Masters*. Richmond, VA: Adolphus Morris, 1857.

Slavery Described

by J. S. Buckingham, 1842

Many Northerners did not believe George Fitzhugh's description of slavery, which you read on page 94. They felt that a slave owner like Fitzhugh could not give a fair report on slavery. But Americans in both the North and South read other descriptions besides Fitzhugh's. In the early 1840s, an Englishman named J.S. Buckingham (1786-1855) visited the South and wrote a book about his travels in 1842. The following excerpt from his book describes life on a rice plantation near Savannah, Georgia. As you read this excerpt, think about how it compares with Fitzhugh's description of slavery. In what ways do these accounts agree? In what ways do they disagree? What do you think might account for the differences between these two views of slavery? When you are finished reading, compare the accounts of both Fitzhugh and Buckingham with the view of Frederick Douglass on pages 97-98.

The slaves are all up by daylight; and every one who is able to work, from eight or nine years old and upwards, **repair** to their several departments of field-labour. They do not return to their houses either to breakfast or dinner; but have their food cooked for them in the field, by negroes appointed to that duty. They continue thus at work till dark, and then return to their dwellings. There is no holiday on Saturday afternoon, or any other time throughout the year, except a day or two at Christmas; but from daylight to dark, every day except Sunday, they are at their labour. Their allowance of food consists of a peck, or two gallons, of Indian corn per week,

repair: go

95

half that quantity for working boys and girls, and a quarter for little children. This corn they are **obliged** to grind themselves, after their hours of labour are over; and it is then boiled in water, and made into **hominey**, but without anything to eat with it, neither bread, rice, fish, meat, potatoes, or butter; boiled corn and water only, and barely a **sufficient** quantity of this for **subsistence**.

Of clothes, the men and boys had a **coarse** woollen jacket and trousers once a year, without shirt or any other garment. This was their winter dress; their summer **apparel** consists of a similar suit of jacket and trousers of the coarsest cotton cloth. Absence from work, or neglect of duty, was punished with **stinted** allowance [of food], imprisonment, and **flogging**. A medical man visited the plantation occasionally, and medicines were **administered** by a negro woman called the sick-nurse. No instruction was allowed to be given in reading or writing, no games or recreations were provided, nor was there indeed any time to enjoy them if they were. Their **lot** was one of continued **toil**, from morning to night, uncheered even by the *hope* of change, or **prospect** of improvement in condition.

obliged: required

hominey: mush

sufficient: enough
subsistence: staying alive
coarse: rough
apparel: clothing

stinted: reduced
flogging: beating, whipping
administered: applied

lot: life
toil: work
prospect: chance

J. S. Buckingham presented a much different side of slavery than the one described by George Fitzhugh. Buckingham's book joined a growing number of works in the middle 1800s that described the horrors and unfairness of life under slavery. But no words were as powerful as those spoken by the people who had experienced slavery themselves. For a firsthand account of slavery, read the next document by Frederick Douglass on pages 97-98.

Source: J. S. Buckingham, *The Slave States of America*, Volume 1. London: Fisher, Son & Co., 1842.

Slavery Denounced

by Frederick Douglass, 1852

No person in the United States spoke out more forcefully against slavery than Frederick Douglass (1817–1895). Born into slavery in Maryland, Douglass escaped to New England in 1838. He became an abolitionist in the 1840s and began touring the North to denounce, or condemn, slavery. He settled in Rochester, New York, and started The North Star, *an anti-slavery newspaper. In 1852 the people of Rochester asked Douglass to give a speech in honor of the Fourth of July. They expected him to speak about Independence Day and the greatness of the United States. But Douglass had a different message—one that shocked his listeners. As you read this excerpt from Douglass's Fourth of July speech, keep in mind the accounts of George Fitzhugh and J. S. Buckingham that you read on pages 94–96. How does Douglass's argument concerning slavery and the equality of African Americans compare with Fitzhugh's? How does he argue for the rights and accomplishments of African Americans?*

Fellow Citizens—Pardon me, and allow me to ask, why am I called upon to speak here today? What have I, or those I represent, to do with your national independence? Are the great **principles** of political freedom and of natural justice, **embodied** in that Declaration of Independence, extended to us? . . .

principles: ideas
embodied: contained

Such is not the state of the case. I say it with a sad sense of the **disparity** between us. I am not included within the **pale** of this glorious anniversary! Your high independence only reveals the immeasurable distance between us. The blessings in which you this day rejoice, are not enjoyed **in common**. The rich inheritance of justice, liberty, prosperity, and independence, **bequeathed** by your fathers, is shared by you, not by me. The sunlight that brought life and healing to you, has brought **stripes** and death to me. This Fourth of July is *yours*, not *mine. You* may rejoice, *I* must mourn. . . .

disparity: difference
pale: boundary

in common: by all
bequeathed: handed down

stripes: whippings

Fellow-citizens, above your national, **tumultuous** joy, I hear the mournful wail of millions, whose chains, heavy and **grievous** yesterday, are to-day **rendered** more **intolerable** by the **jubilant** shouts that reach them. If I do forget, if I do not faithfully remember those bleeding children of sorrow this day, "may . . . my tongue **cleave** to the roof of my mouth!" . . . My subject, then, fellow-citizens, is AMERICAN SLAVERY. I shall see this day and its popular **characteristics** from the slave's point of view. Standing there, identified with the American **bondman**, making his wrongs mine, I do not hesitate to declare, with all my soul, that the character and conduct of this nation never looked blacker to me than on this Fourth of July. Whether we turn to the declarations of the past, or to the **professions** of the present, the conduct of the nation seems

tumultuous: excited
grievous: painful
rendered: made
intolerable: unbearable
jubilant: joyful

cleave: stick

characteristics: features
bondman: slave

professions: beliefs

equally hideous and revolting. America is false to the past, false to the present, and solemnly **binds** herself to be false to the future. Standing with God and the crushed and bleeding slave on this occasion, I will . . . **denounce**, with all the emphasis I can command, everything that serves to **perpetuate** slavery—the great sin and shame of America! . . .

For the present, it is enough to **affirm** the equal manhood of the Negro race. Is it not astonishing that, while we are plowing, planting, and reaping, using all kinds of mechanical tools, erecting houses, constructing bridges, building ships, working in metals of brass, iron, copper, silver, and gold; that, while we are reading, writing, and **cyphering**, acting as clerks, merchants, and secretaries, having among us lawyers, doctors, ministers, poets, authors, editors, **orators**, and teachers; that, while we are engaged in all manner of **enterprises** common to other men—digging gold in California, capturing the whale in the Pacific, feeding sheep and cattle on the hillside, living, moving, acting, thinking, planning, living in families as husbands, wives, and children, and, above all, **confessing** and worshiping the Christian's God, and looking hopefully for life and **immortality** beyond the grave,—we are called upon to prove that we are men! . . .

What! am I to argue that it is wrong to make men **brutes**, to rob them of their liberty, to work them without wages, to keep them **ignorant** of their relations to their fellow-men, to beat them with sticks, to **flay** their flesh with the **lash**, to load their limbs with irons, to hunt them with dogs, to sell them at auction, to **sunder** their families, to knock out their teeth, to burn their flesh, to starve them into obedience and submission to their masters? Must I argue that a system, thus marked with blood and stained with pollution, is wrong? No; I will not. I have better **employment** for my time. . . .

What to the American slave is your Fourth of July? I answer, a day that reveals to him, more than all other days in the year, the **gross** injustice and cruelty to which he is the constant victim. To him, your celebration is a **sham**; . . . your sounds of rejoicing are empty and heartless; . . . your shouts of liberty and equality [are] hollow mockery; your prayers and hymns . . . are to him mere . . . **fraud** . . . and hypocrisy—a thin veil to cover up crimes which would disgrace a nation of savages. There is not a nation on the earth guilty of practices more shocking and bloody, than are the people of these United States, at this very hour.

Frederick Douglass's speech in 1852 made clear that Americans had a long way to go to live up to the ideals of liberty and equality expressed in the Declaration of Independence. The powerful words of Douglass and other abolitionists helped convince many people of the evils of slavery. To learn their effect on three young students in Ohio, read the next document on page 99.

Source: Frederick Douglass, *My Bondage and My Freedom*. New York and Auburn: Miller, Orton & Mulligan, 1855.

binds: forces

denounce: attack
perpetuate: continue

affirm: declare

cyphering: doing mathematics

orators: speakers
enterprises: businesses

confessing: believing in

immortality: life after death

brutes: animals

ignorant: unaware
flay: strip away
lash: whip
sunder: break apart

employment: use

gross: outright
sham: fake

fraud: dishonesty

AFRICAN-AMERICAN CHILDREN SPEAK OUT

by Students in Ohio, 1834

In the 1830s more than 300,000 free African Americans lived in the United States. In both the North and South they ran their own schools, churches, and businesses. Free blacks valued education highly, and in 1834 they opened four new schools in Cincinnati, Ohio. One day near the end of the year, a teacher in one of these schools asked his students to write essays answering the following question: "What do you think most about?" The teacher later gave these essays to the Ohio Anti-Slavery Society, which published them. As you read excerpts from these essays, notice what subject is most on the minds of the students. What are some of their goals?

We are going next summer to buy a farm and to work part of the day and to study the other part if we live to see it. . . . [We hope to] come home part of the day to see our mothers and sisters and cousins . . . and see our kind folks and to be good boys and when we get [to be men] to get the poor slaves from **bondage**.

— ——————— , aged seven years.

bondage: slavery

I now inform you in these few lines, that what we are studying for is to try to get the **yoke** of slavery broke and the chains **parted asunder** and slave holding [to] **cease** for ever. O that God would change the hearts of our fellow men.

— ——————— , aged twelve years.

yoke: burden
parted asunder: torn apart
cease: end

This is to inform you that I have two cousins in slavery who **are entitled** to their freedom. They have done everything that the will requires and now they won't let them go. They talk of selling them **down the river**. If this was your case what would you do? Please give me your advice.

— ——————— , aged ten years.

are entitled: have a right

down the river: much farther south down the Mississippi River, where slavery tended to be harsher

Like many free African Americans, these young students had friends and family members who were still enslaved in the South. The schools, churches, and other organizations that free blacks established helped to unite the African-American community and greatly aided the movement to end slavery.

Source: "Report of the Condition of the Free Colored People of Ohio," in *Proceedings of the Ohio Anti-Slavery Convention Held at Putnam on the Twenty-Second, Twenty-Third, and Twenty-Fourth of April, 1835.*

Go Down, Moses

Spiritual, 1800s

Life under slavery meant hard work, cruelty, and pain. Yet many enslaved African Americans found relief by singing songs together that expressed both their sorrows and their hopes. Many of these songs, called spirituals, were based on stories from the Bible. The spiritual below retells the story of the Jews' enslavement by the pharaoh, the ruler of Egypt, and their escape to freedom. African Americans first began singing Go Down, Moses in Virginia and Maryland, and the song quickly spread across the South. Slave owners often punished slaves for singing this spiritual because they believed its words encouraged rebellion. How does the song express the hopes of enslaved African Americans?

1. When Is-rael was in E-gypt land, Let my peo-ple go, Op-pressed so hard, they could not stand, Let my peo-ple go.

Chorus

"Go down,— Mo-ses,— Way___ down in E-gypt land,___ Tell__old__ Pha-raoh___ To let my peo-ple go."

2. "Thus spoke the Lord," bold Moses said,
   Let my people go,
   "If not, I'll strike your first born dead,"
   Let my people go. *Chorus*

3. When they had reached the other shore,
   Let my people go,
   They sang a song of triumph o'er,
   Let my people go. *Chorus*

4. We need not always weep and mourn,
   Let my people go,
   And wear these Slavery chains forlorn,
   Let my people go. *Chorus*

Sources: John A. Lomax and Alan Lomax, *Folk Song U.S.A.* New York: Signet, 1975; *National Anti-Slavery Standard*, December 21, 1861.

"Ain't I a Woman?"

by Sojourner Truth, 1851

Like Frederick Douglass, whose speech you read on pages 97-98, Sojourner Truth (1797?-1883) was one of the country's leading abolitionists. She also fought strongly for the rights of women. Enslaved in New York State for the first 30 years of her life, Sojourner Truth escaped to freedom in 1827. She became a preacher and a speaker, and published her autobiography (which is shown on page 102) in 1850. One year later she attended a women's rights meeting in Akron, Ohio. As some men in the audience jeered one of the speakers, Truth suddenly stood up and began talking. The meeting's leader, Frances D. Gage, later wrote down Truth's unplanned speech. In her speech, how does Sojourner Truth connect the rights of African Americans to the rights of women?

*W*ell, children, where there is so much racket there must be something out of **kilter**. I think that 'twixt the Negroes of the South and the women of the North, all talking about rights, the white men will be in a fix pretty soon. But what's all this here talking about?

kilter: place
'twixt: between

That man over there says that women need to be helped into carriages, and lifted over ditches, and to have the best place everywhere. Nobody ever helps me into carriages, or over mud-puddles, or gives me any best place! And ain't I a woman? Look at me! Look at my arm! I have plowed, and planted, and gathered [crops] into barns, and no man could **head** me! And ain't I a woman? I could work as much and eat as much as a man—when I could get it—and bear the **lash** as well! And ain't I a woman? I have **borne** thirteen children, and seen them most all sold off to slavery, and when I cried out with my mother's grief, none but Jesus heard me! And ain't I a woman?

head: outdo

lash: whip
borne: given birth to

Then they talk about this thing in the head; what's this they call it? ("**Intellect**," whispered someone near.) That's it, honey. What's that got to do with women's rights or Negroes' rights? If my cup won't hold but a **pint**, and yours holds a quart, wouldn't you be mean not to let me have my little half-measure full?

intellect: ability to think

pint: half-quart

Then that little man in black there, he says women can't have as much rights as men, because Christ wasn't a woman! Where did your Christ come from? Where did your Christ come from? From God and a woman! Man had nothing to do with Him.

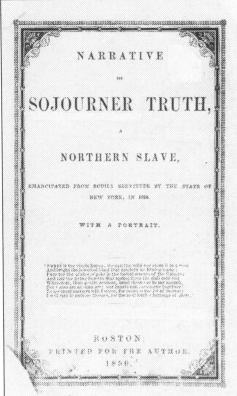

If the first woman God ever made was strong enough to turn the world upside down all alone, these women together ought to be be able to turn it back, and get it right side up again! And now that they are asking to do it, the men had better let them.

Obliged to you for hearing me, and now old Sojourner hasn't got anything more to say.

obliged: many thanks

When Sojourner Truth finished speaking, the audience roared its approval. Truth went on to speak at many other meetings around the country. She was not always welcomed. In Kansas she was clubbed, and in Missouri she was attacked by a mob, yet Truth continued to speak out bravely for the rights of both African Americans and women. During the 1840s and 1850s women abolitionists such as Sojourner Truth helped to make freedom and equal rights for all people some of the major issues in the United States. To learn how other women connected these issues, read the next document on page 103.

Source: Adapted from Elizabeth Cady Stanton, Susan B. Anthony, and Matilda Joslyn Gage, eds., *History of Woman Suffrage*, Volume 1. New York: Fowler & Wells, 1881.

Fighting for Equal Rights,

Poster and Illustrations, 1837-1860

After the first women's rights convention was held in Seneca Falls, New York, in 1848, more and more women began fighting for equal rights. Many of them, such as Sojourner Truth whom you read about on pages 101-102, connected the fight for equal rights for women to the fight to end slavery. On this page are three documents illustrating the struggle for women's rights before the Civil War. The document on the top of the page is an engraving from an 1837 book of abolitionist poetry. The document on the right is a poster announcing a women's rights convention in New York City in 1858. The document below is an illustration from a newspaper in 1860. It shows women shoe workers marching in Lynn, Massachusetts, after they had gone out on strike. How do the three documents show the connection between the fight for women's rights, the fight for equal rights for black people and white people, and the fight to end slavery?

THE EIGHTH

National Woman's-Rights Convention

WILL BE HELD IN

NEW YORK CITY,

AT MOZART HALL, 668 BROADWAY,

On Thursday and Friday, May 13 and 14, 1858,

Commencing at 10 o'clock Thursday A. M.

Lucy Stone, Ernestine L. Rose, Wendell Phillips, Wm. Lloyd Garrison, C. Lenox Remond, Mary F. Davis, Caroline H. Dahl, Rev. T. W. Higginson, Aaron M. Powell, Frances D. Gage, and others,

will address the several sessions of the Convention.

We regret that so many of the noble men and women, who, in spirit, are fully with us, should have so long withheld from us, kind words of recognition and encouragement.

We earnestly ask all those who believe our claims are just, who hope and look for a higher type of womanhood in the coming generations, to assert, now, their faith in the everlasting principles of justice, that have no respect for age, sex, color, or condition. Is it too much to ask that the BRADYS, the CURTIS', the CHAPINS, the BEECHERS, and the BROWNS shall cheer us by their presence at our coming Convention, or by letter make known their position in regard to this movement? Feeling assured that our cause is just, that our positions are tenable, our platform is FREE for all fair discussion.

Communications for the Convention may be addressed to SUSAN B. ANTHONY, ANTI-SLAVERY OFFICE, 138 NASSAU STREET, NEW YORK.

During the middle 1800s many women led the battle to end slavery and gain equal rights for all people. The fight for women's rights would continue for many, many years.

Sources: John Greenleaf Whittier, *Poems During the Progress of the Abolition Question.* Boston: I. Knapp, 1837; *Frank Leslie's Illustrated Newspaper*, March 17, 1860.

103

A Warning to Free Blacks

Poster, 1851

As the documents you have read in this Unit show, slavery remained the most explosive issue in the United States in the middle 1800s. The issue became even more explosive when Congress passed the Fugitive Slave Law in 1850. Under this law, Southerners could seize any African American they had once owned who had escaped to freedom in the North. Slave owners did not need proof to enforce their claims that an African American was an escaped slave, and the law denied blacks who were captured the right to a fair trial. In response to the Fugitive Slave Law, slave catchers began prowling the North in the hopes of kidnapping African Americans and sending them south into slavery. To warn free blacks about this threat, abolitionists put up the following poster in Boston, Massachusetts, in 1851. What does the poster urge African Americans to do to protect themselves?

CAUTION!!

COLORED PEOPLE

OF BOSTON, ONE & ALL,

You are hereby respectfully CAUTIONED and advised, to avoid conversing with the

Watchmen and Police Officers of Boston,

For since the recent ORDER OF THE MAYOR & ALDERMEN, they are empowered to act as

KIDNAPPERS

AND

Slave Catchers,

And they have already been actually employed in KIDNAPPING, CATCHING, AND KEEPING SLAVES. Therefore, if you value your LIBERTY, and the *Welfare of the Fugitives* among you, *Shun* them in every possible manner, as so many *HOUNDS* on the track of the most unfortunate of your race.

Keep a Sharp Look Out for KIDNAPPERS, and have TOP EYE open.

APRIL 24, 1851.

Under the Fugitive Slave Law about 300 African Americans were kidnapped and forced into slavery. Throughout the North, crowds often gathered to rescue blacks from slave catchers, but they could not protect everyone. In Indiana one man was returned to a Southerner who claimed he had owned him 19 years earlier. Others were captured on the streets of Northern cities and taken south before they had a chance to say good-bye to their families. Many Northerners condemned the Fugitive Slave Law and refused to obey it. In the South, African Americans still tried to escape from slavery. For an exciting account of one of these escapes, read the next document on pages 105-106.

Escape to Freedom

by Tom Wilson, 1858

In spite of the Fugitive Slave Law (which you read about on page 104) and the danger of being recaptured, thousands of enslaved African Americans continued trying to escape to freedom in the 1850s. One of these was Tom Wilson. Born in Mississippi in 1813, Wilson had worked as a slave both in cotton fields and on riverboats. In the following interview, printed in a British newspaper in 1858, Wilson describes both his early life and his nightmarish escape to freedom. As you read his story, compare the horrors he endured with George Fitzhugh's description of slavery that you read on page 94. How does Wilson's account help to disprove that of Fitzhugh? What role did free African Americans play in Wilson's escape?

I am slave born. I have been under slave bondage ever since I was born. I am now 45 years old. I belonged to Mr. Henry Fastman, of [New Orleans]. . . . I was under him for the space of seven years. Before then I belonged to Colonel Barr, of Woodford, Mississippi. There I had a wife and three children. . . . I was sold by auction . . . for $2,500, and was taken down to New Orleans, away from my wife and children, and I haven't seen them since. Shortly after I got there, Mr. Fastman's overseer, Burke, **commenced** to **ill-use** me. I didn't understand tying the cotton; it was new to me, and I was awkward, so I was **flogged**. They used to tie me down across a cotton **bale**, and give me 200 or 300 [lashes] with a leather strap. I am marked with the whip from the ankle-bone to the **crown** of my head. Some years before I was sold down from Mississippi, the overseer there, because I resisted punishment once, cut my right arm across the muscle, and then had it stitched up. He did that, as he said, to weaken me, because I was strong in the arm.

About a year and a half after I had been in New Orleans, I ran into the woods. I was followed by Burke and a pack of bloodhounds into the Baddenrush swamp. The dogs soon caught me. They tore

commenced: started
ill-use: mistreat
flogged: whipped
bale: bundle
crown: top

my legs and body with their teeth. Here are the marks yet. Burke rode up to me with his gun, and shot me in the hip with **14 buck-shot**. . . . The dogs continued to pin me with their teeth.

After that I [knew] nothing about what they did to me for about a week. When I got a little strong, they burned my back with a red hot iron, and my legs with strong turpentine, to punish me for escaping. They put an iron collar round my neck, which I wore for eight months, besides two irons, one on each leg. After that I was watched very closely; but one night, about a week after Christmas, I ran away, and hid myself under the saw-dust, in a **saw-mill** pit, below New Orleans. I was followed by Burke, the overseer, and the dogs, but they did not find me. I crept out, and ran away, for more safety, to the Great Salt water Lake, behind Orleans, **secreting** myself under the bushes and vines. There are alligators in the lake, and, as I waded up to the knees in the water, the alligators followed me, grunting and bellowing, and trying to get me. I had several times to climb up trees to escape them; but I felt safer among the alligators than among the white men. In the morning, at four o'clock, I went down to the **wharf**.

On the road I came across some of the men who were out watching for me, with guns and dogs. It was just getting light. I began to whistle and sing and walked close by them, and they paid no attention to me. When I got down to the wharf, some of the coloured crew of the American cotton ship *Metropolis* took me on board, and hid me away among the bales. One of the coloured men **split** on me, and there was a search for me that day; but they did not find me, and I trembled to think I should be taken back and tortured. I was frightened, too, for the coloured men who had **befriended** me.

I was kept out of sight of the white men, and Captain Foster did not know anything about it until after the men had been paid off at **Liverpool**. I remained hid from a week after Christmas until about [late January], when the ship came here. During the time I was secreted I was kept alive by the coloured men, who had been so good to me. They brought me something to eat and drink every night. When I first landed here I was frightened at every white man I passed, and I hid myself about where I could, and begged at night for bread. I was afraid I should be taken into slavery again. I did not know I could not be a slave here.

14 buck-shot: small metal pellets

saw-mill: place where lumber is cut into boards

secreting: hiding

wharf: dock

split: told

befriended: made friends with; protected

Liverpool: city in England

In order to reach freedom, Tom Wilson had to travel more than 4,000 miles (6,400 km) to England. Because of the Fugitive Slave Law, which required free states to return people who had escaped slavery, Wilson would have been in great danger anywhere in the United States. The ongoing disagreements over slavery between the North and South would soon lead to the Civil War. To learn about the beginning of the Civil War, read the next document on page 107.

Source: Liverpool *Albion*, February 20, 1858, reprinted in John W. Blassingame, ed., *Slave Testimony: Two Centuries of Letters, Speeches, Interviews, and Autobiographies*. Baton Rouge, LA: Louisiana State University Press, 1977.

SECESSION AND WAR!

from the *Charleston Mercury* and *The New-York Times*, 1860 and 1861

During the 1850s the United States became more and more divided over the issue of slavery. In 1860 Americans elected Abraham Lincoln President. Lincoln opposed the spread of slavery into the territories of the West. Many Southerners feared that Lincoln might try to end slavery in the South. In December 1860 Southern states began leaving the Union. Less than four months later, in April 1861, the Civil War began. Below are two newspapers—one from the South and one from the North— reporting these two important events. If you had been living at the time, how would you have felt reading these headlines? How might your reactions have differed if you were living in the North, the South, or the West?

The firing on Fort Sumter on April 12, 1861, plunged the country into war. To learn some of the reasons why people enlisted to fight and how the Civil War affected life in both the North and South, read the next three documents on pages 108–111.

Sources: *Charleston Mercury*, December 20, 1860; *The New-York Times*, April 13, 1861.

107

The Gettysburg Address

by Abraham Lincoln, 1863

The Battle of Gettysburg in July 1863 was the bloodiest battle of the Civil War. More than 50,000 soldiers were killed or wounded during three long days of fighting. Four months later, on November 19, 1863, President Abraham Lincoln (1809-1865) went to Gettysburg, Pennsylvania, to dedicate a national cemetery and give a speech in honor of the soldiers who had died there. Another speaker talked first—for about two hours. Then Lincoln stood up and spoke for less than three minutes. As you read Lincoln's Gettysburg Address, look for clues that tell you what Lincoln believed the Civil War was all about. According to Lincoln, what beliefs and values were at stake in the Civil War?

Fourscore and seven years ago our fathers brought forth on this continent a new nation, **conceived** in liberty, and dedicated to the **proposition** that all men are created equal. Now we are **engaged** in a great civil war, testing whether that nation, or any nation so conceived and so dedicated, can long endure. We are **met** on a great battlefield of that war. We have come to dedicate a portion of that field as a final resting place for those who here gave their lives that the nation might live. It is altogether fitting and proper that we should do this.

fourscore and seven: 87
conceived: formed
proposition: idea
engaged: involved

met: meeting

But, in a larger sense, we cannot dedicate—we cannot **consecrate**—we cannot **hallow**—this ground. The brave men, living and dead, who struggled here, have consecrated it, far above our poor power to add or **detract**. The world will little note nor long remember what we say here, but it can never forget what they did here. It is for us, the living, rather, to be dedicated here to the unfinished work which they who fought here have thus far so **nobly** advanced. It is rather for us to be here dedicated to the great task remaining before us—that from these honored dead we take increased **devotion** to that cause for which they gave the last full measure of devotion; that we here highly **resolve** that these dead shall not have died **in vain**; that this nation, under God, shall have a new birth of freedom; and that government of the people, by the people, for the people, shall not **perish** from the earth.

consecrate: make sacred
hallow: make holy
detract: take away

nobly: unselfishly

devotion: loyalty
resolve: promise
in vain: for no reason

perish: die

After Lincoln finished speaking, the audience applauded politely. Lincoln believed that his brief speech had been "a flat failure." Today, however, the Gettysburg Address is considered one of the finest and most poetic statements about freedom and democracy ever written.

Assault on Fort Wagner

by James Henry Gooding, 1863

When the Civil War began in 1861, neither side allowed African Americans to enlist as soldiers. Despite black participation in the American Revolution and other wars, most whites did not believe that blacks were capable of fighting. But after strong pleading by leading abolitionists, such as Frederick Douglass, the North at last allowed one group of black soldiers to be formed in 1863. This all-black regiment, or group of soldiers, was called the Fifty-fourth Massachusetts Voluntary Infantry and became known as the Massachusetts Fifty-fourth. (A picture of the regiment's flag appears on the next page.) This regiment provided African Americans with the opportunity to prove how well they could fight. One of the first people to enlist was 26-year-old James Henry Gooding (1836-1864), a free seaman from New Bedford, Massachusetts, who had worked on whaling ships. A well-educated man, Gooding wrote articles about his regiment for the New Bedford Mercury, his hometown newspaper. Gooding wrote the following article in July 1863, just after the Massachusetts Fifty-fourth had fought two major battles at James Island and Fort Wagner in South Carolina. How does Gooding describe the conduct and willingness to fight of the soldiers in his regiment?

Morris Island [South Carolina], July 20, 1863

At last we have something stirring to record. The 54th, the past week, has proved itself twice in battle. The first was on James Island on the morning of the 16th [of July]. There were four companies of the 54th on **picket** duty at the time. . . . About 3 o'clock in the morning, the rebels began **harassing** our pickets on the right, intending, no doubt, to drive them in, so that by daylight the coast would be clear to rush their main force down on us, and take us by surprise. . . .

picket: guard
harassing: bothering

They made a mistake—instead of returning fire, the officer in charge of the pickets directed the men to lie down under cover of a hedge, rightly expecting the rebels to advance by degrees toward our lines. As he expected, at daylight they were within 600 yards [656 m] of the picket line, when our men rose and poured a **volley** into them. That was something the rebels didn't expect—their line of **skirmishers** was completely broken; our men then began to fall back gradually . . . as the rebels were advancing their main force on to them. On they came, with six pieces of **artillery** and four thousand **infantry**. . . . As their force advanced on our right, the boys held them in check like **veterans**. . . .

volley: round of shots

skirmishers: soldiers

artillery: heavy guns
infantry: soldiers on foot
veterans: experienced soldiers
gallantly: bravely

The men of the 54th behaved **gallantly** on the occasion—so the Generals say. It is not for us to blow our horn; but when a regiment

of white men gave us three cheers as we were passing them, it shows that we did our duty as men should.

I shall pass over the incidents of that day, as regards individuals, to speak of a greater and more terrible **ordeal** the 54th regiment has passed through. . . . Saturday afternoon we were marched up past our **batteries**, amid the cheers of the officers and soldiers.

ordeal: struggle

batteries: groups of large weapons

We wondered what they were all cheering for, but we soon found out. **Gen. [George C.] Strong** rode up, and we halted. Well, you had better believe there was some guessing what we were to do. Gen. Strong asked us if we would follow him into Fort Wagner. Every man said, yes—we were ready to follow wherever we were led . . . [and] we went at it, over the ditch and on to the **parapet** through a deadly fire; but we could not get into the fort.

General George C. Strong: Union officer who led the attack on Fort Wagner

parapet: wall

We met the **foe** on the parapet of Wagner with the **bayonet**—we were exposed to a murderous fire from the batteries of the fort, from our **Monitors** and our land batteries, as they did not cease firing soon enough. **Mortal men** could not stand such a fire, and the **assault** on Wagner was a failure.

foe: enemy
bayonet: steel blade on the end of a rifle
monitors: ships
mortal men: men who can die
assault: attack

The 9th Maine, 10th Connecticut, 63rd Ohio, 48th and 100th New York [regiments] were to support us in the assault; but after we made the first charge, everything was in such confusion that we could hardly tell where the **reserve** was. At the first charge the 54th rushed to within twenty yards [18 m] of the ditches, and, as might be expected of **raw recruits, wavered**—but at the second advance they gained the parapet. The **color bearer** of the State colors was killed on the parapet. **Col. [Robert Gould] Shaw** seized the staff when the standard bearer fell, and in less than a minute after, the Colonel fell himself. When the men saw their gallant leader fall, they made a desperate effort to get him out, but they were either shot down, or **reeled** in the ditch below. One man succeeded in getting hold of the State color staff but the color was completely torn to pieces.

reserve: other regiments

raw recruits: new soldiers
wavered: hesitated
color bearer: flag carrier
Colonel Robert Gould Shaw: commander of the Massachusetts Fifty-fourth
reeled: fell

Almost half of the 600 soldiers of the Massachusetts Fifty-fourth who carried out the attack on Fort Wagner died during the battle. James Henry Gooding was one of the fortunate survivors—as were two of Frederick Douglass's sons, who also fought that day. Gooding remained in the Massachusetts Fifty-fourth and was promoted to corporal in December 1863. He continued to send home articles from the battlefront until he was wounded in 1864 and taken prisoner. He died in prison camp later that year. Thanks to articles by Corporal Gooding and other reporters describing the courage of the Massachusetts Fifty-fourth, Northerners came to realize that black soldiers could fight effectively. Black enlistment boomed. Altogether, more than 200,000 African Americans fought in the Civil War and helped bring victory for the North.

Source: New Bedford *Mercury*, August 1, 1863, reprinted in James Henry Gooding, *On the Altar of Freedom: A Black Soldier's Civil War Letters from the Front*. Amherst, MA: The University of Massachusetts Press, 1991.

Destruction of the South

by Eliza Frances Andrews, 1864

Fierce fighting during the Civil War left much of the South in ruins. In November 1864 General William Tecumseh Sherman and 60,000 Union soldiers began a march from Atlanta, Georgia, to Savannah, Georgia, aiming to destroy everything in their path. In the following journal excerpt from December 1864, a Georgia woman named Eliza Frances Andrews (1840-1931) describes some of the destruction they caused. How does Andrews feel about the damage done to the South?

About three miles from **Sparta** we struck the "Burnt Country," . . . and then I could better understand the **wrath** and desperation of these poor people. I almost felt as if I should like to hang a **Yankee** myself. There was hardly a fence left standing all the way from Sparta to **Gordon**. The fields were trampled down and the road was lined with **carcasses** of horses, hogs, and cattle that the invaders, unable either to consume or to carry away with them, had **wantonly** shot down to starve out the people and prevent them from making their crops. The **stench** in some places was unbearable; every few hundreds yards we had to hold our noses or stop them with the cologne Mrs. Elzey had given us, and it proved a great **boon**.

The dwellings that were standing all showed signs of **pillage**, and on every plantation we saw the **charred** remains, . . . while here and there, lone chimney-stacks, "**Sherman's Sentinels**," told of homes laid in ashes. The **infamous** wretches! I couldn't wonder now that these poor people should want to put a rope round the neck of every [one of them that] they could lay their hands on.

Hay ricks and **fodder stacks** were demolished, **corn cribs** were empty, and every bale of cotton that could be found was burnt by the savages. I saw no grain of any sort, except little patches they had spilled when feeding their horses and which there was not even a chicken left in the country to eat. A bag of oats might have lain anywhere along the road without danger from the beasts of the field, though I cannot say it would have been safe from the assaults of hungry man. . . .

I saw [soldiers] seated on the roadside greedily eating raw turnips, meat skins, **parched** corn—anything they could find, even picking up the loose grains that Sherman's horses had left.

Sparta: town in central Georgia

wrath: deep anger

Yankee: Southern term for a Northerner

Gordon: town about 30 miles (48 km) from Sparta

carcasses: dead bodies

wantonly: without caring

stench: bad smell

boon: help

pillage: destruction, robbery

charred: burned

"Sherman's Sentinels": name for chimneys left standing after Sherman's troops had destroyed the rest of the house

infamous: wicked

hay ricks: haystacks

fodder stacks: stacks of food for livestock

corn cribs: containers for storing corn

parched: dried

General William Tecumseh Sherman's march through Georgia in 1864 weakened the will of many Southerners to keep fighting. On April 9, 1865, the South surrendered, ending the bloodiest war in the nation's history. Southerners spent many years rebuilding their war-torn region.

Source: Eliza Frances Andrews, *The War-Time Journal of a Georgia Girl*. Boston: D. Appleton and Co., 1908.

Teaching Freed People

by Charlotte Forten, 1864

Before the 1860s it was against the law to teach enslaved African Americans how to read and write. Some slaves went to school secretly—and illegally—but most were prevented from getting an education. As the world of slavery crumbled during the Civil War, however, one of the first things African Americans did was set up schools and begin holding classes throughout the South. They hired teachers, both black and white, to teach them. One of the first to head south to educate these newly freed people was a 25-year-old African-American abolitionist from Philadelphia named Charlotte Forten (1837-1914). Forten arrived at St. Helena, an island along the coast of South Carolina, in October 1862, just after Union troops had taken control of the area. Forten began teaching at once—to classes sometimes as large as 140 students! Two years later she wrote two magazine articles about her experiences as a teacher. An excerpt from these articles is printed below. According to Forten, how important was education to the freed people of the South?

The first day at school was rather trying. Most of my children were very small, and **consequently** restless. Some were too young to learn the alphabet. These little ones were brought to school because the older children—in whose care their parents leave them while at work—could not come without them. We were therefore willing to have them come, although they seemed to have discovered the secret of **perpetual** motion, and **tried** one's patience sadly. But after some days of positive, though not **severe** treatment, order was brought out of **chaos**, and I found but little difficulty in managing and quieting the tiniest and most restless spirits. I never before saw children so eager to learn, although I had several years' experience in New-England schools. Coming to school is a constant delight and recreation to them. They come here as other children go to play. The older ones, during the summer, work in the fields from early morning until eleven or twelve o'clock, and then come into school, after their hard toil in the hot sun, as bright and as anxious to learn as ever. . . .

consequently: as a result

perpetual: constant
tried: tested
severe: harsh
chaos: confusion

The majority learn with wonderful **rapidity**. Many of the grown people **are desirous of** learning to read. It is wonderful how a people who have been so long crushed to the earth . . . can have so great a desire for knowledge, and such a **capability** for **attaining** it. . . .

The tiniest children are delighted to get a book in their hands. Many of them already know their letters. The parents are eager to have them learn. . . .

They are willing to **make many sacrifices** [so] that their children may attend school. One old woman, who had a large family of children and grandchildren, came regularly to school in the winter, and took her seat among the little ones. She was at least sixty years old. Another woman—who had one of the best faces I ever saw— came daily, and brought her baby in her arms.

rapidity: speed
are desirous of: want to

capability: ability
attaining: reaching

make many sacrifices: give up many things

Charlotte Forten returned home to Philadelphia in 1864. She later became a writer and translator, and also worked for the United States Treasury Department. With the help of teachers like Charlotte Forten, African Americans built hundreds of schools that were open to both black and white students during the period of Reconstruction that followed the Civil War. African Americans also donated more than $1 million to education in the South. The Freedmen's Bureau, an agency of the federal government, also built schools to teach freed people. This vast system of education became one of the major achievements of Reconstruction.

Source: Charlotte Forten, "Life on the Sea Islands," *Atlantic Monthly*, Volume 13, May and June 1864.

113

Many Thousands Gone

Freedom Song, 1860s

The most important result of the Civil War was the freedom of almost 4 million African Americans from slavery. For the rest of their lives, former slaves never forgot that moment in their lives when they learned they were free. Many celebrated by singing songs of joy. The freedom song below, also called No More Auction Block For Me, was first sung by freed African Americans in South Carolina. It soon became a popular marching song for black soldiers in the Union army, such as those in the Massachusetts Fifty-fourth Regiment. The meaning of the term "peck of corn" can be found in the description of slavery by J. S. Buckingham on pages 95–96. How does this song express both the sorrow of slavery and the joy of freedom?

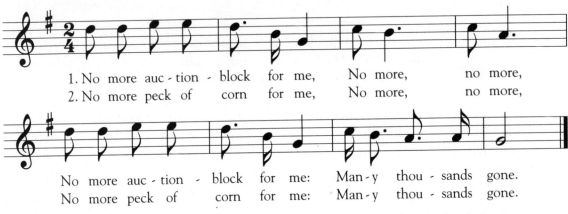

1. No more auc-tion-block for me,   No more,   no more,
2. No more peck of   corn   for me,   No more,   no more,

No more auc-tion-block for me: Man-y thou-sands gone.
No more peck of   corn   for me: Man-y thou-sands gone.

3. No more driver's lash for me,
   No more, no more,
   No more driver's lash for me:
   Many thousands gone.

4. No more pint of salt for me,
   No more, no more,
   No more pint of salt for me:
   Many thousands gone.

5. No more hundred lash for me,
   No more, no more,
   No more hundred lash for me,
   Many thousands gone.

6. No more mistress' call for me,
   No more, no more,
   No more mistress' call for me:
   Many thousands gone.

Source: Henry Edward Krehbiel, *Afro-American Folksongs*. New York: Ungar, 1962.

UNIT

8

A CHANGING NATION

The word liberty makes me think of the fact that this country is the land of liberty for all men of all nations except the Chinese.

Saum Song Bo, 1885

A BUFFALO HUNT

by Waheenee-wea, 1921

For hundreds of years, the Hidatsa Indians lived on the Great Plains. They relied on both farming and buffalo hunting for survival. In the following oral history from 1921, a Hidatsa woman named Waheenee-wea, or Buffalo-Bird Woman, describes a buffalo hunt she went on around the 1860s. Born about 1839, Waheenee-wea lived near the Missouri and Knife rivers in what is today North Dakota. Years later, as an old woman, she told her life story to a researcher. As you read her oral history, note the different skills needed to hunt buffalo. What roles did women and men play in the buffalo hunt she describes?

Spring had come. . . . Our hunters had not killed many deer the winter before, and our **stores** of corn were getting low. As ours was a large family, **Son-of-a-Star** thought he would join a hunting party that was going up the river for buffaloes. "Even if we do not find much game," he said, "we shall kill enough for ourselves. We younger men should not be eating the corn and beans that old men and children need."

stores: supplies

Son-of-a-Star: Waheenee-wea's husband

Small Ankle thought the plan a good one. I was glad also, for I was to be one of the party. Corn planting time would not come for a month yet; and, after the weeks in our narrow winter quarters, I longed to be out again in the fresh air. . . .

Small Ankle: Waheenee-wea's father

My tribe now owned many horses, and fewer dogs were used than when I was a little girl. A party of buffalo hunters usually took both hunting and pack horses; but our village herd was weak and poor in flesh after the **scant** winter's feeding, and we thought it better to take only dogs. There was yet little pasture, and the ground was wet and spongy from the spring thaws. Only a strong, well-fed pony could go all day on wet ground. . . .

scant: small

We were **clad** warmly, for the weather was chill. All had robes. I wore a dress of two deer skins sewed edge to edge; the hind legs, thus sewed, made the sleeves for my arms. . . .

clad: dressed

We all wore winter moccasins, fur lined, with high tops. The men carried guns. Buffalo hunters no longer used bows except from horseback.

We started off gaily, in a long line. Each woman was followed by her dogs. Two women, having no dogs, packed their camp stuff on their backs.

We made our first camp late in the afternoon, at a place called Timber-Faces-across-River. There was a spring here, of good water.

Crow-Flies-High and Bad Brave went hunting, while we women pitched our tent. We cut forked poles and stacked them with tops together like a tepee. We covered this frame with skins . . .; and small logs, laid about the edges, held the tent to the ground. We could not use tent pins, for the ground was frozen. . . . We were some time building, as the tent had to be large enough for twelve persons.

[The next day] . . . Son-of-a-Star and **Scar** came in to say they had killed a stray buffalo not far away. They had packed part of the meat to camp on their shoulders, and Son-of-a-Star had cut out the buffalo's **paunch** and filled it with fresh blood. While the two hunters went back for the rest of the meat, I put on my copper kettle and made blood pudding. It was hot and ready to serve by the time they came back. I had stirred the pudding with a green **chokecherry stick**, giving it a pleasant, cherry flavor.

We were a jolly party as we sat around the evening fire. The hot pudding felt good in our stomachs, after the long march. . . .

We were up the next morning before the sun, and, after a hasty breakfast, the men went out to look for buffaloes. "The one we killed yesterday may have strayed from a herd," Son-of-a-Star said. He was hopeful that they might find the herd near. . . .

While we women busied ourselves with things in camp, the men went to hunt, and five miles farther on they discovered a herd of buffaloes crossing the Missouri [River] from the south side. Our hunters, creeping close on the down-wind side, shot five fat **cows** as they landed. Buffaloes are rather stupid animals, but have **keen scent**. Had our hunters tried to come at them from the **windward side**, the herd would have **winded** them a half mile away. As it was, no more buffaloes crossed after the shots were fired, and some that were in the water swam back to the other side. . . .

The next morning Crow-Flies-High called a council, and we decided to cross over to the other side of the river. "The main herd is there," said Crow-Flies-High. "We should hunt the buffaloes before they move to other pasture." We thought he spoke wisely, and men and women seized axes to cut a road through the willows for our **travois**. . . .

It was evening and getting dusk when Son-of-a-Star came into the tent, saying, "Buffaloes are on a bluff a quarter of a mile up the river. I can see them moving against the sky line." We listened and heard the **bulls** roaring; so we knew a herd was coming in.

We were careful to chop no wood that evening, nor do anything to make a noise. We smothered our fires, and we fed our dogs; for, with **gorged** stomachs, they would be sleepy and not bark. If a dog stirred in the night, one of us went out and quieted him. . . .

We hastened into camp [the next morning] and saw the buffaloes a quarter of a mile away, **swarming** over a **bluff**. There was a bit of **bad-land formation** below, round-topped **buttes** with grassy stretches between. In these lower levels the sun had started warming

Crow-Flies-High and Bad Brave: two Hidatsa men in the hunting party

Scar: a Teton Sioux man in the hunting party who was visiting the Hidatsa

paunch: belly

chokecherry stick: branch from a type of cherry tree

cows: female buffaloes

keen: sharp

scent: sense of smell

windward side: direction from which the wind blows

winded: smelled

travois: A-shaped frame made of poles and pulled by animals to carry supplies

bulls: male buffaloes

gorged: full

swarming: crowding

bluff: high cliff

bad-land formation: strangely shaped hills

buttes: flat, steep-sided hills

117

up the grass, and I think the buffaloes were coming down into them to seek pasture.

Our hunters had come up from the boats, guns in hand, and set off at once, creeping up the **coulees** from the **lee side**, that the buffaloes might not wind them. Presently I saw a flash and a puff of smoke; then another, and another; and the reports came echoing down the river basin, *poh-poh-poh, poh, poh, poh!* like thunder, away off. The herd took to their heels . . . swerved off and went tearing away toward the north.

The hunters returned before evening. Son-of-a-Star was the first to come in. "I shot two fat cows," he cried. "I have cut up the meat and put it in a pile, covered with the skins." He had brought back the choice cuts, however, the tongues, kidneys and hams. . . .

We remained in the camp about ten days. The men would hunt until they made a kill. Then we harnessed our dogs, and all went out to fetch in the meat. To do this took us about half a day. At other times, when not drying meat, we women busied ourselves making **bull boats**, to **freight** our meat down the river. . . .

While our hunters were **stalking** the herd, we women stayed in camp, keeping very quiet, and stilling the dogs if they whined or barked. Before long we heard the *poh-poh-poh!* of guns, and knew the herd was started. We now arose and began gathering sticks for a fire. . . .

We did not trouble to set up our tent. "The weather is not cold," said Crow-Flies-High's wife. "We can sleep in the open air." I cut buckbrush bushes and spread a robe over them for my bed. Dry grass stuffed under one end of the robe did for a pillow. My covering was a pair of buffalo skins. We were weary and went to bed early. The night was clear; and, with the fresh river air blowing in my face, I soon fell asleep. . . .

The rest of us stayed one more day, to finish drying and packing our meat. Then we loaded our boats and started down the river.

As she became older, Waheenee-wea continued to grow corn and hunt buffalo. By the late 1800s, however, white settlers had killed off almost all the buffalo herds on the Great Plains, and the United States government had forced the Hidatsa to live on reservations. Like other Plains Indians, the Hidatsa had to change their way of life.

Source: Waheenee, *An Indian Girl's Story Told by Herself to Gilbert L. Wilson*. St. Paul, MN: Webb Publishing Company, 1927; reprinted Lincoln, NE: University of Nebraska Press, 1981.

coulees: dry streambeds
lee side: side protected from the wind

bull boats: boats made from wood and bull hides
freight: carry
stalking: searching for

The Battle of Little Bighorn

by Two Moon, 1898

In 1868 the Sioux signed a treaty with the United States government, giving them ownership of the Black Hills region of what is today South Dakota. (You can see a record of this treaty in Lone Dog's Winter Count on pages 8-10.) When gold was discovered in the Black Hills in 1874, the United States government demanded that the Sioux sell their land. The Sioux refused. In order to regain this land and force all the Plains Indians onto reservations, the United States went to war against the Sioux and their neighbors, the Cheyenne. The first major battle took place in the spring of 1876 on the Rosebud River in present-day Montana, and the Indians defeated the United States army. An even larger battle, known as the Battle of Little Bighorn, or Custer's Last Stand, took place on June 25, 1876, along the banks of the nearby Little Bighorn River. Chief Two Moon (1847-1917) of the Cheyenne—who is pictured on page 121— fought in these two battles. More than 20 years later, in 1898, he described these battles to a magazine reporter. As you read an excerpt from this article, think about the scenes Chief Two Moon describes. How did the Sioux and the Cheyenne feel about fighting? How did they feel after the Battle of Little Bighorn?

That spring [1876] I was camped on **Powder River** with fifty lodges of my people—Cheyennes. . . . One morning soldiers charged my camp. . . . We were surprised and scattered, leaving our ponies. The soldiers ran all our horses off. That night the soldiers slept, leaving the horses [on] one side; so we crept up and stole them back again, and then we went away.

Powder River: river in southeast Montana

We traveled far, and one day we met a big camp of Sioux at **Charcoal Butte**. We camped with the Sioux, and had a good time, plenty [of] grass, plenty [of] game, [and] good water. **Crazy Horse** was head chief of the camp. **Sitting Bull** was camped a little ways below, on the **Little Missouri River**.

Charcoal Butte: steep-sided flat hill in southeast Montana

Crazy Horse: a Sioux leader

Sitting Bull: a Sioux leader

Crazy Horse said to me, "I'm glad you [have] come. We are going to fight the white man again."

Little Missouri River: river in southeast Montana

The camp was already full of wounded men, women, and children.

I said to Crazy Horse, "All right. I am ready to fight. I have fought already. My people have been killed, my horses stolen; I am satisfied to fight." . . .

119

About May, when the grass was tall and the horses strong, we broke camp and started [west] across the country to the mouth of the **Tongue River**. Then Sitting Bull and Crazy Horse and all went up the **Rosebud [River]**. There we had a big fight with **General [George] Crook**, and whipped him. Many soldiers were killed—few Indians. It was a great fight, much smoke and dust.

From there we all went over the divide, and camped in the valley of [the] **Little [Bighorn River]**. Everybody thought, "Now we are out of the white man's country. He can live there, we will live here." After a few days, one morning when I was in camp north of Sitting Bull, a Sioux messenger rode up and said, "Let everybody paint up, cook, and get ready for a big dance."

Cheyennes then went to work to cook, cut up tobacco, and get ready. We all thought to dance all day. We were very glad to think we were far away from the white man.

I went to water my horses at the creek, and washed them off with cool water, then took a swim myself. I came back to the camp afoot. When I got near my lodge, I looked up the Little [Bighorn] towards Sitting Bull's camp. I saw a great dust rising. It looked like a whirlwind. Soon [a] Sioux horseman came rushing into camp shouting: "Soldiers come! Plenty [of] white soldiers."

I ran into my lodge, and said to my brother-in-law, "Get your horses; the white man is coming. Everybody run for horses."

Outside, far up the valley, I heard a battle cry, *Hay-ay, hay-ay!* I heard shooting, too. . . . I couldn't see any Indians. Everybody was getting horses and saddles. After I had caught my horse, a Sioux warrior came again and said, "Many soldiers are coming."

Then he said to the women, "Get out of the way, we are going to have [a] hard fight."

I said, "All right, I am ready."

I got on my horse, and rode out into my camp. I called out to the people all running about: "I am Two Moon, your chief. Don't run away. Stay here and fight. You must stay and fight the white soldiers. I shall stay even if I am to be killed."

I rode swiftly toward Sitting Bull's camp. There I saw the white soldiers fighting in a line. Indians covered the **flat**. They began to drive the soldiers all mixed up—Sioux, then soldiers, then more Sioux, and all shooting. The air was full of smoke and dust. I saw the soldiers fall back and drop into the river-bed like buffalo fleeing. They had no time to look for a crossing. The Sioux chased them up the hill, where they met more soldiers in wagons, and then messengers came saying more soldiers were going to kill the women, and the Sioux turned back. **Chief Gall** was there fighting, Crazy Horse also.

I then rode toward my camp. . . . While I was sitting on my horse I saw flags come up over the hill to the east. . . . Then the soldiers

Tongue River: Montana river west of the Powder and Little Missouri rivers

Rosebud River: Montana river west of the Tongue River

General George Crook: a United States army officer

Little Bighorn River: Montana river west of the Rosebud River

flat: valley

Chief Gall: a Sioux leader

120

rose all at once, all on horses. . . . They formed into three bunches with a little ways between. Then a bugle sounded, and they all got off horses, and some soldiers led the horses back over the hill.

Then the Sioux rode up the ridge on all sides, riding very fast. The Cheyennes went up the left way. Then the shooting was quick, quick. Pop—pop—pop very fast. Some of the soldiers were down on their knees, some standing. Officers all in front. The smoke was like a great cloud, and everywhere the Sioux went the dust rose like smoke. We circled all round them—swirling like water round a stone. We shoot, we ride fast, we shoot again. Soldiers drop, and horses fall on them. Soldiers in line drop, but one man rides up and down the line—all the time shouting. He rode a **sorrel** horse. . . .

Indians keep swirling round and round, and the soldiers killed only a few. Many soldiers fell. At last all horses [were] killed but five. Once in a while some man would break out and run toward the river, but he would fall. At last about a hundred men and five horsemen stood on the hill all bunched together. All along the bugler kept blowing his commands. He was very brave. . . . Then a chief was killed. I hear it was **Long Hair**, I don't know; and then the five horsemen and the bunch of men, may be . . . forty, started toward the river. The man on the sorrel horse led them, shouting all the time. He wore a **buckskin** shirt, and had long black hair and [a] mustache. He fought hard with a big knife. His men were all covered with white dust. I couldn't tell whether they were officers or not. One man all alone ran far down toward the river, then round up over the hill. I thought he was going to escape, but a Sioux fired and hit him in the head. He was the last man. . . .

All the soldiers were now killed, and the bodies were stripped. After that no one could tell which were officers. The bodies were left where they fell. We had no dance that night. We were sorrowful.

Next day four Sioux chiefs and two Cheyennes and I, Two Moon, went upon the battlefield to count the dead. One man carried a little bundle of sticks. When we came to dead men, we took a little stick and gave it to another man, so we counted the dead. There were 388. There were thirty-nine Sioux and seven Cheyennes killed, and about a hundred wounded.

The Battle of Little Bighorn in 1876 marked the greatest military victory by American Indians against the United States army. It would also be one of the last Indian triumphs. In 1877 the army defeated the Sioux and the Cheyenne and forced them onto reservations. One of those forced to surrender was Chief Two Moon, who later served as a scout for the United States army.

Source: Hamlin Garland, "General Custer's Last Fight as Seen by Two Moon," *McClure's Magazine*, September 1898.

sorrel: light brown

Long Hair: nickname for Colonel George Armstrong Custer, a United States army officer

buckskin: antelope or deer hide

RESETTLING THE GREAT PLAINS Poster, 1870s

Even before the United States army had removed the Sioux, who were also known as the Dakota, from their lands on the Great Plains, the area was opened to new settlers. This area was called the Dakota Territory. Under the terms of the Homestead Act, passed in 1862, the United States government offered this land for free. To encourage homesteaders to settle the Dakota Territory, railroad companies put up posters throughout the eastern United States and in Europe. The poster on this page was used by the Chicago and North-Western Railway Company in the 1870s. How does the poster try to attract homesteaders? Why do you think the railroad company was eager for new settlers to come west?

Attracted by posters such as the one above, thousands of people headed west to the Great Plains in the 1870s and 1880s. Some of these posters were aimed at people called Exodusters. To learn about Exodusters, read the next document on page 123.

122

EXODUSTERS

Poster, 1877

As a result of the Civil War, slavery was ended in the United States in 1865. Although free, African Americans faced many hardships. With little money to buy land, many blacks in the South became sharecroppers and fell deeply into debt. Unfair laws denied them equal rights, and secret groups such as the Ku Klux Klan attacked and killed blacks throughout the South. To escape these conditions, many African Americans moved west to the Great Plains. A large migration, or movement, of people is called an exodus, and the Southern blacks who moved west after the Civil War were called Exodusters. Most Exodusters headed to Kansas because it had been one of the first free states in the Great Plains to enter the Union. This is a poster from 1877 encouraging African Americans to move to Kansas. Why do you think the poster is urging Exodusters to move in colonies, or groups?

All Colored People

THAT WANT TO

GO TO KANSAS,

On September 5th, 1877,

Can do so for $5.00

IMMIGRATION.

WHEREAS, We, the colored people of Lexington, Ky,. knowing that there is an abundance of choice lands now belonging to the Government, have assembled ourselves together for the purpose of locating on said lands. Therefore,

BE IT RESOLVED, That we do now organize ourselves into a Colony, as follows:— Any person wishing to become a member of this Colony can do so by paying the sum of one dollar ($1.00), and this money is to be paid by the first of September, 1877, in installments of twenty-five cents at a time, or otherwise as may be desired.

RESOLVED, That this Colony has agreed to consolidate itself with the Nicodemus Towns, Solomon Valley, Graham County, Kansas, and can only do so by entering the vacant lands now in their midst, which costs $5.00.

RESOLVED, That this Colony shall consist of seven officers—President, Vice-President, Secretary, Treasurer, and three Trustees. President—M. M. Bell; Vice-President—Isaac Talbott; Secretary—W. J. Niles; Treasurer—Daniel Clarke; Trustees—Jerry Lee, William Jones, and Abner Webster.

RESOLVED, That this Colony shall have from one to two hundred militia, more or less, as the case may require, to keep peace and order, and any member failing to pay in his dues, as aforesaid, or failing to comply with the above rules in any particular, will not be recognized or protected by the Colony.

Spurred on by the hope of cheap land and a freer life, thousands of Exodusters left the South and settled in Kansas in the 1870s and 1880s. Farming in the Great Plains, however, was anything but easy. To learn about some of the challenges facing new settlers—whether they were black or white—read the documents on pages 124-129.

123

GRASSHOPPER SUMMER

by Ann Turner, 1989

After the Civil War, posters like those on pages 122-123 helped persuade thousands of homesteaders to head west and settle on the Great Plains. Turning the vast, treeless prairies into productive farmland, however, took years of hard work. Homesteaders had to dig deep wells for water, build houses out of sod, and endure long, harsh winters. Grasshopper Summer, a novel by Ann Turner, written in 1989, follows a homesteading family that leaves Kentucky and settles in the Dakota Territory in 1874. When they first arrive, 11-year-old Sam White and his younger brother Billy help to build their family's house and to plant a field of corn. Sam's parents, Walter and Ellen, hope that they have made the right decision in coming west. But suddenly, during their first summer on the Great Plains, something happens that they never expected. As you read the following excerpt from Turner's novel, note the fear that grips the White family. How do they try to protect themselves?

Billy made a face at me. "Want to go fishing?"

"Nope. Too hot. Too many flies." Down by the creek it would be cooler, but the bugs'd be worse.

Billy flicked at the flies with one hand. "Poor horses," he sighed. We watched Pa **tethering** Ham and Duke in the shade of the sod barn. Their tails swished back and forth. They stamped, and Ham's big sides shuddered to keep the flies off.

tethering: tying

Pa came and flopped down beside us. "It's too hot to work today. Hope it won't hurt the corn," he worried.

"Now, Walter, the corn can survive a little heat. As long as we keep getting some rain."

"Haven't had much of *that*!" Pa said.

None of us said any more. It felt like bad luck to talk too much about the corn crop and what might go wrong. It was like looking backward over your shoulder when you went past a graveyard; as long as you *didn't* look, no ghosts could get you.

"Everything'll be just fine," **Mrs. Grant** said. I wanted to hush her, not to say more, but she went on. "We'll harvest the crops and get a good price, **Pete** says. Then we'll all be riding in **buggies** and dressing in silks, isn't that so, Ellie?"

"I hope so, Mary." She pushed at her wet hair and fanned baby **Ben**. He lay on the grass, looking up at the sky and played with his toes.

Allan and I had it all worked out. Once the crops were sold, we were both going to get rifles and go hunting together—maybe for coyotes. With what we could shoot and trap come winter, we'd have money of our own next spring.

Then the baby began to cry, a high, **fretful** sound. Mrs. Grant picked him up and **joggled** him back and forth.

"Here." Ma handed her a wet cloth, and Mrs. Grant patted Ben's face. He just cried harder.

Then the horses began to stamp and shy. First Ham—the nervous one—then Duke. Pa pointed to the sky. It was dark and smoky.

"Must be a storm coming. Quick, boys, help with the horses." We ran to the barn and Pa got Ham inside while Billy and I untethered Duke and put him in the barn. Once inside, they calmed down a bit, but Ham still tossed his head and rolled his eyes.

"They're spooked," Pa said, wiping his brow. "Don't know why, but something's got into them. I don't like the look of that sky. Maybe there's a thunderstorm coming."

We went back to the **dugout**, and Ma gave us water in a tin cup. The baby still cried.

"Shhh, let me have Ben," Billy said. Mrs. Grant hesitated, then handed him over. Billy snuggled the baby against his shoulder and walked up to the top of the dugout. "Maybe there's a breeze up here," he called down. The baby's head bobbed against his shoulder, and the crying stopped.

Billy watched the sky, and I watched him. He looked nervous, too, like the horses. The sun dimmed as the clouds came up. Suddenly, Billy cricked his neck back and shouted. He ran downhill to us, holding tight to the baby.

"There's something in those clouds, Pa, can't you see?" He pointed.

The clouds rolled toward us, like a big wind pushed them. The light was a strange, hard gray. At first they looked like everyday clouds, but then I began to see things in them.

Mrs. Mary Grant: a neighbor

Pete: Mrs. Grant's husband

buggies: carriages

Ben: Mrs. Grant's baby

Allan: Sam's friend

fretful: worried

joggled: rocked

dugout: sod house

125

"There's something moving in them!" Mrs. Grant yelled. "Small things."

"Insects!" Pa said in an awful voice. "**Locusts!**" They began to fall from the sky. Brown things falling, *plunk!* on Ma's bonnet. *Plunk!* on the baby's head and on Mrs. Grant's striped dress. *Thunk!* they landed on the garden.

locusts: grasshoppers

We just stood there a moment, frozen, then Ma shouted, "My garden!" She ran into the dugout and came back with **gunnysacks.** Mrs. Grant took her baby from Billy, rushed him into the dugout, tied him to the bedpost, and shut the door. They ran to the garden and ripped out the rows of lettuce and tiny, new carrots. The grasshoppers rained down on us, and it was hard to see. Ma and Mrs. Grant looked like people working in clouds of smoke.

gunnysacks: sacks made of gunny, a rough, heavy fabric

Pa shouted. "My rifle! Boys, you grab shovels, anything you can find from the barn and get out to the cornfield!"

Billy and I ran to the barn and grabbed rakes and shovels and raced out to the cornfield. Pa ran around the edge, shooting his rifle.

Capow! A small cloud lifted, then settled. He threw his hat on the ground and set off another volley. *Capow! Capow! Capow!*

I hit at them with the shovel, but for every ten I squished, another twenty fell from the sky. Brown bodies hanging on green leaves. Brown jaws tearing into the unripe corn. Billy struck at them with the spade, but nothing made any difference. All the time we raced around, trying to scare them off, no one said a word. Their crunching filled our ears.

Pa fired until all his bullets were gone. Then he shouted, "Sam, we'll dig a **trench** as far as we can in the plowed edge of the field. Billy, grab all the grass and twigs you can find. Pile them in the trench."

trench: ditch

Pa and I dug as fast as we could in the hard ground. The dirt flew to the side, and the grasshoppers fell on my hat, chewed on my collar. Their **raspy** claws poked through my shirt, but I couldn't stop digging.

raspy: scratchy

Billy ran up with arms full of grass and threw it into the trench. Pa pulled out his matches and lit the grass. It flared and caught, sending smoke up in dark clouds. The grasshoppers seemed to rise over the smoke for a moment. Pa put his hat on and cheered.

clamped: shut

Then the grasshoppers fell into the trench, *plunk!* They fell on top of each other, again and again. The fire sputtered and died. Pa just looked at it. He turned but did not see us.

"It's no use. Nothing will scare them. There's too many." He picked up his hat, wiped the grasshoppers off, and jammed it on his head. "Come back to the dugout, boys."

He turned, and we followed, Billy dragging the shovel behind. His face looked green, and his jaws were **clamped** tight. I clamped mine, too, afraid that I'd eat one of them if I breathed through my mouth. I felt sick and greasy inside, with those little claws clutching at my shirt and back and their bodies squishing under my feet. They were so deep now, it was like walking through a pile of leaves—brown, moving leaves.

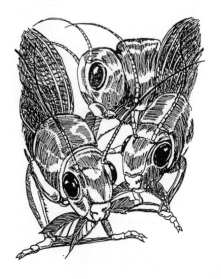

126

Mrs. Grant and Ma were still outside, flapping at the garden with those sacks. Pa yelled, "Come inside! It's no good, Ellen."

I went to help carry in the sacks of vegetables they'd picked, when Mrs. Grant began to scream.

"Ellen! Ellen! They're eating my dress. Get them off me!"

All along the green stripes of her dress, the grasshoppers were chewing. Pieces of white cloth fell to the ground. Pa ran into the dugout, and brought out Grandma's quilt. He wrapped it tight around her and pulled it off, taking most of the grasshoppers with it. She yelled, with loud, rising screams, and Pa hurried her inside. I slammed the door shut behind us. We brushed the grasshoppers off each other and stamped them dead.

"Ooooh, ooooh, get them off me!" Mrs. Grant beat at her tattered dress. "Get them off me!"

"They're off, Mary, it's all right," Ma soothed her, brushing the last grasshoppers from her and squishing them with a shovel. . . .

Billy went over and untied Ben, holding him tight against his chest. His eyes, over Ben's shoulder, looked . . . wide and scared. Pa stood in the middle of the room as wet as if he'd been in a rainstorm. Ma dabbed at her face with a handkerchief and kept repeating, "My heavens. Who would've ever thought. Who!" She shook herself, patted Mrs. Grant's hand, and drew out the water pail from under the table. She skimmed grasshoppers from it and filled a tin cup.

"Here. Drink this, Mary." Mrs. Grant hiccupped and drank.

"Ooooh, ooooh," she kept sighing. "Ooooh, their little feet." Ma drank some water, then Pa, and Billy, and I swallowed it down. Just to make the taste of them go away.

Bits of white clung to the seams around Mrs. Grant's shoulders and waist, along with a few ragged pieces of green. . . .

She blew her nose, and I could see she was trying hard not to cry. Suddenly, she buried her face in her arms and began to sob. "We have nothing, Ellen, nothing at all. We borrowed to buy the seed. Don't you see what this means?" She turned a terrible face toward Ma.

Quietly, Ma took a deep breath and said, " 'The locusts have no king, yet go they forth all of them by bands.' Oh, Mary, I am so sorry."

My mouth felt dusty and raw. My stomach hurt. I couldn't even look at Billy. We sat in that dugout, and even the thick walls could not keep out the sound of them chewing, eating up all we'd worked for.

The grasshoppers destroy the Whites' crops and force the family to borrow money to survive the following winter. The grasshopper attack of 1874, along with drought, tornadoes, hailstorms, and blizzards, forced thousands of homesteaders to give up farming on the Great Plains. Many stayed, however, and through hard work helped to turn this vast region into the nation's breadbasket. For a firsthand account of pioneer life, read the next document on pages 128–129.

Source: Ann Turner, *Grasshopper Summer.* New York: Macmillan Publishing Company, 1989.

THE STORY OF A PIONEER

by Anna Howard Shaw, 1915

Was life as a pioneer really as challenging as that described by novelist Ann Turner in the story on pages 124-127? You can judge for yourself by reading the excerpt below from The Story of a Pioneer, an autobiography by Anna Howard Shaw (1847-1919) written in 1915. When Anna was a girl in 1859, her father traveled to Michigan and built a log cabin deep in the woods. He then returned to Massachusetts and sent his wife, oldest son, and four youngest children to live in Michigan. Mrs. Shaw and her oldest son soon became sick and could not work. This left the care of the family to 12-year-old Anna. As you read her autobiography, notice the different tasks Anna has to do and the hardships she must overcome. What skills does Anna need to survive?

We all had an idea that we were going to a farm, and we expected some resemblance at least to the **prosperous** farms we had seen in New England. . . .What we found awaiting us were the four walls and the roof of a good-sized log-house, standing in a small cleared strip of the wilderness, its doors and windows represented by square holes, its floor also a thing of the future, its whole effect achingly **forlorn** and **desolate.**

prosperous: successful, flourishing

[When my father sent us] to live there alone until he could join us eighteen months later, he gave no thought to the manner in which we were to make the struggle and survive the hardships before us. He had furnished us with land and the four walls of a log cabin. . . .We were one hundred miles [160 km] from a railroad, forty miles [64 km] from the nearest post-office, and half a dozen miles [10 km] from any neighbors. . .; we were wholly unlearned in the ways of the woods as well as in the most primitive methods of farming; we lacked not only every comfort, but even the bare necessities of life. . . .

forlorn: sad, lonely
desolate: deserted

We faced our situation with clear and unalarmed eyes the morning after our arrival. . . .We had brought with us enough coffee, pork, and flour to last for several weeks; and the one necessity father had put inside the cabin walls was a great fireplace, made of mud and stones, in which our food could be cooked. [We found] a creek a long distance from the house; and for months we carried from this creek, in pails, every drop of water we used, save that which we caught in **troughs** when the rain fell. . . .

troughs: containers

Obviously the first thing to do was to put doors and windows into the yawning holes father had left for them, and to lay a board flooring over the earth inside our cabin walls, and these duties we accomplished before we had occupied our new home a **fortnight**. . . .We began by making three windows and two doors; then, inspired by these achievements, we ambitiously constructed an attic and divided the ground floor with **partitions**, which gave us four rooms. . . .

fortnight: two weeks

partitions: walls

The boards which formed the floor were never even nailed down; they were fine, wide planks without a **knot** in them, and they looked so well that we merely fitted them together as closely as we could. . . . Neither did we properly **chink** the house. Nothing is more comfortable than a log cabin which has been carefully built and finished; but for some reason—probably because there seemed always a more urgent duty calling to us around the corner—we never plastered our house at all. The result was that on many future winter mornings we awoke to find ourselves. . .blanketed by snow, while the only warm spot in our living-room was that directly in front of the fireplace, where great logs burned all day. Even there our faces **scorched** while our spines slowly **congealed**, until we learned to **revolve** before the fire like a bird upon a **spit**. . . .

knot: hole

chink: fill in the gaps between the logs of

scorched: burned
congealed: froze
revolve: turn
spit: metal pole on which meat is roasted

My brothers and I [did] the work out of doors. . . .It was too late in the season for plowing or planting, even if we had possessed anything with which to plow, and, moreover, our so-called "cleared" land was thick with sturdy tree-stumps. . . .

Harry and I gathered. . .gooseberries, raspberries, and plums. . .on the banks of our creek. Harry also became an expert fisherman. We had no hooks or lines, but he took wires from our **hoop-skirts** and made **snares** at the ends of poles. My part of this work was to stand on a log and frighten the fish out of their holes by making horrible sounds, which I did with **impassioned earnestness**. When the fish hurried to the surface of the water to investigate the **appalling** noises they had heard, they were easily snared by our small boy, who was very proud of his ability to contribute in this way to the family table.

Harry: Anna's 8-year-old brother

hoop-skirts: old-fashioned skirts held up with hoops
snares: traps
impassioned earnestness: great seriousness
appalling: horrible

During our first winter we lived largely on **cornmeal**, making a little journey of twenty miles [32 km] to the nearest mill to buy it; but even at that we were better off than our neighbors, for I remember one family in our region who for an entire winter lived solely on **coarse-grained** yellow turnips, gratefully changing their diet to **leeks** when these came in the spring.

cornmeal: ground corn

coarse-grained: rough
leeks: onion-like vegetables

Anna Howard Shaw continued to take care of her family throughout the 1860s. She later taught school and became one of the first women in the United States to graduate from both divinity, or religious-training, school and medical school. Shaw worked as a minister and a doctor and later became one of the nation's leading speakers and organizers for women's suffrage. Shaw's harsh pioneer life had certainly taught her how to survive and overcome any challenges she faced.

Source: Anna Howard Shaw, *The Story of a Pioneer.* New York: Harper, 1915.

FOR SALE BY MAIL

Advertisements from the *Sears, Roebuck Catalogue*, 1897

In the late 1800s factories in the United States were producing more goods than ever before. But factory owners had a problem. Two out of three Americans lived in rural areas, far from stores and businesses. Getting into town to buy goods was often hard and time-consuming. In the 1890s business leaders came up with a new way to reach customers—by mail. Large companies such as Sears, Roebuck began printing huge catalogs—some of them over 1,000 pages—filled with products for sale. These catalogs featured new items such as refrigerators and "magic lanterns." Look at some of the items advertised in the 1897 Sears, Roebuck Catalogue. Why might people have wanted these products? How do the advertisements try to encourage shoppers to buy the products? How do these advertisements compare with advertisements today?

No. 65011.
CALENDAR WATCH.
If you own one of these watches you will not find it necessary to consult an almanac or ask some one to tell you the day of the month. The case is nickel plated, and fitted with a heavy beveled edge glass.
The movement is imported, stem wind and stem set, jeweled, cylinder escapement, hard enameled dial, and in addition to being complete in every respect as a timekeeper, it has a complete calendar, which works automatically, always indicating correctly the day of the month.
Price..................$4.45

OUR $58.00 B GRADE COLUMBUS PHAETON.

This is a Genuine Columbus, O. Phaeton,

With care they will Last a lifetime.

MADE BY

One of the Oldest and Most Reliable Manufacturers in Columbus, Ohio.

A BINDING TWO YEAR'S GUARANTY GOES WITH EVERY PHAETON.

OUR REGULAR B GRADE
Guaranteed
Work

We Offer a Cheap Special B Grade Phaeton at $39.90.

No. 92816. Order by Number.

We have many other grades of Phaeton's in our Special Vehicle Catalogue which will be mailed free to any Address upon application.

Juvenile Magic Lanterns and Outfit.
We believe that money cannot be spent to better advantage for the amusement of children than for a magic lantern and outfit. They derive a great deal of pleasure from giving magic lantern exhibitions, posting circulars, and all of the detail connected with an amateur entertainment.

No. 61000.
No. 61000. The "Home" Magic Lantern for parlor entertainments; has metal body, handsomely japanned, with gilt decorations, and has kerosene lamp with six colored slides, with views 1½ inches wide, magnifying picture to about one foot. Each..................75c

PRESERVED MEATS.

No family should be without a nice supply of these preserved meats. Handy for quick lunches, outings, traveling and very palatable. As usual, we keep only the best, and you must be sure to include some in your freight order.

Tongue.
Doz. Each.
G 1472 1-lb. Lunch Tongue.........$2 75 $0 25
Ham.
G 1473 Potted ¼-lb. tins.........$1 00 $0 10

POTTED HAM
SEARS ROEBUCK & CO
CHICAGO

Boys' Blouse Waists.

Sizes 4 to 12 Years.
EVERY ONE A GREAT BARGAIN. New and Handsome Patterns; Nobby Effects and Rich Colorings. You cannot afford to overlook them.
No. 21471 Boys' Extra Quality Fast Colored Percale Blouse, with large ruffled sailor collar, ruffled front and cuffs. Assorted colors and patterns; pinks, blues, etc. All combination colors. Sizes 4 to 12 years.
Price each...$0.43
Three for... 1.20

130

SPALDING'S BASEMEN'S AND INFIELDERS' MITTS.

No. 8924. Mitt, made of the very best and softest light tanned buckskin; the thumb and at wrist are extra well padded with the highest quality felt, making it a very safe and easy fitting mitt combined with strength and durability. The mitt throughout is of the best workmanship, as indicated by our "Highest Quality" trade mark. Made in rights and lefts. Each $2.55

No. 8924.

...stained and polished, and decorated with gilt stripes. Extra value and worth double the money. Each..$0.10

No. 8910. Spalding's Black End, Boys' Maple Bat, plain finish with gilt stripes, a dandy bat for a few pennies. Each...............$0.04 Per dozen............$0.45

D 184 Worm Cakes. This is a very satisfactory remedy for destroying worms and removing them from the system. It is in convenient form for children to take, which they readily do, thinking it is a candy. Full instructions how to give them and other useful information in each box. Price 20c; Doz.....................$2.25

RELIABLE WORM CAKES Pleasant and Effective

Our $1.99 Leader.

No. 23469 A style made Hat, one of the lovely productions of '97. Wire frames entirely covered with handsome lace, finished with a jet edge and a very pretty jet crown, trimmed on right side with loops of lace and on left side with a handsome bunch of flowers and loops...red lace...

Tricycles and Velocipedes.

Notwithstanding the immense popularity of the bicycle, the tricycle and velocipede still remain in favor. Many parents prefer them for their children by reason of their safety, convenience and the ease with which they can be run by the little girl or boy. The tricycle, which we illustrate, is made for girls or boys from two to fifteen years. They are constructed with especial care and will stand the abuse they very frequently receive. They are very easy running and handsomely finished. The improved spring seat takes all vibration, and being upholstered in plush and furnished with back, makes riding easy and comfortable. Frame is enameled black. Quoted with iron tire wheels or C plate rubber tire wheels. The illustration shows the tricycle with fenders. We quote without fenders. The following are our special prices with iron tire wheels:

No. 85018 Rear wheels 18 inch, for girls 2 to 4 years	$3.35
No. 85019 Rear wheels 20 inch, for girls 3 to 5 years	4.45
No. 85020 Rear wheels 22 inch, for girls 4 to 7 years	5.30
No. 85021 Rear wheels 26 inch, for girls 7 to 10 years	6.35
No. 85022 Rear wheels 30 inch, for girls 10 to 15 years	7.35

..Perfection in Fine Footwear..

No. 3607 THIS ELEGANT BOOT is the very latest production in fine footwear, and is one of the most popular shoes we have ever sold. Made from finest selection of VICI KID, Coin Toe with Patent Leather Tips, Patent Leather Lace Stay, fancy vamp and heel foxing. AND NEVER WAS EQUALED FOR THIS PRICE.

SIZES, 2 1-2 to 7. WIDTHS, B, C, D, E and EE.

OUR SPECIAL PRICE, PER PAIR $2.85

Rich's Patent "Julia Marlowe" Lace Boot

THE RICH SHOE CO.

A FEW OF ITS GOOD POINTS.....

Produced Through Having Elastic Coring Over the Instep.

IT FITS like a glove. IT IS BEAUTIFUL in design. IT NEVER PINCHES the foot. FITS either high or low instep. IT YIELDS to every action of the foot. IT CONFORMS in vital points to the shape of the wearer's foot instead of pressing the foot...

NONE GENUINE Unless bearing this Stamp on every Sole.

Pat. Aug 11 -96. JULIA MARLOWE

Kazoos.

No. 7778. The Kazoo is the simplest musical 'nstrument made. No trouble to learn. Insert some noise at the one end, the pleasing music is emitted from the other. Made of maple with metal ring.

Each $0.08
Per dozen 0.85

Our Combined Acme Dry Air Refrigerator and Sideboard at from $11.47 to $18.67.

One of our very finest ..

REFRIGERATORS

It is made of solid oak.

Finished antique, highly polished, heavily paneled on front, sides, back and bottom; is fitted with a sideboard attachment with a heavy beveled French plate mirror. The whole is beautifully carved and decorated with raised carved ornamentations. This is a very large refrigerator and one of the most popular styles we have. All but the two smaller sizes have an ice chest large enough to take artificial ice.

Has lift-out Ice Reservoir.

Ice Rack is made entirely of metal.

Sears, Roebuck quickly became the biggest mail-order company in the world. Goods that had once been available only in towns and cities could now be bought anywhere in the United States. In this way, mail-order catalogs helped to bridge the gap between country and city. How might these new products have changed people's lives?

Source: *Sears, Roebuck Catalogue.* Chicago, 1897.

131

CHILD LABOR IN THE MINES

by John Spargo, 1906

The products in the Sears, Roebuck Catalogue that you read about on pages 130-131 were sold all over the country in the late 1800s and early 1900s. Almost all of these goods were made in factories, and most of these factories ran on coal. Coal also powered railroads and heated people's homes across the United States. But coal, the nation's most important source of energy at the time, was buried deep in the ground, and coal miners had to work hard to get it out. Many coal miners were children under the age of ten. Day in, day out, these children worked in dangerous places for long hours. In the early 1900s, a writer named John Spargo (1876-1966) visited some of these coal mines and wrote a book called The Bitter Cry of the Children. *Below is an excerpt from Spargo's book. As you read this excerpt, notice the different tasks performed by children in the mines. How does Spargo feel about child labor? What evidence does he present to support his view?*

According to the **census** of 1900, there were 25,000 boys under sixteen years of age employed in and around the mines and quarries of the United States. In the state of Pennsylvania alone . . . there are thousands of little "**breaker boys**" employed, many of them not more than nine or ten years old. . . . During the . . . coal strike of 1902, I attended the Labor Day demonstration at **Pittston** and witnessed the parade of another at **Wilkes-Barre**. In each case there were hundreds of boys marching, all of them wearing their "working buttons," **testifying to** the fact that they were *bona fide* workers. **Scores** of them were less than ten years of age, others were eleven or twelve.

Work in the coal **breakers** is exceedingly hard and dangerous. Crouched over the **chutes**, the boys sit hour after hour, picking out the pieces of slate and other **refuse** from the coal as it rushes past to the washers. From the cramped position they have to assume, most of them become more or less **deformed** and bent-backed like old men. . . . The coal is hard, and accidents to the hands, such as

census: population count

breaker boys: boys who separate coal from waste products

Pittston: town in Pennsylvania

Wilkes-Barre: town in Pennsylvania

testifying to: proving

bona fide: real

scores: many

breakers: rooms where coal is separated

chutes: sloping platforms

refuse: waste products

deformed: misshapen

cut, broken, or crushed fingers, are common among the boys. Sometimes there is a worse accident: a terrified shriek is heard, and a boy is **mangled** and torn in the machinery, or disappears in the chute to be picked out later smothered and dead. Clouds of dust fill the breakers and are **inhaled** by the boys, laying the foundations for **asthma** and miners' **consumption**. I once stood in a breaker for half an hour and tried to do the work a twelve-year-old boy was doing day after day, for ten hours at a stretch, for sixty cents a day. The gloom of the breaker **appalled** me. Outside the sun shone brightly, the air was **pellucid**, and the birds sang in chorus with the trees and the rivers. Within the breaker there was blackness, clouds of deadly dust **enfolded** everything, the harsh, grinding roar of the machinery and the **ceaseless** rushing of coal through the chutes filled the ears. I tried to pick out the pieces of slate from the hurrying stream of coal, often missing them; my hands were bruised and cut in a few minutes; I was covered from head to foot with coal dust, and for many hours afterwards I was **expectorating** some of the small particles of **anthracite** I had swallowed.

I could not do that work and live, but there were boys of ten and twelve years of age doing it for fifty and sixty cents a day. Some of them had never been inside of a school; few of them could read a child's **primer**. True, some of them attended the night schools, but after working ten hours in the breaker the educational results from attending school were practically *nil*. . . .

Nor is it in Pennsylvania only that these conditions exist. In the **bituminous** mines of West Virginia, boys of nine or ten are frequently employed. I met one little fellow ten years old in Mt. Carbon, West Virginia, last year, who was employed as a "trap boy." Think of what it means to be a trap boy at ten years of age. It means to sit alone in a dark mine passage hour after hour, with no human soul near; to see no living creature except the mules as they pass with their loads, or a rat or two seeking to share one's meal; to stand in water or mud that covers the ankles, chilled to the **marrow** by the cold **draughts** that rush in when you open the trap-door for the mules to pass through; to work for fourteen hours—waiting—opening and shutting a door—then waiting again—for sixty cents; to reach the surface when all is wrapped in the **mantle** of night, and to fall to the earth exhausted and have to be carried away to the nearest "shack" to be **revived** before it is possible to walk to the farther shack called "home."

mangled: injured, crippled

inhaled: breathed in

asthma: breathing disease

consumption: lung disease, tuberculosis

appalled: shocked

pellucid: clear

enfolded: surrounded

ceaseless: endless

expectorating: coughing up

anthracite: hard coal

primer: schoolbook

nil: nothing

bituminous: soft coal

marrow: bone

draughts: drafts

mantle: covering

revived: brought back to life

At the time John Spargo wrote this description in 1906, more than 300,000 children, age 15 and under, were working in mines, factories, and mills across the country. Many people were horrified to learn of these conditions and worked both to outlaw child labor and to reduce the number of hours people worked each day. Leading this effort were labor unions and working people. For a look at their goals and beliefs, read the song on page 134.

Source: John Spargo, *The Bitter Cry of the Children*. New York: The Macmillan Company, 1906.

Eight Hours

Words by I. G. Blanchard and Music by Jesse H. Jones, 1866

As the document on pages 132-133 showed, children often worked in mines and factories for 10 hours a day in the 1800s. Adults worked even longer—as many as 16 hours a day. Workers formed labor unions to gain better working conditions and a shorter workday. In 1866 a newspaper called the Workingman's Advocate printed a poem by I. G. Blanchard called Eight Hours. A minister named Jesse H. Jones later set the words to music. How does this song express some of the hopes, goals, and accomplishments of American workers and unions?

1. We mean to make things o - ver, we are tired of toil for naught,
2. Hur - rah, hur - rah, for La - bor! for it shall a - rise in might;

With barely e - nough to live up - on, and nev - er an hour for thought;
It has filled the world with plen - ty, it shall fill the world with light;

We want to feel the sun - shine, and we want to smell the flowers,
Hur - rah, hur - rah, for La - bor! it is muster - ing all its powers,

We are sure that God has will'd it, and we mean to have eight hours.
And shall march a - long to vic - tor - y with the ban - ner of Eight Hours!

We're sum - mon - ing our for - ces from the ship - yard, shop and mill,
Shout, shout the ec - ho - ing ral - ly till all the hea - vens thrill,

Eight hours for work, eight hours for rest, eight hours for what we will!

Eight hours for work, eight hours for rest, eight hours for what we will!

Source: Adapted from the *Workingman's Advocate*, August 18, 1866, reprinted in Philip S. Foner, *American Labor Songs of the Nineteenth Century*. Chicago: University of Illinois Press, 1975.

The Promised Land

by Mary Antin, 1911

In one of the greatest waves of immigration in history, more than 28 million people from all over the world came to the United States between 1860 and 1920. Many immigrants came for freedom and for opportunity, and they called America "the promised land." One of these immigrants was a 13-year-old Russian Jew named Mary Antin (1881–1949). Speaking no English, she and her family arrived in Boston, Massachusetts, in 1894 to join Mary's father, who had come to the United States three years earlier. In 1911 she wrote her autobiography, which she titled The Promised Land. *In the following excerpt, Antin describes her first days in the United States. How does she feel about her new country? What are her first thoughts about going to school?*

Our **initiation** into American ways began with the first step on the new soil. My father found occasion to instruct or correct us even on the way from the pier to **Wall Street**, which journey we made crowded together in a rickety cab. He told us not to lean out of the windows, [and] not to point. . . .

The first meal was an object lesson of much variety. My father produced several kinds of food, ready to eat, without any cooking, from little tin cans that had printing all over them. He attempted to introduce us to a queer, slippery kind of fruit, which he called [a] "banana," but [he] had to give it up for the time being. After the meal, he had better luck with a curious piece of furniture on runners, which he called [a] "rocking-chair." There were five of us newcomers, and we found five different ways of getting into the American machine of **perpetual** motion, and as many ways of getting out of it. One born and **bred** to the use of a rocking-chair cannot imagine

initiation: introduction

Wall Street: street in Boston

perpetual: constant
bred: raised

135

how **ludicrous** people can make themselves when attempting to use it for the first time. We laughed **immoderately** over our various experiments with the **novelty**, which was a **wholesome** way of letting off steam after the unusual excitement of the day.

In our **flat** we did not think of such a thing as storing the coal in the bathtub. There was no bathtub. So in the evening of the first day my father conducted us to the **public baths**. As we moved along in a little **procession**, I was delighted with the **illumination** of the streets. So many lamps, and they burned until morning, my father said, and so people did not need to carry lanterns. In America, then, everything was free, as we had heard in Russia. Light was free; the streets were as bright as a **synagogue** on a holy day. Music was free; we had been **serenaded**, to our gaping delight, by a brass band of many pieces, soon after our **installation** on **Union Place**.

Education was free. That subject my father had written about repeatedly, as **comprising** his chief hope for us children, the **essence** of American opportunity, the treasure that no thief could touch, not even misfortune or poverty. It was the one thing that he was able to promise us when he sent for us; surer, safer than bread or shelter. On our second day I was thrilled with the **realization** of what this freedom of education meant. A little girl from across the alley came and offered to **conduct** us to school. My father was out, but we five between us had a few words of English by this time. We knew the word school. We understood. This child, who had never seen us till yesterday, who could not pronounce our names, who was not much better dressed than we, was able to offer us the freedom of the schools of Boston! No application made, no questions asked, no **examinations**, rulings, **exclusions**; no **machinations**, no fees. The doors stood open for every one of us. The smallest child could show us the way.

This incident impressed me more than anything I had heard in advance of the freedom of education in America. It was a concrete proof—almost the thing itself. One had to experience it to understand it.

As was the case in many immigrant families, Mary Antin's older sister could not go to school because she needed to work to help the family earn money. Because of the sacrifices of both her sister and her parents, Mary was able to attend school and go to college. She later became a poet and an author, and worked for women's rights. Antin never forgot her immigrant roots, and she later fought against efforts to limit the number of immigrants to the United States. For an account of another immigrant's very different experience in America, read the next document on pages 137-138.

Source: Mary Antin, *The Promised Land*. Boston: The Atlantic Monthly Company, 1911; reprinted Boston: Houghton Mifflin Company, 1969.

ludicrous: silly, ridiculous
immoderately: very much
novelty: new item
wholesome: healthy
flat: apartment

public baths: places where people can bathe
procession: group
illumination: lighting

synagogue: Jewish house of worship
serenaded: sung to
installation: settling in
Union Place: street in Boston
comprising: making up
essence: heart, basis

realization: understanding

conduct: lead

examinations: tests
exclusions: keeping people out
machinations: tricks

A Chinese Immigrant and the Statue of Liberty

by Saum Song Bo, 1885

Not all immigrants were as lucky as Mary Antin, whom you read about on pages 135-136. In 1882 Congress passed a law preventing almost all Chinese people from coming to the United States. Congress also prevented Chinese immigrants already in the country from becoming American citizens. At the same time, Americans were building a base for a giant new statue given to the United States by France—the Statue of Liberty. In order to raise money to finish building this base, fund-raisers sent out letters to people across the country. One of these letters was sent to Saum Song Bo, a Chinese immigrant. In response, he sent out his own letter in 1885 to the New York Sun, a daily newspaper. Below is an excerpt from this letter. How does Saum Song Bo feel about the Statue of Liberty and the way Chinese people were being treated in the United States?

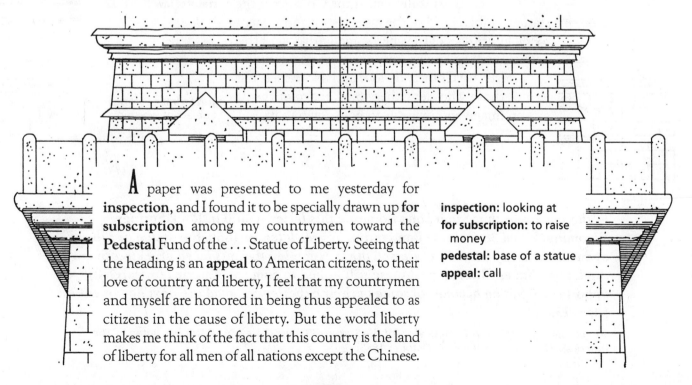

A paper was presented to me yesterday for **inspection**, and I found it to be specially drawn up **for subscription** among my countrymen toward the **Pedestal** Fund of the ... Statue of Liberty. Seeing that the heading is an **appeal** to American citizens, to their love of country and liberty, I feel that my countrymen and myself are honored in being thus appealed to as citizens in the cause of liberty. But the word liberty makes me think of the fact that this country is the land of liberty for all men of all nations except the Chinese.

inspection: looking at
for subscription: to raise money
pedestal: base of a statue
appeal: call

137

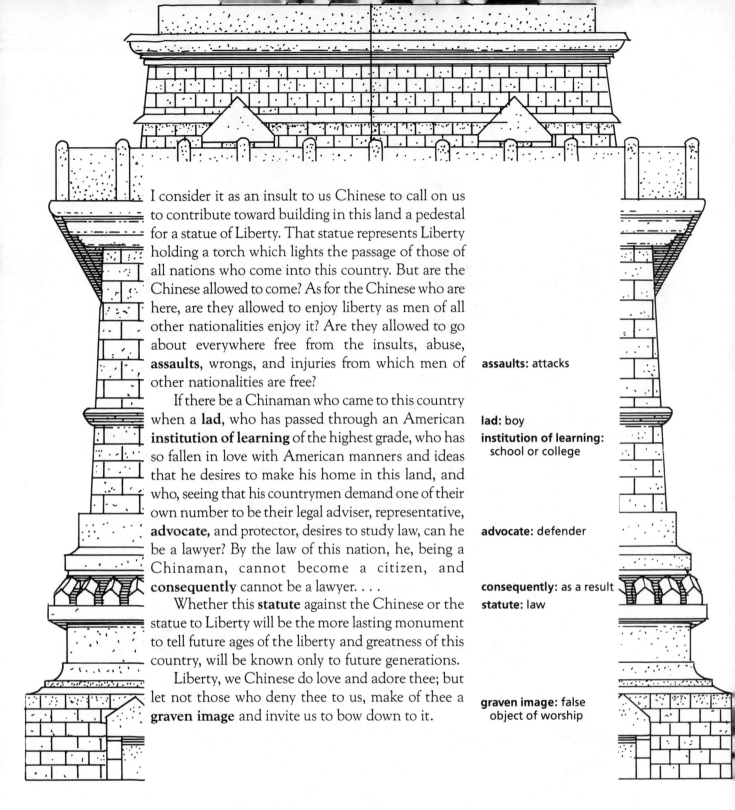

I consider it as an insult to us Chinese to call on us to contribute toward building in this land a pedestal for a statue of Liberty. That statue represents Liberty holding a torch which lights the passage of those of all nations who come into this country. But are the Chinese allowed to come? As for the Chinese who are here, are they allowed to enjoy liberty as men of all other nationalities enjoy it? Are they allowed to go about everywhere free from the insults, abuse, **assaults**, wrongs, and injuries from which men of other nationalities are free?

assaults: attacks

If there be a Chinaman who came to this country when a **lad**, who has passed through an American **institution of learning** of the highest grade, who has so fallen in love with American manners and ideas that he desires to make his home in this land, and who, seeing that his countrymen demand one of their own number to be their legal adviser, representative, **advocate,** and protector, desires to study law, can he be a lawyer? By the law of this nation, he, being a Chinaman, cannot become a citizen, and **consequently** cannot be a lawyer. . . .

lad: boy

institution of learning: school or college

advocate: defender

consequently: as a result

Whether this **statute** against the Chinese or the statue to Liberty will be the more lasting monument to tell future ages of the liberty and greatness of this country, will be known only to future generations.

statute: law

Liberty, we Chinese do love and adore thee; but let not those who deny thee to us, make of thee a **graven image** and invite us to bow down to it.

graven image: false object of worship

In the same year that Saum Song Bo wrote this letter, a mob in Rock Springs, Wyoming, killed 28 Chinese immigrants. A year later, in 1886, the Statue of Liberty opened. For many years Chinese and other Asian immigrants faced cruel treatment in the United States. But many Chinese still hoped to come to America in search of opportunity. For an account of some of their experiences, read the next document on pages 139-140.

Source: Saum Song Bo, "A Chinese View of the Statue of Liberty," New York *Sun*, reprinted in *The American Missionary*, Volume 39, October 1885.

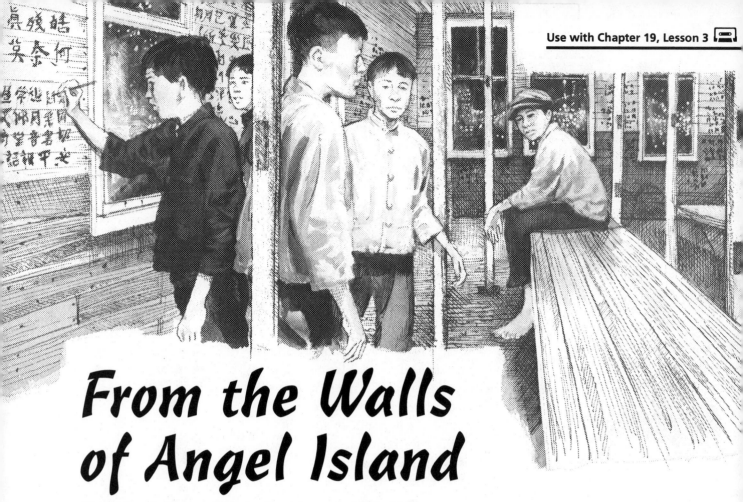

From the Walls of Angel Island

Poems by Unknown Chinese Immigrants, 1910–1940

Congress passed a law in 1882 limiting immigration from China. But many Chinese, seeking a better life, still tried to come. In 1910 the United States opened a new immigration center for Chinese immigrants on Angel Island in San Francisco Bay. As soon as their boats docked, Chinese men and women were separated from each other and taken to a wooden building on Angel Island. On this island, Chinese immigrants had to take medical tests and answer many questions before they could leave. Some were forced to stay on Angel Island for a few weeks, others for as long as three years. This lack of freedom, along with poor food, poor health care, and lack of privacy, made Angel Island seem like a prison. During their long hours of waiting, many of the immigrants wrote poems on the walls of the building expressing their feelings about their condition. Most of these poems were written by teenage boys and young men who did not sign their names. Five of their poems are printed below in the original Chinese and in English translation. In what ways do these poems describe how the immigrants felt about their treatment in America?

困囚木屋常愁悶：
憶別家鄉月幾圓。
家人倚望音書切：
憑誰傳語報平安？

Imprisoned in this wooden building,
   I am always sad and bored.
I remember since I left my native village,
   it has been several **full moons**.
The family at home is leaning on the
   door, urgently looking for letters.
Whom can I count on to tell them I
   am well?

full moons: months

139

美有強權無公理，
囹圄吾人也罹辜。
不由分説真殘酷，
俯首回思莫奈何。

America has power, but not justice.
In prison, we were **victimized** as if we were guilty.
Given no opportunity to explain, it was really brutal.
I bow my head in **reflection** but there is nothing I can do.

victimized: treated badly

reflection: deep thought

凤慕花旗幾優哉，
即時籌款動程來。
風波閱月已歷盡。
監牢居所受災磨。
仰望屋崙相咫尺，
願回祖國負耕鋤。
滿腹牢騷難寢寐，
聊書數句表心裁。

I used to admire the **land of the Flowery Flag** as a country of **abundance**.
I immediately raised money and started my journey.
For over a month, I have experienced enough winds and waves.
Now on an extended **sojourn** in jail, I am subject to the **ordeals** of prison life.
I look up and see **Oakland** so close by.
I wish to go back to my motherland to carry the farmer's hoe.
Discontent fills my belly and it is difficult for me to sleep.
I just write these few lines to express what is on my mind.

land of the Flowery Flag: Chinese term for the United States

abundance: plenty

sojourn: stay

ordeals: struggles

Oakland: city near San Francisco

壁上題詩過百篇，
看來皆是嘆迍邅。
愁人曷向愁人訴，
自古英雄每厄先。

Over a hundred poems are on the walls.
Looking at them, they are all **pining** at the delayed progress.
What can one sad person say to another?
Unfortunate travellers everywhere wish to **commiserate**....
From ancient times, heroes often were the first ones to face **adversity**.

pining: suffering

commiserate: share their feelings of sadness

adversity: hardship

埃屋三椽聊保身，
崙麓積懷不堪陳。
待得飛騰順遂日，
劃除關税不論仁。

The low building with three **beams** merely shelters the body.
It is unbearable to relate the stories **accumulated** on the Island slopes.
Wait till the day I become successful and fulfill my wish!
I will not speak of love when I **level** the immigration station!

beams: heavy pieces of lumber

accumulated: gathered

level: destroy

Between 1910 and 1940, about 100,000 Chinese passed through Angel Island. Some were allowed to enter the United States but many were forced to return to China. Some of the Chinese imprisoned on the island banded together and successfully fought for better conditions. Angel Island was closed in 1940. Today Angel Island is a state park open to the public and the poems can still be seen on the building's walls.

Source: Him Mark Lai, Genny Lim, and Judy Yung, *Island: Poetry and History of Chinese Immigrants on Angel Island, 1910–1940.* Seattle, WA: University of Washington Press, 1980.

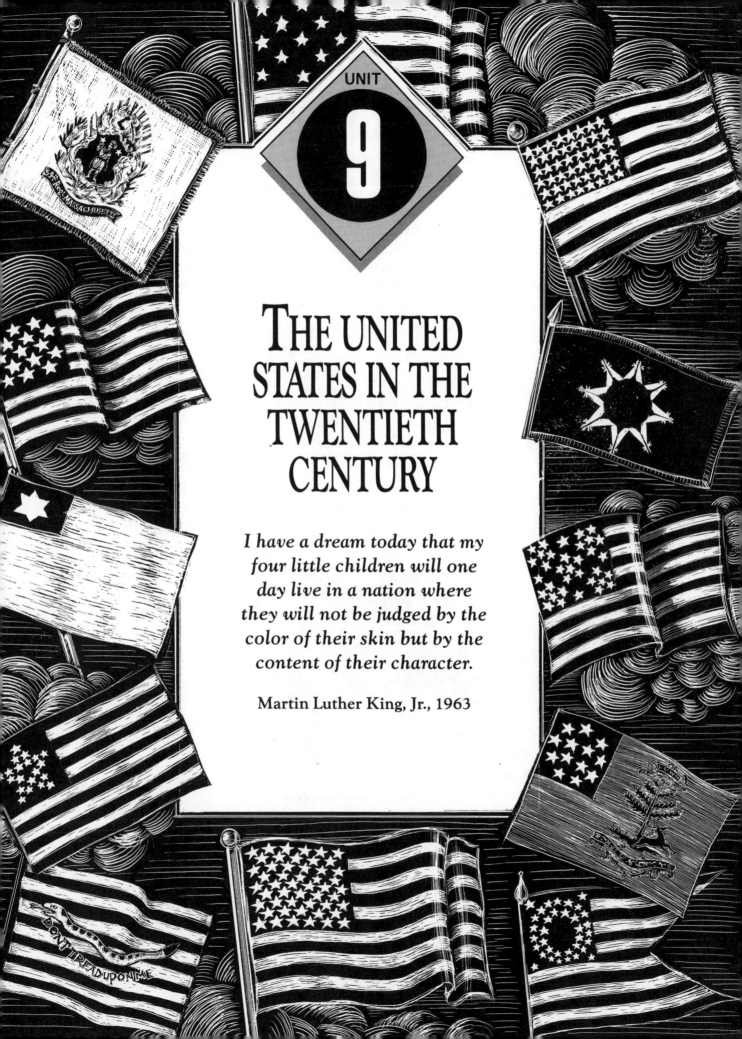

UNIT

9

THE UNITED STATES IN THE TWENTIETH CENTURY

I have a dream today that my four little children will one day live in a nation where they will not be judged by the color of their skin but by the content of their character.

Martin Luther King, Jr., 1963

EXPLOSION OF THE *MAINE*

from the *New York Journal*, 1898

In 1895 Cuban colonists began fighting for their independence from Spain. For the next three years many newspapers in the United States reported shocking stories of bloody battles and Spanish cruelty in Cuba. Not all these stories were true, but they sold newspapers. They also helped to increase tensions between the United States and Spain, and some Americans wanted the United States to declare war. Suddenly, on February 15, 1898, the American battleship Maine mysteriously blew up in Cuba's

port city of Havana, killing 260 sailors. Was the explosion an accident or did someone plan it? No one knew for sure, but some newspapers rushed to assign blame. Take a close look at the front page of the New York Journal, which was printed two days after the explosion. According to the newspaper, what caused the disaster? How do the headlines try to shape readers' opinions?

In April 1898, two months after the explosion of the Maine, the United States declared war on Spain. By summertime the Spanish-American War was over. By defeating Spain, the United States gained control of the Philippines, Puerto Rico, and Guam, and Cuba gained its independence. For many years the United States maintained control over Cuba. No one ever discovered why the Maine blew up. To this day the cause of the explosion remains a mystery.

Source: *New York Journal*, February 17, 1898.

Faith that Moved a Dump Heap

by Mary McLeod Bethune, 1941

In the early 1900s education opened up new opportunities for many people in the United States. In the South, however, several states denied African Americans the right to attend the same schools as white students. Few public schools for blacks existed so African Americans had to build schools of their own. As the following magazine article written in 1941 by educator Mary McLeod Bethune (1875–1955) shows, building a school required much hard work—especially if the only place available to build was on a garbage dump! How does Bethune's will and determination lead her to succeed? How does she manage to get help from others?

I was born in Maysville, South Carolina, a country town in the midst of rice and cotton fields. . . . Mother worked in the fields at Father's side, cutting rice and cotton, and chopping **fodder**. Each of us children had tasks to perform, according to our **aptitudes**. Some milked the cows, others helped with the washing, ironing, cooking, and house-cleaning. I was my father's champion cotton picker. When I was only nine, I could pick 250 pounds [93 kg] of cotton a day. . . .

fodder: food for animals
aptitudes: abilities

[Back then] it was almost impossible for a Negro child, especially in the South, to get [an] education. There were hundreds of square miles, sometimes entire states, without a single Negro school, and colored children were not allowed in public schools with white children. . . .

A knock on our door changed my life over-night. There stood a young woman, a colored missionary sent by the Northern Presbyterian Church to start a school near by. She asked my parents to send me. Every morning I picked up a little pail of milk and bread, and walked five miles [8 km] to school; every afternoon, five miles [8 km] home. . . .

By the time I was fifteen I had taken every subject taught at our little school and could go no farther. . . . I used to kneel in the cotton fields and pray that the door of opportunity should be opened to me once more. . . . My prayers were answered. A white dressmaker . . . had become interested in the work of our little neighborhood school and had offered to pay for the higher education of some worthy girl. My teacher selected me, and I was sent to Scotia Seminary in Concord, North Carolina. . . . When I was graduated, I . . . [received] another scholarship, and I spent two years at the Moody Bible School, in Chicago. . . .

143

In 1904 I [went to]. . . Daytona Beach, a beautiful little village, shaded by great oaks and giant pines. . . . I found a shabby four-room cottage, for which the owner wanted a rental of eleven dollars a month. My total **capital** was a dollar and a half, but I talked him into trusting me until the end of the month for the rest. This was in September. A friend let me stay at her home, and I plunged into the job of creating something from nothing. I spoke at churches, and the ministers let me take up collections. . . .

capital: funds

On October 3, 1904, I opened the doors of my school, with an enrollment of five little girls, aged from eight to twelve, whose parents paid me fifty cents' weekly **tuition**. My own child was the only boy in the school. Though I hadn't a penny left, I considered cash money as the smallest part of my resources. I had faith in a loving God, faith in myself, and a desire to serve. . . .

tuition: cost of schooling

We burned logs and used the **charred** splinters as pencils, and mashed elderberries for ink. I begged strangers for a broom, a lamp, a bit of **cretonne** to put around the packing case which served as my desk. I haunted the city dump and the trash piles behind hotels, **retrieving discarded** linen and kitchenware, cracked dishes, broken chairs, pieces of old lumber. Everything was **scoured** and mended. . . . As parents began gradually to leave their children overnight, I had to provide sleeping **accommodations**. I took corn sacks for mattresses. Then I picked Spanish moss from trees, dried and cured it, and used it as a substitute for mattress hair.

charred: burnt

cretonne: cotton cloth

retrieving: finding
discarded: thrown-out
scoured: scrubbed and cleaned
accommodations: places to sleep

The school expanded fast. In less than two years I had 250 pupils. In desperation I hired a large hall next to my original little cottage, and used it as a combined **dormitory** and classroom. I concentrated more and more on girls, as I felt that they especially were **hampered** by lack of educational opportunities. . . .

dormitory: building for students to live in
hampered: kept back

I had many volunteer workers and a few regular teachers, who were paid from fifteen to twenty-five dollars a month and **board**. I was supposed to keep the balance of the funds for my own pocket, but there was never any balance—only a yawning hole. I wore old clothes sent me by **mission boards**, recut and redesigned for me in our dress-making classes. At last I saw that our only solution was to stop renting space, and to buy and build our own college.

board: meals

mission boards: religious organizations

Near by was a field . . . which was used as a dumping ground. I approached the owner, determined to buy it. The price was $250. In a daze, he finally agreed to take five dollars down, and the balance in two years. I promised to be back in a few days with the **initial** payment. He never knew it, but I didn't have five dollars. I raised this sum selling ice cream and sweet-potato pies to the workmen on construction jobs, and I took the owner his money in small change wrapped in my handkerchief.

initial: first

That's how the Bethune-Cookman college campus started. . . . But what use was a plot [of land] without a building?. . . I went to all the carpenters, mechanics, and plasterers in town, pleading with

them to contribute a few hours' work in the evening in exchange for sandwiches and tuition for their children and themselves.

Slowly the building rose from its foundations. The name over the entrance still reads Faith Hall.

I had learned already that one of my most important jobs was to be a good beggar! I rang doorbells and tackled cold prospects without a lead. I wrote articles for whoever would print them, distributed leaflets, rode **interminable** miles of dusty roads on my old bicycle; invaded churches, clubs, lodges, **chambers of commerce**. . . .

interminable: endless
chambers of commerce: groups of local business leaders

Strongly **interracial** in my ideas, I looked forward to an advisory board of **trustees** composed of both white and colored people. . . .

Do you wonder I have faith?

I never stop to plan. I take things step by step. For thirty-five years we have never had to close our doors for lack of food or fuel, although often we had to live from day to day. . . .

interracial: believing in whites and blacks working together
trustees: directors

As the school expanded, whenever I saw a need for some training or service we did not supply, I **schemed** to add it to our **curriculum**. Sometimes that took years. When I came to Florida, there were no hospitals where a Negro could go. A student became **critically** ill . . . so I went to a local hospital and begged a white **physician** to take her in and operate. My pleas were so desperate he finally agreed. A few days after the operation, I visited my pupil.

schemed: planned
curriculum: course of study
critically: seriously
physician: doctor

When I appeared at the front door of the hospital, the nurse ordered me around to the back way. I **thrust** her aside—and found my little girl segregated in a corner of the porch behind the kitchen. Even my toes clenched with rage.

thrust: moved

That decided me. I called on three of my faithful friends, asking them to buy a little cottage behind our school as a hospital. They agreed, and we started with two beds.

From this humble start grew a fully equipped twenty-bed hospital—our college **infirmary** and a refuge for the needy throughout the state. It was staffed by white and black physicians and by our own student nurses. . . .

infirmary: medical clinic

When I [now] walk through the campus, with its stately palms and well-kept lawns, and think back to the dump-heap foundation, I rub my eyes and pinch myself. And I remember my childish visions in the cotton fields.

Mary McLeod Bethune later worked in other areas besides education. A great speaker and organizer, she helped register black women to vote in the 1920s and founded the National Council of Negro Women in 1935. For many years she worked for the federal government, tirelessly fighting for equal rights for African Americans in education, the workplace, and government. Bethune-Cookman College, the school she founded on a "dump heap," remains open today, a testament to her spirit and determination.

Source: Mary McLeod Bethune, "Faith that Moved a Dump Heap," *Who, The Magazine About People,* Volume 1, June 1941.

145

Hitting the Road

Advertisements, 1902 and 1924

The first automobiles were invented in the late 1800s. These early cars took a long time to build and cost anywhere from $1,000 to $3,000. Most Americans at this time earned less than $1,000 a year. As a result, only wealthy people could afford to buy cars. But in 1913 Henry Ford came up with a new way to build automobiles. He set up an assembly line on which each worker performed the same job over and over again as cars rolled by on a moving platform. The assembly line speeded up production time and greatly reduced costs. Look at the two automobile advertisements printed below.

The one on the left is from 1902, and the one on the right is from 1924. How do the cars compare in price and looks? What differences do you see in them? How do these car advertisements compare to car ads today?

Henry Ford's automobiles changed life in the United States forever. At such low prices, almost anyone could afford to buy a car. Soon new highways—dotted with gasoline stations, motels, and restaurants—crisscrossed the nation. People used cars to get to work, to go shopping, and to visit friends. With automobiles now available for transportation, many Americans began leaving cities and moving to new nearby areas called suburbs. Today more people live in suburbs than ever before. How do automobiles affect your life?

146

The Trial of Susan B. Anthony

Trial Transcript, 1873

In the early 1900s women's suffrage leaders worked hard to gain women the right to vote. The fight for women's suffrage had actually begun many years earlier when women had gathered for a large convention in Seneca Falls, New York, in 1848. At the time it was against the law for women to vote. One of the most important suffrage leaders in the late 1800s was a former school teacher named Susan B. Anthony (1820-1906). On November 5, 1872, Anthony did something that shocked people— she voted in an election in Rochester, New York! She was arrested and put on trial in June 1873. The judge denied Anthony the right to have a trial by jury. He decided the case himself and found her guilty. Just as he was about to announce her punishment for breaking the law, Anthony stood up to defend herself. Below is an excerpt of Anthony's comments and the judge's response. Their statements are taken from a transcript, or written record, of the trial. As you read this transcript, notice why Anthony believes her trial has been unfair. Why does she feel she has the right to vote? How does she compare the condition of women to the enslavement of African Americans before the Civil War?

Judge: The prisoner will stand up. Has the prisoner anything to say why **sentence** shall not be pronounced?

Anthony: Yes, your honor, I have many things to say; for in your ordered **verdict** of guilty, you have trampled underfoot every **vital** principle of our government. My natural rights, my civil rights, my political rights, are all alike ignored. Robbed of the **fundamental** privilege of citizenship, I am **degraded** from the status of a citizen to that of a **subject**; and not only myself individually, but all of my sex, are, by your honor's verdict, doomed to political **subjection**. . . .

Judge: The Court can not listen to . . . arguments [that] the prisoner's **counsel** has already **consumed** three hours in presenting.

Anthony: May it please your honor, I am not arguing the question, but simply stating the reasons why sentence can not, in justice, be pronounced against me. Your denial of my citizen's right to vote is the denial of my right of consent as one of the governed, the denial of my right of representation as one of the taxed, the denial of my right to a trial by a jury of my **peers** as an offender against law, therefore, the denial of my sacred rights to life, liberty, property, and—

Judge: The Court can not allow the prisoner to go on.

Anthony: But your honor will not deny me this one and only poor privilege of protest against this **high-handed** outrage upon my

sentence: punishment

verdict: decision
vital: important

fundamental: basic
degraded: reduced
subject: person ruled by others
subjection: second-class citizenship
counsel: lawyer
consumed: spent

peers: equals

high-handed: harsh, overwhelming

147

citizen's rights. May it please the Court to remember that since the day of my arrest last November, this is the first time that either myself or any person of my **disfranchised** class has been allowed a word of defense before judge or jury—

Judge: The prisoner must sit down; the Court can not allow it.

Anthony: All my **prosecutors**, from the [neighborhood] politician, who **entered** the complaint [against me], to the United States Marshal, Commissioner, District Attorney, District Judge, [and] your honor on the bench, not one is my peer, but each and all are my political **sovereigns**; and had your honor submitted my case to the jury, as was clearly your duty, even then I should have had just cause of protest, for not one of those men was my peer; but, native or foreign, white or black, rich or poor, educated or ignorant, awake or asleep, sober or drunk, each and every man of them was my political superior; hence, in no sense, my peer. . . . Precisely as no disfranchised person **is entitled** to sit upon a jury, and no woman is entitled to the **franchise**, so, none but a regularly **admitted** lawyer is allowed to practice [law] in the courts, and no woman can gain admission to the **bar**—hence, jury, judge, counsel, must all be of the superior class.

Judge: The Court must insist—the prisoner has been tried according to the established forms of law.

Anthony: Yes, your honor, but by forms of law all made by men, interpreted by men, administered by men, in favor of men, and against women; and hence, your honor's ordered verdict of guilty, against a United States citizen for the exercise of "that citizen's right to vote," simply because that citizen was a woman and not a man. But, yesterday, the same man-made forms of law declared it a crime punishable with $1,000 fine and six months' imprisonment, for you, or me, or any of us, to give a cup of cold water, a crust of bread, or a night's shelter to a panting fugitive [slave] as he was tracking his way to Canada. And every man or woman in whose veins **coursed** a drop of human sympathy violated that wicked law, **reckless** of consequences, and was justified in so doing. As then the slaves who got their freedom must take it over, or under, or through the unjust forms of law, precisely so now must women, to get their right to a voice in this Government, take it; and I have taken mine [my rights], and mean to take it at every possible opportunity.

Judge: The Court orders the prisoner to sit down. It will not allow another word.

Anthony: When I was brought before your honor for trial, I hoped for a broad and **liberal** interpretation of the Constitution . . . that should declare all United States citizens under its protecti[on] . . . equality of rights [which is] the national guarantee to all persons born or **naturalized** in the United States. But failing to get this justice—failing, even, to get a trial by a jury *not* of my peers—I ask not **leniency** at your hands—but rather the full **rigors** of the law.

disfranchised: denied the right to vote

prosecutors: accusers
entered: filed

sovereigns: rulers

is entitled: has the right
franchise: vote
admitted: qualified
bar: court system

coursed: flowed
reckless: regardless

liberal: open-minded

naturalized: made citizens
leniency: easy treatment
rigors: force

Judge: The Court must insist—(Here the prisoner sat down.) The prisoner will stand up. (Here Miss Anthony arose again.) The sentence of the Court is that you pay a fine of one hundred dollars and the costs of the **prosecution.**

Anthony: May it please your honor, I shall never pay a dollar of your unjust penalty. All . . . I possess is a $10,000 debt, **incurred** by publishing my [news]paper—[named] ***The Revolution***—. . . the sole object of which was to educate all women to do precisely as I have done, rebel against your man-made, unjust, unconstitutional forms of law, that tax, fine, imprison, and hang women, while they deny them the right of representation in the Government; and I shall work on with **might and main** to pay every dollar of that honest debt, but not a penny shall go to this unjust claim. And I shall earnestly and **persistently** continue to urge all women to the practical recognition of the old revolutionary maxim, that "Resistance to **tyranny** is obedience to God."

prosecution: trial

incurred: brought about

The Revolution: newspaper on women's rights, started by Anthony in 1868

might and main: all my strength

persistently: constantly

tyranny: oppressive rule

Susan B. Anthony never paid the $100 fine charged by the judge. Six years later, in 1878, Anthony persuaded the United States Senate to debate an amendment to the Constitution granting women the right to vote. Although the amendment failed, Anthony spent the rest of her life fighting for it. Her bold actions inspired millions of women to fight for women's suffrage in the late 1800s and early 1900s. Finally, in 1920, the Nineteenth Amendment to the Constitution was approved, granting women the right to vote. In honor of her lifelong efforts, many people have called this the "Anthony Amendment."

Source: Elizabeth Cady Stanton, Susan B. Anthony, and Matilda Joslyn Gage, eds., *History of Woman Suffrage*, Volume 1. New York: Fowler & Wells, 1881.

I Didn't Raise My Boy to Be a Soldier

**Words by Alfred Bryan and
Music by Al Piantadosi, 1915**

When World War I broke out in Europe in 1914, many Americans wanted to remain neutral. They did not feel that either side was fighting for any great beliefs or values, and they wanted the United States to stay out of the war. In 1915 songwriters Alfred Bryan (1895-1984) and Al Piantadosi (1884-1955) wrote the following song. As you read or sing this song, notice how the writers feel about war. In what ways do they suggest future wars might be prevented? When you are finished, compare this song to the one on pages 152-153, which presents a different view toward fighting and World War I.

1. Ten mil-lion sol-diers to the war have gone, Who may nev-er re-turn a-gain._____ Ten mil-lion moth-ers' hearts must break For the ones who died in vain._____

2. What vic-tor-y can cheer a moth-er's heart, When she looks at her blight-ed home?_____ What vic-tor-y can bring her back All she cared to call her own?_____

150

Head bowed down in sor - row In her lone - ly years, I
Let each moth - er an - swer In the year to be, Re -

heard a moth - er mur - mur thro' her tears:_____
mem - ber that my boy be - longs to me!_____

Chorus

"I did - n't raise my boy to be a sol -

dier, I brought him up to be my pride and joy,_____ Who

dares to place a mus - ket on his shoul - der, To shoot some oth - er

moth - er's dar - ling boy?_____ Let na - tions ar - bi - trate their fu - ture

trou - bles, It's time to lay the sword and gun a - way,_____ There'd

be no war to - day, If moth - ers all would say, "I

1.
did - n't raise my boy to be a sol - dier." "I
2.
dier."____

Source: David C. Olsen, ed., *Nostalgia, Volume 2.* Miami, FL: Columbia Pictures Publications, 1987.

151

OVER THERE

by George M. Cohan, 1917

In 1915, the same year that Alfred Bryan and Al Piantadosi wrote the song I Didn't Raise My Boy to Be a Soldier—which you read on pages 150-151—German submarines sank the British ship Lusitania, killing many American passengers on board. Despite this, many Americans still remained neutral and hoped the United States would stay out of World War I. Then, in March 1917, Germany began sinking American ships. The next month the United States declared war on Germany and entered World War I. Within weeks songwriter George M. Cohan (1878-1942) wrote the song below. As you read this song, notice how Cohan feels about World War I. What does he ask American soldiers to do? How does Cohan's song, which became one of the most popular war songs ever written, compare with the song by Bryan and Piantadosi?

1. John-nie get your gun, get your gun, get your gun,
2. John-nie get your gun, get your gun, get your gun,

Take it on the run, on the run, on the run;
John-nie show the Hun, you're a son-of-a-gun,

Hear them call-ing you and me; Ev-'ry son of lib-er-ty.
Hoist the flag and let her fly, Like true he-roes do or die.

Hur-ry right a-way, no de-lay, go to-day,
Pack your lit-tle kit, show your grit, do your bit,

Make your dad-dy glad, to have had such a lad,
Sol-diers to the ranks from the towns and the tanks,

152

Tell your sweet - heart not to pine, To be
Make your moth - er proud of you, And to

proud her boy's in line._____
lib - er - ty be true._____

Chorus

O - ver there,_____ o - ver there,_____ Send the word, send the

word o - ver there,_____ That the {Yanks / boys} are com - ing, the

{Yanks / boys} are com - ing, The drums rum - tum - ming ev - 'ry

where_____ So pre - pare,_____ say a pray'r,_____ Send the

word, send the word to be - ware,_____ We'll be

o - ver, we're com - ing o - ver, And we won't come

1. back till it's o - ver o - ver there. 2. O - ver there.

Source: David C. Olsen, ed., *Nostalgia, Volume 2.* Miami, FL: Columbia Pictures Publications, 1987.

Signs of Despair

Signs, 1930s

The Great Depression of the 1930s threw millions of people out of work. Both rich people and poor people lost their jobs, and by 1933 one out of every four Americans was unemployed. Hunger, poverty, and despair hit every region of the country. Desperate for money, people sold anything they owned for a few dollars—or a few pennies. Others walked the streets carrying signs, seeking jobs and economic changes. Some of these signs, many of them hand-painted, are shown below. How does each of these homemade documents from the 1930s tell a story? What do they show about life during the Great Depression?

City and town dwellers across the United States suffered much during the Great Depression. But they were not the only people who were struggling to survive. As the next two documents on pages 155-157 show, people living on farms and in rural communities also faced hard times in the 1930s.

154

LINEAGE

by Margaret Walker, 1941

As the document on page 154 showed, people in towns and cities across the United States hunted everywhere for work during the Great Depression. Throughout the farming communities of the South, however, the main problem was how to make a living from one's hard work. Farm prices fell to an all-time low in the 1930s and farmers received only pennies for their crops. The situation was even harder for African-American farmers, who faced prejudice when they tried to market their crops. African-American poet Margaret Walker was born in Birmingham, Alabama, in 1915. In the poem below she compares farm troubles during the Great Depression to those her grandmothers had faced years earlier. How does Walker feel about her ancestors?

My grandmothers were strong.

They followed plows and bent to toil.

They moved through fields **sowing** seed.   **sowing:** planting

They touched earth and grain grew.

They were full of **sturdiness** and singing.   **sturdiness:** firmness, strength

My grandmothers were strong.

My grandmothers are full of memories.

Smelling of soap and onions and wet clay

With veins rolling roughly over quick hands

They have many clean words to say.

My grandmothers were strong.

Why am I not as they?

Black and white farmers in the South were not the only farmers in the United States who faced hard times during the Great Depression. On the Great Plains of the Middle West and Southwest, farmers watched as their farms literally blew away, leaving them with nothing. To understand some of the horrors of the Dust Bowl, read the next document on pages 156-157.

Source: Margaret Walker, *For My People*. New Haven, CT: Yale University Press, 1942.

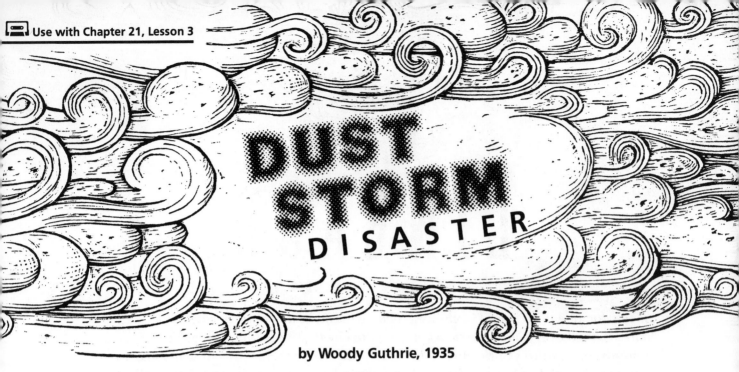

DUST STORM DISASTER

by Woody Guthrie, 1935

As you read in the two documents on pages 154-155, farmers in the South and people in towns and cities across the United States struggled to survive during the Great Depression. Farmers on the Great Plains faced a different kind of disaster in the 1930s—the Dust Bowl. For many years little rain had fallen on this region of the country. Crops died and the farmland became very dry. Then huge winds began blowing across the Great Plains. These winds picked up the loose topsoil and created massive black clouds of dust and dirt that stretched for miles. The Dust Bowl was born. In the song below, folksinger Woody Guthrie (1912-1967), one of the country's best-known songwriters, describes a Dust Bowl scene from 1935. As you read this song, notice all the different places Guthrie mentions. According to Guthrie, what did the Dust Bowl do? How did farmers in the Great Plains react to the Dust Bowl?

1. On the four-teenth day of A-pril Of nine-teen thir-ty-five There struck the worst of dust-storms That ev-er filled the sky. 2. You could

(3. From) O-kla-ho-ma Cit-y To the Ar-i-zo-na line Da-ko-ta and Ne-bras-ka To the la-zy Ri-o Grande. 4. It

(5. The) ra-di-o re-port-ed We lis-tened with a-larm The wild and wind-y ac-tions Of this great mys-ter-ious storm. 6. From

156

see that dust storm com-ing____ The cloud looked death-like
fell a-cross our cit-y____ Like a cur-tain of black rolled
Al-bu-quer-que and Clo-vis____ And all New Mex-i-

black____ And through our might-y na-tion____ It
down____ We thought it was our judg-ment____ We
co____ They said it was the black-est____ That

left a dread-ful track.____ 3. From gain.____
thought it was our doom.____ 5. The
ev-er they had saw.____ (7. From)

7. From old Dodge City, Kansas,
The dust had rung their knell,
And a few more comrades sleeping
On top of old Boot Hill.

8. From Denver, Colorado,
They said it blew so strong,
They thought that they could hold out,
They didn't know how long.

9. Our relatives were huddled
Into their oil-boom shacks,
And the children they were crying
As it whistled through the cracks.

10. And the family, it was crowded
Into their little room,
They thought the world had ended,
And they thought it was their doom.

11. The storm took place at sundown.
It lasted through the night.
When we looked out next morning
We saw a terrible sight.

12. We saw outside our window
Where wheatfields they had grown,
Was now a rippling ocean
Of dust the wind had blown.

13. It covered up our fences,
It covered up our barns,
It covered up our tractors
In this wild and dusty storm.

14. We loaded our jalopies
And piled our families in,
We rattled down that highway
To never come back again.

Source: Woody Guthrie, "Dust Storm Disaster," in Harold Levanthal and Marjorie Guthrie, eds., *The Woody Guthrie Songbook*. New York: Grosset & Dunlap, 1976.

FIGHTING WORLD WAR II

Posters, early 1940s

On December 8, 1941, one day after Japan bombed Pearl Harbor, Hawaii, the United States entered World War II. Millions of American men and women joined the armed forces and went overseas to serve and to fight. Millions more stayed at home to work in factories and to build supplies needed to win the war. How do these two posters show the nation's commitment to winning World War II?

The combined efforts of millions of Americans helped the United States and the Allies to win World War II. To learn how one group of American citizens was treated during the war, read the next document on pages 159-161.

Life in a Japanese-American Prison Camp

by Yuri Tateishi, 1984

Soon after the United States entered World War II in 1941, some people feared that Japanese Americans might serve as spies for Japan, one of the nations the United States was fighting. In response to this fear, the United States government began a program in 1942 that forced all Japanese Americans who lived on the West Coast to leave their homes. Many Japanese Americans were citizens who had been born in the United States and had never been to Japan. Japanese Americans protested this unfair treatment and claimed they were being mistreated because of prejudice. But the government took away their citizenship rights, and more than 110,000 Japanese Americans were taken to prison camps for the rest of the war. One of those imprisoned was Yuri Tateishi (ur' ē ta tā' shē), a 28-year-old woman living in West Los Angeles, California. In 1984 she described the three and a half years she had spent in Manzanar, a prison camp located in Inyo County, California, near the Sierra Nevada mountains. Manzanar, which became the home for 10,000 Japanese Americans, was surrounded by armed guards, searchlight towers, and barbed-wire fences. As you read this oral history by Tateishi (shown above with four of her children), think of what it was like for innocent people to suddenly be placed in prison. How did some Japanese-American prisoners band together at Manzanar to fight for better treatment?

When the **evacuation** came, we were renting a home and had four kids. It was terrible because you had to sell everything. We were just limited to what we could take with us, and so everything was just sold for whatever we could get. Our furniture was rather new at that time because we had just bought a living-room and dining-room set. I just finished paying for a refrigerator when I had to sell that. Of course, we got nothing for it, because we had such a limited time...[and] we had to rush to sell everything. . . .

The day of the evacuation was April 26 [1942]. The day before, we had to sleep on the floor because all the furniture was gone. We all slept on the floor, ate on the floor, and cooked what we could with what few utensils we had. I recall we had to get up very early in the morning, and I think we all walked to the Japanese school because no one had a car then. And everybody was just all over the

evacuation: forced removal

159

place, the whole Japanese community was there, the West **L.A.** community. The Westwood Methodist Church had some hot coffee and doughnuts for us that morning, which helped a lot, and we were loaded in a bus.

Just about the time we were ready to load, my youngest son broke out with measles that morning, and I had him covered up, and then a nurse came to me and said, "May I see your baby?" He was almost three, . . . and she said, "I'm sorry but I'm going to have to take him away.". . . When I thought about how he might wake up and be in a strange place, with strange people, I just really broke down and cried. I cried all morning over it, but there was nothing we could do but leave him. He stayed at the general hospital and joined us at Manzanar in three weeks.

When we got to Manzanar, it was getting dark and we were given numbers first. We went to the **mess hall**, and I remember the first meal we were given in those tin plates and tin cups. It was canned **wieners** and canned spinach. It was all the food we had, and then after finishing that we were taken to our **barracks**. It was dark and **trenches** were here and there. You'd fall in and get up and finally got to the barracks. The floors were boarded, but they were about a quarter to a half inch apart, and the next morning you could see the ground below. What hurt most I think was seeing those hay mattresses. We were used to a regular home atmosphere. [I still remember] seeing those hay mattresses—so **makeshift**, with hay sticking out—a barren room with nothing but those hay mattresses. It was depressing, such a primitive feeling. We were given army blankets and army cots. Our family was large enough that we didn't have to share our barrack with another family but all seven of us were in one room.

The next morning was very cold. I went out to brush my teeth. There was a faucet at the front of each building, and it was so cold, so painful it was so cold. You felt like a prisoner. You know, you have to stay inside and you have a certain amount of freedom within the camp I suppose, but . . . it's not a comfortable feeling. You had to stay within the **confines** of that camp, not in the sense that you're in a jail or anything, but you're kept inside a barbed-wire fence, and you know you can't go out.

And you don't know what your future is, going into a camp with four children. You just have to trust God that you will be taken care of somehow. It's scary—not in the sense that you would be hurt or anything but not knowing what your future will be. You don't know what the education for the children will be or what type of housing or anything like that. Of course, you don't know how you're going to be able to raise the children.

After we had been in Manzanar for about a year . . . someone by the name of Mr. Ueno was treated unfairly and was taken out of the camp to jail, and some of the men felt that they should try to get him released. They didn't think it was right that they should

L.A.: Los Angeles

mess hall: dining room

wieners: hot dogs
barracks: living places
trenches: deep ditches

makeshift: poorly made

confines: boundaries

take him, and a few men were chosen. My husband was one of them, and these men went to the **administration** to **negotiate** this man's release, but while they were negotiating a crowd gathered, and it got larger and larger and it just got out of control. The men came out of the meeting and told the crowd to quiet down and go home, but they just wouldn't listen, and that's when the trouble started outside. Well, somebody got shot. The people that were negotiating were taken. They were kept at the jail in **Independence**, and then after that they were transferred to **Lone Pine** and then sent to Utah. They stayed there quite a while, and then they were transferred from one place to another.

administration: prison camp authorities
negotiate: bargain for

Independence: town near Manzanar
Lone Pine: town near Manzanar

When my husband was arrested, someone came and told me, but I didn't try to go see him because there was no chance of seeing him. They had already taken him. I didn't think I'd have a chance; I don't think they ever would have given me the chance. It wasn't that kind of a situation. I hoped that he would be released soon but, again, you really didn't know what was going to happen. It occurred to me that I might not ever see him again. He wrote letters, but they were all **censored**. He came back, I think [about] eight months later.

censored: inspected and had words blotted out by the authorities

When I think back on the evacuation, that's something you'd like to erase if you can, but it's a fact; we went through it. I'm unhappy about it, but I don't think I was really bitter. You feel like you can't do anything against the government. They tell you, You go or else. You just had to go.

You hurt. You give up everything that you worked for that far, and I think everybody was at the point of just having gotten out of the Depression and was just getting on his feet. And then all that happens! You have to throw everything away. You feel you were betrayed.

Years later Yuri Tateishi's son—who had been taken away from her because he had the measles—interviewed many Japanese Americans imprisoned during the war. His mother's oral history is taken from his book. During their years in Manzanar, prisoners grew their own food, set up their own schools, and even published their own newspaper. In 1945, when World War II ended, Japanese Americans were freed from prison. Many had lost everything they owned. No Japanese-American spies were ever discovered. In 1988 the United States government apologized and admitted it had made a great mistake in putting Japanese Americans in prison camps.

Source: John Tateishi, *And Justice for All: An Oral History of the Japanese American Detention Camps.* New York: Random House, 1984.

Signs of Segregation

Signs, 1950s

In the late 1800s and early 1900s, states in the South began passing segregation laws. These unfair laws, which remained in force for many years, separated black people from white people. Segregated places for blacks—such as schools, restaurants, or sections of buses—were usually in worse shape or of poorer quality than places for whites. Segregation laws denied African Americans equal rights and limited their opportunities. How do the signs below illustrate segregation in the South? How would you have felt if you had seen such signs every day?

During the 1950s many African Americans and other Americans began working together to fight segregation and to end these unfair laws. Their struggle for equal rights came to be known as the civil rights movement. For a description of the goals of this movement, read the next document on pages 163-166.

162

I Have a Dream

by Martin Luther King, Jr., 1963

As the document on page 162 showed, segregation existed throughout the South during the first half of the 1900s. Discrimination against African Americans also existed in other parts of the United States. In the 1950s, however, African Americans began organizing to end laws of segregation and to fight for the equal rights of all Americans. One of the leaders of this growing civil rights movement, which included both blacks and whites, was Dr. Martin Luther King, Jr. (1929-1968). King was a powerful speaker whose voice stirred people's hearts. On August 28, 1963, King delivered a speech to a crowd of 250,000 people who had gathered at the Lincoln Memorial in Washington, D.C., to urge Congress to pass a strong civil rights law. As you read King's speech, notice how he often uses forceful words and images to get across his ideas. How do these words and images help you to see both the problems King identifies and the goals he hopes the civil rights movement will achieve? How does King urge his listeners to struggle for equal rights?

Five score years ago, a great American, in whose symbolic shadow we stand, signed the **Emancipation Proclamation**. This **momentous decree** came as a great beacon light of hope to millions of Negro slaves who had been **seared** in the flames of withering injustice. It came as a joyous daybreak to end the long night of **captivity**.

But one hundred years later, we must face the tragic fact that the Negro is still not free. One hundred years later, the life of the Negro is still sadly crippled by the **manacles** of segregation and the chains of discrimination. One hundred years later, the Negro lives on a lonely island of poverty in the midst of a vast ocean of material **prosperity**. One hundred years later, the Negro is still **languishing** in the corners of American society and finds himself an **exile** in his own land. So we have come here today to dramatize an **appalling** condition.

In a sense we have come to our nation's capital to cash a check. When the architects of our republic wrote the magnificent words of the Constitution and the Declaration of Independence, they were signing a **promissory note** to which every American was to **fall heir**. This note was a promise that all men would be guaranteed the inalienable rights of life, liberty, and the pursuit of happiness.

five score: 100

Emancipation Proclamation: order signed by Abraham Lincoln in 1863 banning slavery in Confederate states

momentous decree: important order

seared: burned

captivity: enslavement

manacles: chains

prosperity: wealth

languishing: being neglected

exile: stranger

appalling: terrible

promissory note: promise to be repaid later

fall heir: be entitled to

163

It is obvious today that America has **defaulted on** this promissory note insofar as her citizens of color are concerned. Instead of honoring this sacred **obligation**, America has given the Negro people a bad check; a check which has come back marked "**insufficient** funds." But we refuse to believe that the bank of justice is **bankrupt**. We refuse to believe that there are insufficient funds in the great vaults of opportunity of this nation. So we have come to cash this check—a check that will give us upon demand the riches of freedom and the security of justice. We have also come to this **hallowed** spot to remind America of the fierce urgency of now. This is no time to engage in the luxury of cooling off or to take the **tranquilizing** drug of **gradualism**. *Now* is the time to rise from the dark and **desolate** valley of segregation to the sunlit path of racial justice. *Now* is the time to open the doors of opportunity to all of God's children. *Now* is the time to lift our nation from the quicksands of racial injustice to the solid rock of brotherhood.

It would be fatal for the nation to overlook the urgency of the moment and to underestimate the determination of the Negro. This sweltering summer of the Negro's **legitimate** discontent will not pass until there is an **invigorating** autumn of freedom and equality. Nineteen sixty-three is not an end, but a beginning. Those who hope that the Negro needed to blow off steam and will now be content will have a rude awakening if the nation returns to business as usual. There will be neither rest nor **tranquility** in America until the Negro is granted his citizenship rights. The whirlwinds of revolt will continue to shake the foundations of our nation until the bright day of justice emerges.

But there is something that I must say to my people who stand on the warm **threshold** which leads into the palace of justice. In the process of gaining our rightful place we must not be guilty of wrongful deeds. Let us not seek to satisfy our thirst for freedom by drinking from the cup of bitterness and hatred.

We must forever conduct our struggle on the high plane of dignity and discipline. We must not allow our creative protest to **degenerate** into physical violence. Again and again we must rise to the **majestic** heights of meeting physical force with soul force. The marvelous new **militancy** which has engulfed the Negro

defaulted on: failed to pay

obligation: promise

insufficient: not enough

bankrupt: empty

hallowed: sacred

tranquilizing: calming
gradualism: slowness
desolate: barren

legitimate: rightful
invigorating: lively; filled with energy

tranquility: peace

threshold: entrance

degenerate: break down
majestic: grand; glorious
militancy: fighting spirit

164

community must not lead us to distrust of all white people, for many of our white brothers, as **evidenced** by their presence here today, have come to realize that their **destiny** is tied up with our destiny and their freedom is **inextricably** bound to our freedom. We cannot walk alone.

And as we walk, we must make the pledge that we shall march ahead. We cannot turn back. There are those who are asking the **devotees** of civil rights, "When will you be satisfied?" We can never be satisfied as long as the Negro is the victim of unspeakable horrors of police **brutality**. We can never be satisfied as long as our bodies, heavy with the **fatigue** of travel, cannot gain lodging in the motels of the highways and the hotels of the cities. We cannot be satisfied as long as the Negro's basic **mobility** is from a smaller **ghetto** to a larger one. We can never be satisfied as long as a Negro in Mississippi cannot vote and a Negro in New York believes he has nothing for which to vote. No, no, we are not satisfied, and we will not be satisfied until justice rolls down like waters and righteousness like a mighty stream.

I am not unmindful that some of you have come here out of great **trials and tribulations**. Some of you have come fresh from narrow cells. Some of you have come from areas where your **quest** for freedom left you battered by the storms of **persecution** and staggered by the winds of police brutality. You have been the veterans of creative suffering. Continue to work with the faith that unearned suffering is **redemptive**.

Go back to Mississippi, go back to Alabama, go back to Georgia, go back to Louisiana, go back to the slums and ghettos of our northern cities, knowing that somehow this situation can and will be changed. Let us not **wallow** in the valley of despair.

I say to you today, my friends, that in spite of the difficulties and frustrations of the moment, I still have a dream. It is a dream deeply rooted in the American dream.

I have a dream that one day this nation will rise up and live out the true meaning of its **creed**: "We hold these truths to be self-evident: that all men are created equal."

I have a dream that one day on the red hills of Georgia the sons of former slaves and the sons of former slaveowners will be able to sit down together at the table of brotherhood.

I have a dream that one day even the state of Mississippi, a desert state, sweltering with the heat of injustice and oppression, will be transformed into an **oasis** of freedom and justice.

I have a dream that my four little children will one day live in a nation where they will not be judged by the color of their skin but by the content of their character.

I have a dream today.

I have a dream that one day the state of Alabama, whose governor's lips are presently dripping with the words of **interposition and nullification**, will be transformed into a situation where little

evidenced: shown
destiny: future
inextricably: inseparably

devotees: supporters

brutality: cruel violence
fatigue: tiredness

mobility: movement
ghetto: poor, segregated section of a city

trials and tribulations: sufferings and troubles
quest: search
persecution: unfair treatment

redemptive: of value; worthwhile

wallow: rest; remain helpless

creed: stated belief

oasis: safe place

interposition and nullification: opposition to integration and the federal government

165

black boys and black girls will be able to join hands with little white boys and white girls and walk together as sisters and brothers.

I have a dream today.

I have a dream that one day every valley shall be **exalted**, every hill and mountain shall be made low, the rough places will be made plain, and the crooked places will be made straight, and the glory of the Lord shall be revealed, and all **flesh** shall see it together.

This is our hope. This is the faith with which I return to the South. With this faith we will be able to **hew** out of the mountain of despair a stone of hope. With this faith we will be able to transform the **jangling discords** of our nation into a beautiful symphony of brotherhood. With this faith we will be able to work together, to pray together, to struggle together, to go to jail together, to stand up for freedom together, knowing that we will be free one day.

This will be the day when all of God's children will be able to sing with a new meaning, "My country, 'tis of thee, sweet land of liberty, of thee I sing. Land where my fathers died, land of the pilgrim's pride, from every mountainside, let freedom ring."

And if America is to be a great nation this must become true. So let freedom ring from the **prodigious** hilltops of New Hampshire. Let freedom ring from the mighty mountains of New York. Let freedom ring from the heightening Alleghenies of Pennsylvania!

Let freedom ring from the snowcapped Rockies of Colorado!

Let freedom ring from the **curvaceous** peaks of California!

But not only that; let freedom ring from Stone Mountain of Georgia!

Let freedom ring from Lookout Mountain of Tennessee!

Let freedom ring from every hill and molehill of Mississippi. From every mountainside, let freedom ring.

When we let freedom ring, when we let it ring from every village and every **hamlet**, from every state and every city, we will be able to speed up that day when all of God's children, black men and white men, Jews and Gentiles, Protestants and Catholics, will be able to join hands and sing in the words of the old Negro spiritual, "Free at last! free at last! thank God Almighty, we are free at last!"

Soon after Dr. Martin Luther King, Jr., delivered this speech in 1963, Congress passed two of the strongest civil rights laws in American history. Ongoing work by people in the civil rights movement helped end many segregation laws in the South during the 1960s. King continued leading marches and speaking out for the equality of all people until 1968, when he was murdered. His dream for a better and fairer America lives on.

Source: Martin Luther King, Jr., "I Have a Dream," 1963.

exalted: raised

flesh: people

hew: carve

jangling discords: angry sounds and disagreements

prodigious: great

curvaceous: curving

hamlet: small town

The Endless War

by Jules Feiffer, 1972

During the 1960s the United States became deeply involved in a war between North Vietnam and South Vietnam. The United States sent more than 8 million men and women overseas to serve and to fight. At first some Americans believed they would win a quick victory, but as the war dragged on, many Americans began to oppose United States involvement. They believed that the war in Vietnam was wrong and was costing too many American lives. Three United States Presidents—John F. Kennedy, Lyndon Johnson, and Richard Nixon—supported the war effort. In this political cartoon from 1972, Jules Feiffer, one of the nation's leading cartoonists, shows these three Presidents trying to convince Americans that the war will end soon. How does Feiffer show that the war seems to have no end in sight? What happens to the person who is watching these Presidents on television?

In 1973, one year after Jules Feiffer drew this cartoon, the United States signed a peace agreement with North Vietnam and South Vietnam. Fighting continued, however, for another two years. The Vietnam War divided the American people and strongly affected the millions of American men and women who served overseas. Many of these effects are still felt today. For a description of some of these effects, read the next document on pages 168-172.

Source: Syd Hoff, *Editorial and Political Cartooning*. New York: Stravon Educational Press, 1976.

Charlie Pippin

by Candy Dawson Boyd, 1987

As the document on page 167 showed, United States involvement in the Vietnam War dragged on for many years. More than 58,000 Americans died in the war. The men and women who survived saw many of their friends die in battle. When Vietnam veterans returned home to a nation still divided over the war, many tried to forget the fighting and the pain it had caused. The selection below is from Candy Dawson Boyd's novel, Charlie Pippin. Charlie is an 11-year-old girl whose father and uncle both fought in the Vietnam War. Charlie's father is a short-tempered man who refuses to talk about the war. When he fails to answer Charlie's questions, she sets out to learn as much about the Vietnam War as possible. Charlie finds out that two of her father's best friends, Fred Hansen and Gerald Moer, were killed in battle. In the following scene, Charlie, her Uncle Ben, and her Aunt Jessie visit the Vietnam Veterans Memorial in Washington, D.C. The names of all the Americans who died in the war are engraved on the walls of this memorial. As you read this excerpt, notice what gift Charlie seeks to bring home to her father. How does her visit to the memorial make her feel sad? How does it also make her feel better?

The moment Aunt Jessie had parked, Charlie leaped eagerly from the car. Ahead of her, on a mound of winter grass, Charlie saw a tent, a stand, a sign, and flags flapping in the wind. Blown-up photographs of men were hung on wooden racks near the flags. She walked over and read the large sign: VETERAN'S **VIGIL** OF HONOR. Below that were the words *You Are an American. Your voice can make the difference.* Charlie recognized the initials POW MIA. **Prisoners of War. Missing in Action.** Then she saw pamphlets, buttons, and other items about POWs and MIAs at the stand.

"Uncle Ben, that stands for the soldiers some people believe are in prison in Vietnam or dead, but the Vietnam government won't give us back their bodies. Right?" she asked, snapping two pictures.

He nodded, "Charlie, please don't take any of me. I don't feel like posing for pictures today."

"Okay, I won't."

"Ben, you want to go on? Charlie and I will wait for you," said Aunt Jessie.

He nodded again. Charlie recognized the distant, **mournful** expression in his eyes. She knew he had friends on the wall, just as Daddy did.

vigil: watch

Prisoners of War: captured soldiers some believe are still in Vietnam

Missing in Action: soldiers whose whereabouts are unknown

mournful: sad

"Sure, Jess. This is something I have to do." He started walking up the mound to a path to the left.

"Charlie, let him alone," Aunt Jessie said.

"No, Aunt Jessie. I have to go, too!" And Charlie ran after her uncle, grabbing his hand. "That's why I came!" Her aunt followed.

There were other people on the long, curved path, some with small children. To her left, Charlie saw a Black family, the father, mother, and two children. One girl was about her age. An older white man huddled around a wooden stand. Charlie waited with her aunt and uncle while the family turned the pages of a book, then moved away. The **elderly** man did the same.

elderly: old

Charlie read the title of the large book, *Directory of Names*. From her research, she knew that in this book were the names of all of the women and men who had died or were listed as missing in action during the Vietnam War. That included the first deaths in 1959 and the last deaths in 1975. It was a thick book with many single-spaced pages.

Uncle Ben took a piece of crumpled paper out of his wallet. It looked as if it had been there a long time. The paper was so creased that he had to unfold it slowly.

Aunt Jessie showed her brother how to locate the names of the friends he was seeking. She reached into her purse and handed him a pen. After searching, his finger leading him, he paused, writing down a panel number and a line number. These would tell him exactly where on the 492-foot-long [150-m] granite wall the names of the men he knew were engraved. Then he wrote down two more sets of numbers before giving Charlie the pen.

Charlie found Fred Hansen by the date of his death. Then Gerald Moer. She copied the numbers.

The pathway **meandered** through a parklike setting. Stark, bare trees lined both sides. There was light snowfall on the ground that crunched beneath her boots. Charlie had expected to see the wall immediately, but instead, the path led down a gradual **incline**. To her left, in the distance, she saw the grand **spire** of the Washington Monument.

meandered: wandered

incline: slope
spire: pointed top

At last they reached one end of the wall. Charlie remembered that the Vietnam Memorial wall was made of polished black granite. It was V-shaped, with one arm pointed toward the Washington Monument and the other arm aimed at the Lincoln Memorial. She was at the end of the wall that pointed toward the Washington Monument, which explained why she could see the tall spire. The long wall was divided into one hundred and fifty panels, each forty inches wide. On each panel were carved the names of the dead and missing in action. Charlie had to squat down to read the names on the panels at the end. That was because the panels decreased in height from the center of the wall, where they were almost eleven feet [3.4 m] high, to the ends of the wall, where they were only eight inches [.2 m] high.

As the path proceeded downward, toward the center of the V, the panels got taller, until they towered above Charlie. She had to stare up to see the names at the top. The wall was like a huge wide V built into the earth, opening its arms in welcome, **beckoning** her to enter. The black granite panels were so highly polished that she could see her face in them.

beckoning: signaling

Walking along the path, she saw small American flags stuck into the ground below. And taped to a panel was one red, **shriveled** rose.

shriveled: dried up

The Vietnam Memorial was real. Real. Scary. Beautiful. Each time Charlie looked at a panel she saw her face, Uncle Ben, the naked trees and sky. In front of her, a woman paused. Her fingers ran down the wall, counting the small dots on the side of each panel that marked ten rows. Next to her a man and a little girl **fidgeted**. The child was watching the woman. Charlie heard her ask, "What is Mommy looking for, Papa?" And she heard him reply, "The name of someone she loves."

fidgeted: moved nervously

Uncle Ben stopped, his eyes sweeping the panel numbers and letters. "Rows and rows of names," Charlie heard him mutter, shaking his head. "Rows and rows." From her report, she knew how many names were cut into the stone that had been quarried not far from Bangalore, India—58,007 names.

While Uncle Ben's hand searched, Charlie watched. Then, as if a cold wind had swept over him, she saw his body begin to tremble. His fingers touched the letters of a name. Afraid, Charlie stood there, wishing that her aunt were closer. But Aunt Jessie was talking to the couple with the little girl.

170

His hand moved again, this time down and to the left. It stopped, and this time he froze. Charlie couldn't see her uncle's face. There were other people around them. He stood there a long time. Finally, she touched his arm. Clearly she saw the two of them and the snow on the ground and the dull, cold sky and the faded red rose. And she saw tears streaming down her uncle's face.

He reached out and held her close, his eyes never leaving the panel. Charlie looked up at him. And she knew that he didn't see her. For a second she thought she was standing there with her father, holding him while he cried.

"Were they your best friends, too, Uncle Ben?" she whispered, thinking of Gerald Moer and Fred Hansen. She had to repeat the question twice before he heard her.

"They were my men," he said. He wiped at his face with his free hand, sniffing. From the way he held his body, Charlie realized that he wanted to stay, so she gently **disengaged** herself. She had work to do.

disengaged: freed

A few panels down she discovered the names she sought: Gerald Moer and Fred Hansen. One name was too high for her to touch, but she could see it. Charlie faced her panel.

"Hi, I'm Charlie, Oscar Pippin's daughter," she whispered. "I came to see you. My daddy is fine. I know he still misses you." She took a deep breath and squeezed back the tears. This was not the time to cry. Then she saw the person she needed, the park ranger.

"Mister," Charlie asked, "please make a rubbing of two names for me."

The white-haired man **ambled** over and took a pencil and two strips of white paper out of his coat pocket. Charlie pointed to the names and repeated them while he laid a piece of white paper over each name. Next, he rubbed the pencil over the raised letters underneath the paper. He handed her the first strip, then started on the second. Charlie stared at the elegant, engraved letters. She thanked the ranger when he handed her the second strip. He moved on to help someone else.

ambled: strolled

With care, Charlie took the **origami flower** out of her pocket and wedged the stem into the slight break in the panel midway between the two names. "For you two to remember me and Daddy," she whispered. "And for us to remember you, Fred Hansen and Gerald Moer." Then Charlie bent her head and said a prayer, letting the tears fall. Moments later, she composed herself and took several photographs, making sure to get their names.

origami flower: flower made of beautifully folded paper

"Charlie, you ready? It's getting cold out here," her aunt called. Charlie looked around for her uncle. He was still where she'd left him. . . .

"So many names," Uncle Ben murmured to himself, staring back.

Aunt Jessie whirled around. "That's most of the men of my generation on that wall! And too many sent home torn up, on drugs, or with their hearts and minds messed up! What good are memorials when so many of them need medical help and jobs today? Tell me, Ben!"

Aunt Jessie's bitterness startled Charlie. Gone was the laughter, replaced by anger and sorrow. What surprised Charlie was that Mama never talked like that. Mama just loved Daddy and tried to hold the family together. For the first time, Charlie wondered if her mother shared any of Aunt Jessie's feelings.

Uncle Ben sighed and kissed his sister's cheek. Then he took her arm. "Calm down, Jess. I came home. So did Oscar. A lot of us survived."

Charlie wanted to point back to the wall and say, "They didn't." She remembered her family's happy Thanksgiving dinner. And she thought that for every name on the wall there had been an empty space at some family's table.

Charlie later gives the rubbings to her father, and he begins to tell her about the Vietnam War. The pain caused by the Vietnam War—and the divisions it caused among the American people—still exist today. The Vietnam Veterans Memorial in Washington, D.C., is a powerful monument to the men and women who served and died in the war.

Source: Candy Dawson Boyd, *Charlie Pippin*. New York: Macmillan Publishing Company, 1987.

Reaching the Moon

from *The New York Times*, 1969

During the 1960s the United States space program made some spectacular achievements. In 1961 the first American astronauts soared high above the planet Earth. Four years later, astronauts left their spacecraft and walked in space! But the most spectacular feat of all occurred on July 20, 1969. On this page is a report on the moon landing from the front page of The New York Times. *In what ways does the Times describe this amazing feat?*

From 1969 to 1972 American astronauts landed on the moon six different times. Since then, the United States space program has focused on building reusable space shuttles and on sending rockets carrying scientific equipment to study other planets. What's next for the space program? Some people talk of sending astronauts to visit the planet Mars. This could happen in your lifetime! Even if it does, people will still remember the first moon landing in 1969 as one of the greatest scientific accomplishments of all time.

Source: *The New York Times*, July 21, 1969.

173

César Chávez

by Consuelo Rodriguez, 1991

César Chávez, who was born in 1927, has long been fighting to end the use of dangerous pesticides that harm farm workers and the environment. In the 1960s Chávez led a major battle to improve the health and lives of migrant farm workers in California. These workers, many of them Mexican Americans, are people who move from harvest to harvest with the seasons to pick crops. Many migrant farm workers lack health care, work long hours, and receive very low wages. In 1962 Chávez formed a labor union to fight for better pay, safer working conditions, and protection from pesticides. In 1965 grape pickers in the union went on strike against the grape growers in California. The strike began peacefully, but three years later violence broke out, and some workers feared the strike would fail. Then, in 1968, Chávez did something bold to stop the violence and inspire the workers. To find out what Chávez did, read the excerpt below from a biography about the the union leader. How do Chávez's ideas and goals compare with those of Martin Luther King, Jr., and the civil rights movement that you read about on pages 163-166?

On March 10, 1968, 4,000 people filled a county park in Delano, California. Most of them were farm workers: Mexican Americans, Mexicans, Puerto Ricans, Filipinos, blacks, southern whites. Since 1965, they had been on strike against California's grape growers. But they had not come to the park to attend a meeting of their union, the United Farm Workers Organizing Committee (UFWOC). They had come to attend a **mass**. A **makeshift** altar had been set up on a flatbed truck in the center of the park, and a Catholic priest was preparing to offer **Holy Communion**. Rabbis and Protestant ministers were also on hand to participate.

> **mass:** Catholic religious service
> **makeshift:** quickly built
> **Holy Communion:** main part of the mass

The center of attention was a small man bundled in a hooded **parka**. He was seated on a chair in front of the altar with his wife and children. Though only 41 years old, he had needed 2 men to help him to his seat. His supporters, seeing his weakness and his **gauntness**, were deeply concerned for his life. The man was César Chávez, leader of the farm workers' union, and he had not eaten for 25 days.

> **parka:** coat
>
> **gauntness:** thinness

Why had Chávez willfully placed himself near death? Why had he **steadfastly** refused to touch food while his weight plunged from 175 to 140 pounds? Even some of those who had worked with him closely were confused and disturbed. They wondered if Chávez was merely trying to call attention to himself, trying in effect to **martyr himself**. Others who shared Chávez's political goals but not his

> **steadfastly:** firmly
>
> **martyr himself:** sacrifice his life for a cause

174

La Desgracia de los Pesticidas

The Scourge of Pesticides

religious faith were put off by the **mystical** element of the **fast** and the involvement of the **clergy**. The grape growers, locked in a bitter struggle with the UFWOC, considered Chávez's fast nothing more than a publicity stunt designed to **elicit** sympathy from the American public. But those who knew Chávez best—those who had worked with him to build a union from the ground up—knew that everything he did was directed toward a single purpose: to better the lot of the American farm worker.

The farm workers had begun their strike in 1965, refusing to labor in the **vineyards** of California's grape growers. Though farm workers had struck in the past, few of the strikes had ever been successful: The growers, with the local politicians and the police on their side, had almost always beaten down the strikers. Chávez, the son of **migrant workers**, knew this history well. He was totally committed to the philosophy of nonviolence, which had been applied successfully in the Deep South by black civil rights **activists**. As the leader of the farm workers, Chávez was determined to use these **tactics** against the grape growers. He saw no other way to win the strike. "If we had used violence," he told the writer Peter Matthiessen, "we would have won contracts long ago, but they wouldn't be lasting, because we wouldn't have won respect."

Chávez emphasized his belief in nonviolence at many union meetings, but he may have expressed himself most **eloquently** in a letter to the American Farm Bureau Federation, a growers' association: "If to build our union required the **deliberate** taking of

mystical: spiritual
fast: not eating
clergy: religious leaders
elicit: gain

vineyards: grape fields

migrant workers: farm workers who move from harvest to harvest
activists: workers
tactics: methods

eloquently: clearly and beautifully
deliberate: planned

175

life, either the life of a grower or his child or the life of a farm worker or his child then I would choose not to see the union built. . . . We hate the **agribusiness** system that seeks to keep us enslaved, and we shall overcome and change it not by **retaliation** or bloodshed, but by a determined nonviolent struggle carried on by those masses of farm workers who intend to be free and human."

Chávez's approach yielded dramatic results. The **picketing** of the fields, a nationwide boycott of California grapes, and skillful use of the **mass media** won the farm workers the sympathy of the nation and pressured several large growers into signing contracts with the union. But the growers were a **tenacious** group who had never before given in to a union. They fought back with threats, violence, court orders, and **maneuvers** such as using different labels on their boxes to **evade** the boycott. With pressures on the union mounting, it became harder and harder for Chávez to restrain those members of his union who wanted to destroy the growers' property or beat up **strikebreakers**. As the violence began to break out, he knew he had to put an end to it. As Chávez described it to journalist Jacques Levy several years later: "I thought I had to bring the Movement to a halt, to do something that would force them and me to deal with the whole question of violence and ourselves. We had to stop long enough to take account of what we were doing. . . . So I stopped eating." . . .

Finally, [after almost a month,] at the urging of his doctor, Chávez ended his fast. On the flatbed truck, he prepared to receive bread from the Reverend C. Wayne Hartmire, one of the many local clergy who supported the farm workers' cause. It was an emotional moment for the farm workers, intensified still more by the presence of Senator Robert F. Kennedy of New York. Kennedy, having heard that Chávez was ending his fast, had **chartered** a plane in Los Angeles and arrived in Delano to be present. The crowd was so **enthused** at the sight of him that he could barely make his way to the flatbed without being swept off his feet. Five years after the **assassination** of his brother President John F. Kennedy, Robert Kennedy was considering a bid for the presidency in the 1968 election. He had gained a reputation as a champion of America's poor and had come out in favor of the farm workers' struggle in Delano as early as 1966. During the fast, Kennedy had sent Chávez a telegram of support. Now he had come to take part in the Holy Communion, in this case by means of the *semita*, or poor man's bread, in accordance with the Mexican ritual.

In front of the television cameras, Kennedy gave César Chávez a piece of bread. Then, in the Boston accent which his brother had made familiar to the nation years before, he delivered a simple message: "The world must know that the migrant farm worker, the Mexican American, is coming into his own right." . . .

The next to speak was the Reverend Jim Drake. He had been a friend and ally of Chávez's from the very beginning of the union

agribusiness: agricultural big business
retaliation: getting even

picketing: marching with signs of protest

mass media: newspapers, television, and radio

tenacious: strong, stubborn

maneuvers: tricks
evade: avoid

strikebreakers: people who take the job of striking workers

chartered: hired

enthused: excited

assassination: murder

struggle. Drake read a speech that César Chávez had penned earlier that day:

"Our struggle is not easy. Those who oppose our cause are rich and powerful, and they have many allies in high places.

"We are poor. Our allies are few. But we have something the rich do not own.

"We have our own bodies and spirits and [the] justice of our cause as our weapons.

"When we are honest with ourselves, we must admit that our lives are all that really belong to us. So it is how we use our lives that determines what kind of men we are. It is my deepest belief that only by giving our lives do we find life.

"I am convinced that the truest act of courage, the strongest act of manliness, is to sacrifice ourselves for others in a totally nonviolent struggle for justice. To be a man is to suffer for others. God help us to be men!"

César Chávez's fast in 1968 marked a turning point in the farm workers' strike. The violence ended, and more people began to support the union's cause. Finally, in 1970, the farm workers won the strike and gained better wages and health insurance. They also gained protection from the use of pesticides. Chávez and the farm workers' union have played a leading role in alerting Americans to the dangers of pesticides and pollution. To see other views of these dangers, read the next two documents on pages 178-181.

Source: Consuelo Rodriguez, *Cesar Chavez*. New York: Chelsea House Publishers, 1991.

DROWNING IN POLLUTION

by Draper Hill, 1973

For more than 100 years American industry and workers have helped to make the United States one of the wealthiest nations in the world. But this wealth has not come without a high cost. Factories, automobiles, and deadly pesticides have caused pollution in many parts of the country. César Chávez and the California farm workers, whom you read about on pages 174-177, have long fought against pollution. So have many other Americans. The political cartoon below, drawn by cartoonist Draper Hill in 1973, features one of our nation's best-known symbols. How is this symbol responding to the danger of pollution? How might the raised torch of freedom suggest hope for the environment in the United States? What else is featured in the political cartoon?

Cartoons such as this one have helped to show Americans how pollution threatens the environment. Beginning in the late 1960s and 1970s, Americans began working together to clean up the environment. New anti-pollution laws were passed, and people started to recycle goods and stop wasting energy. But pollution still remains a major problem. To learn what you can do to help clean up the environment, read the next document on pages 179-181.

Source: Syd Hoff, *Editorial and Political Cartooning.* New York: Stravon Educational Press, 1976.

Save the EARTH
(It's Not Too Late)

by Professor Rap, 1991

As the political cartoon on page 178 showed, many Americans started to become aware of the dangers of pollution in the 1970s. What can you do to help clean up the environment? A musician living in Michigan named Professor Rap has a few ideas. In 1991 Professor Rap wrote a song called Save the Earth (It's Not Too Late). As you read or sing this song, notice the different types of geographic features and the forms of pollution that he mentions. What are some of Professor Rap's suggestions you can use to help save the earth?

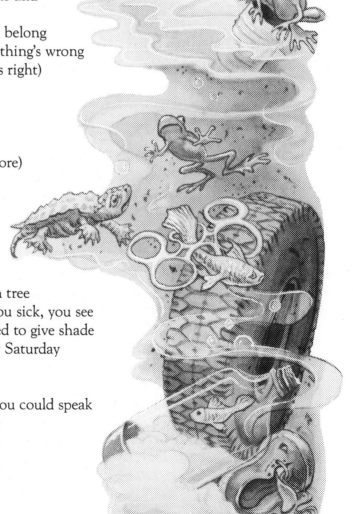

Just suppose you were a crystal blue lake and
   through bad decisions and mistakes
People filled you with things that don't belong
Now you're not so blue no more, something's wrong
'Cause people won't swim in you (that's right)
And the fish can't live in you
Your shore was once filled with sand
And now it's a garbage can
D'ya see what I'm sayin'?
It's not a game that we're playin' (no more)

(Chorus)
It's not too late
Let's not hesitate
Let us all work together
To protect the earth we treasure

Just imagine you were a beautiful green tree
And the air that's around you made you sick, you see
The kids used to climb in you, you used to give shade
   to someone reading a book on a lazy Saturday
Now the kids can't climb in you, your
   limbs have gone weak
You can't give shade no more, if only you could speak
The birds can't nest in you, do you see
   what I'm sayin'?
We've got to start living right, it's not a
   game we're playing

(Chorus)

179

Now, if we all work together, and get involved
Our environmental problems will one day be solved
No we're not preaching, or blaming you alone
We just want these problems to be better known
Now, no one could ever be too educated
And to those who want to learn, this song is dedicated
So, take it from me, the hip-hop cat
You just can't argue when it comes to facts
Pollution is everywhere and often hides
In factory smokestacks and pesticides
It's time we got serious and lend a hand
With things like not using aerosol cans
The things you can do are debatable
But, it's always good to use **biodegradable**...
Products...to stop the growth of **landfills**
And help clean up the litter on the sides of our hills.
The **ozone layer** protects us from...
harmful rays sent down by the sun
After years of polluting, it's formed a hole
It grows every day over the South Pole
We are only adding to its growing rate
It's been said to be three times the size of the U.S.A.
To me, that's a problem, and to you it should too
It's time we decided what we want to do
It's a real scary fact, yet hardly known
We're **deteriorating** our ozone...
Layer upon layers of garbage sits...
   in landfills...I mean, if it fits
We need to recycle, all of us, and soon
So we can help control our planet's doom
It's as simple as that...ten minutes a day
And help save the next generation on the way

(Chorus)

biodegradable: able to be broken down by nature
landfills: garbage dumps
ozone layer: layer of air high above the earth

deteriorating: breaking down

180

Now, if everybody, from the richest to the poorest...
Helps out...we can save the rain forest
We're losing our trees, one by one
We need the trees to make oxygen
Did you know that? That's what we breathe
I like to breathe! So help out—please!
It's not going to take you that much time
You do your share and I'll do mine
Okay, but, polluted air hurt states like Maine
Where, like in many other places, has **acid rain**
Factory smoke can take some of the blame, (but)
Laws aren't that stiff, and that's a shame
Acid rain is formed from **toxins** in the air...
   falling down in rain drops here and everywhere
Slowly, but surely, these things come back to haunt
Now tell me...is that what you really want?

acid rain: poisonous rain caused by pollution

toxins: poisons

(Chorus)

I am tired of things that make me cough
Like the smell of smoke, or car exhaust
Every day stuff adds up to ruin our planet
It's these things that we all take for granted
Unrecyclable plastic bags add up to a lot
It takes hundreds of years before they rot
And Styrofoam...we see it everyday
When you throw it out, you think it's gone, it never goes away
We've got to get serious, and want to win
So let's stick together through thick and thin
Like stop using aerosol and Styrofoam cups
Believe me, all the little things will soon add up
Be a part...set a goal and pursue it
We're in too deep to "let the other guy do it"
So...to every man, woman, boy and girl
Let's share a goal to make our earth a better world.

(Chorus)

Source: Professor Rap, *Save the Earth (It's Not Too Late)*. Utica, MI: Dalka Studios, 1991.

181

Let America Be America Again

by Langston Hughes, 1936

As many of the documents in this book have shown, the United States is a nation based on such great ideals as freedom, liberty, and equality. But as you have also read, a major theme of American history has been the struggle of Americans to live up to these great ideals and to make them real. In the poem below, called Let America Be America Again, poet Langston Hughes (1902-1967) reaches back into American history to describe the ongoing struggle of all the people who have worked to make our country a land of liberty and justice. What are some of the different types of people that he mentions? Which of these types of people can you connect to other documents you have read in this book?

Let America be America again.
Let it be the dream it used to be.
Let it be the pioneer on the plain
Seeking a home where he himself is free.

(America never was America to me.)

Let America be the dream the dreamers dreamed—
Let it be that great strong land of love
Where never kings **connive** nor tyrants scheme   **connive**: plot
That any man be crushed by one above.

(It never was America to me.)

O, let my land be a land where Liberty
Is crowned with no false patriotic **wreath**,   **wreath**: circular bouquet
But opportunity is real, and life is free,   of flowers
Equality is in the air we breathe.

(There's never been equality for me,
Nor freedom in this "homeland of the free.")

Say who are you that mumbles in the dark?
And who are you that draws your veil across the stars?

I am the poor white, fooled and pushed apart,
I am the Negro bearing slavery's scars.
I am the **red man** driven from the land,
I am the immigrant clutching the hope I seek—
And finding only the same old stupid plan
Of dog eat dog, of mighty crush the weak.

red man: Indian, Native American

I am the young man, full of strength and hope,
Tangled in that ancient endless chain
Of profit, power, gain, of grab the land!
Of grab the gold! Of grab the ways of satisfying need!
Of work the men! Of take the pay!
Of owning everything for one's own greed!

I am the farmer, **bondsman** to the soil.
I am the worker sold to the machine.
I am the Negro, servant to you all.
I am the people, worried, hungry, mean—
Hungry yet today despite the dream.
Beaten yet today—O, Pioneers!
I am the man who never got ahead,
The poorest worker **bartered** through the years.

bondsman: servant

bartered: traded

Yet I'm the one who dreamt our basic dream
In that Old World while still a **serf** of kings,
Who dreamt a dream so strong, so brave, so true,
That even yet its mighty daring sings
In every brick and stone, in every **furrow** turned
That's made America the land it has become.
O, I'm the man who sailed those early seas
In search of what I meant to be my home—
For I'm the one who left dark Ireland's shore,
And Poland's plain, and England's grassy **lea**,
And torn from Black Africa's **strand** I came
To build a "homeland of the free."
The free?

serf: slave

furrow: plowed field

lea: pasture
strand: shore

A dream—
Still **beckoning** to me!

beckoning: reaching out

183

O, let America be America again—
The land that never has been yet—
And yet must be—
The land where *every* man is free.
The land that's mine—
The poor man's land, Indian's, Negro's, ME—
Who made America,
Whose sweat and blood, whose faith and pain,
Whose hand at the **foundry**, whose plow in the rain,   **foundry:** metal factory
Must bring back our mighty dream again.

Sure, call me any ugly name you choose—
The steel of freedom does not stain.
From those who live like **leeches** on the people's lives,   **leeches:** worms that suck blood
We must take back our land again,
America!

O, yes,
I say it plain,
America never was America to me,
And yet I swear this oath—
America will be!
An ever-living seed,
Its dream
Lies deep in the heart of me.

We, the people, must **redeem**   **redeem:** free, win back
Our land, the mines, the plants, the rivers,
The mountains and the endless plain—
All, all the stretch of these great green states—
And make America again!

This poem by Langston Hughes reminds us that American history is an ongoing story in which we all play a part. The poem also reminds us that the struggles of people who lived before us must never be forgotten. Many challenges lie ahead, and it is up to all of us to work together to help America achieve its great ideals.

Source: Langston Hughes and Arna Bontemps, eds., *The Poetry of the Negro, 1746-1949*. Garden City, NY: Doubleday & Company, Inc., 1949.

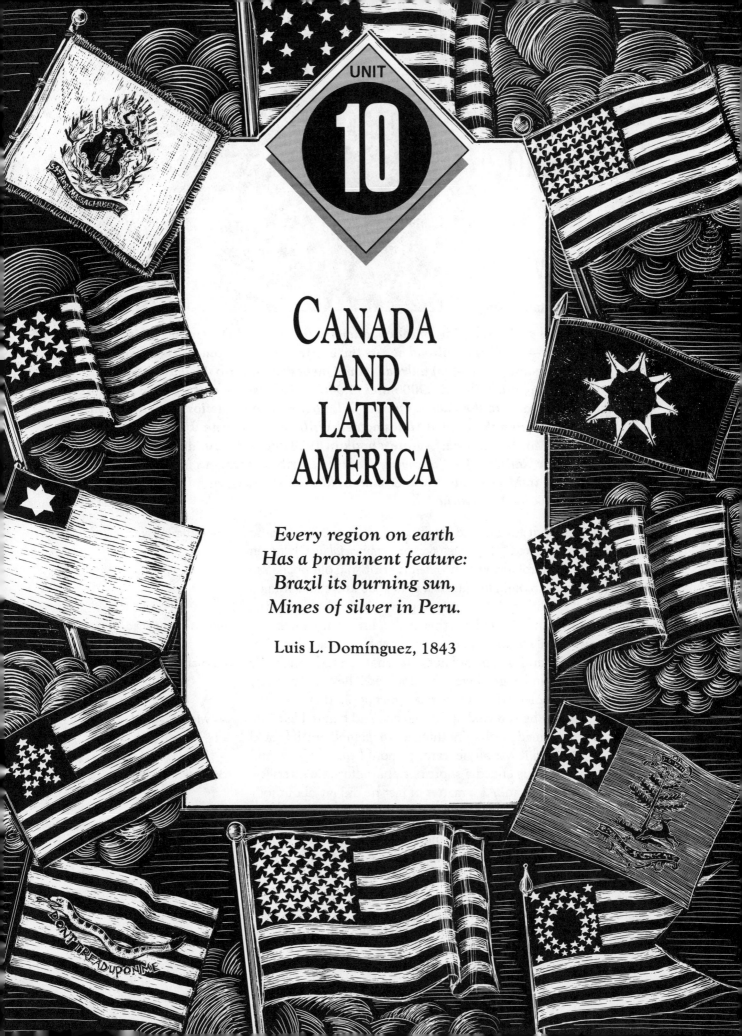

UNIT

10

CANADA AND LATIN AMERICA

*Every region on earth
Has a prominent feature:
Brazil its burning sun,
Mines of silver in Peru.*

Luis L. Domínguez, 1843

Building the Canadian Pacific Railway

by J. H. E. Secretan, 1924

In 1881, 14 years after becoming an independent nation, Canada began one of its greatest projects—building a railroad across the entire country. Canadians had already built a 1,100-mile-long (1,770-km) railroad from Quebec to Ontario. Now the great task began of extending this railroad 1,900 miles (3,040 km) across the vast western prairies and Rocky Mountains to the Pacific Ocean. To help direct construction, Canada hired a railroad builder from the United States named William Van Horne. J. H. E. Secretan, an engineer on Van Horne's staff, wrote a book in 1924 about the building of the Canadian Pacific Railway. The following excerpt describes Secretan's first meeting with Van Horne in Moose Jaw Creek, Saskatchewan, in 1882. What might it have been like to work for Van Horne?

Van Horne sent for me and announced in a most **autocratic** manner that he wanted *"The shortest possible commercial line"* between Winnipeg [in Manitoba] and Vancouver [in British Columbia], also that he intended to build *five hundred miles* [800 km] that summer, lay the track, and have trains running over it. In discussing the **projected** location I pointed out that such a line would often run through an infertile country, and made many other objections; but he was **adamant** and said he did not care what it ran through. He was evidently bound to get there. . . . I doubted if he could possibly construct five hundred miles in a short summer (it was then probably about April), but he **scowled** at me fiercely, and before I left "the presence" he informed me that "nothing was *impossible* and if I could show him the road it was all he wanted and if I *couldn't* he would have my scalp." Thus ended a short but **characteristic** interview with the great magician! As a matter of fact he did lay about four hundred and eighty miles [770 km] of track that summer.

autocratic: bossy

projected: planned

adamant: firm

scowled: frowned

characteristic: typical

Thousands of railroad workers, many of them Chinese immigrants, worked hard to build the Canadian Pacific Railway in the early 1880s. Thanks to their efforts and those of William Van Horne, the railroad was finished in 1885 and immediately became the main transportation route across Canada.

Source: J. H. E. Secretan, *Canada's Great Highway: From the First Stake to the Last Spike.* London: John Lane the Bodley Head Ltd.; and Ottawa: Thornburn and Abbott, 1924.

Skybird to the High Heavens

by Nancy White Carlstrom, 1990

Central America is a region of great beauty, containing lush rain forests, soaring green mountains, and deep blue lakes. It is also a region of great pain. For the past 200 years Central American countries have been rocked by unstable governments, bloody wars, and devastating earthquakes. These events have shaped the lives of the people living in this region, and governments run by dictators and military leaders have sometimes forced people to flee from their homes and families. The following story is about a young girl named Rosa who lives with her family in the highlands of Guatemala. As you read this story, think of the land and the culture of the people who live there. Why are the pieces of weaving made by Rosa's grandmother so important? How does having these pieces make Rosa feel at the end of the story?

My name is Rosa. Rosa Lucas Paíz (pä ēs'). I once lived in a land where footbridges dangled high above rushing streams and mountains stretched up green to the sky. Somehow the cows kept from falling off the steep cliffs.

"Grandmother, who keeps the cows in place?" I asked when I was a young girl.

"The same one who keeps the sun in the sky," my grandmother answered as she sat weaving on the floor of our house.

187

Corn grew in my land. Corn grew in patches on the side of the mountains where the cows did not fall. Grandmother said corn was one of the most important things we had. Corn gave us life.

My grandmother taught me how to weave. She had pieces of old weavings her grandmother gave to her when she was a girl. One day, she took them out and showed me.

"Rosa, these are the designs of our people." And she explained to me how each village used certain colors and designs in the weaving of cloth.

"I have saved these samples for many years, so I could pass them on to you. When I die, you will have them to use as patterns, so our own special weaving will live on."

As Grandmother taught me to weave, she told me stories about our land and its living things.

"Grandmother, tell me again about the time you saw the quetzal (ket säl')."

And Grandmother told me yet another time about when she was a girl and traveled far to the lowlands with her family. There, as they passed through the jungle, Grandmother had glimpsed the most beautiful bird in the world. The quetzal had blue-green feathers that stretched out three feet long. On its head was a tuft of gold and its chest wore a blood-red vest.

"If only I could see a quetzal someday, Grandmother."

"Maybe you will, my child. Maybe you will."

That night, I dreamed I rode on the back of a quetzal. I felt the rush of the wind as we soared to the high heavens. In the morning, I told my grandmother about my dream.

"How could I ride a quetzal, Grandmother?" I asked. "Did the bird become large, or did I become small?"

"Perhaps the dream was telling you that soon you must become small and hide from the danger wandering through our land. No matter what happens, may you always remember the sweet smell of the earth, my child."

I knew my grandmother was talking about the war that was tearing our country apart, like a **hideous** beast. But still, I did not fully understand her warning.

And so, all morning as I did my chores, I daydreamed about becoming small. Small enough to hide behind the clay cooking pots my mother kept by the fire. Maybe if I jumped out I could surprise her and make her laugh.

I could be small enough to hide in an ear of corn and watch the sun glow on my father's back as he lifted the hoe.

"Father, why do you spend so many hours weeding the corn?" I asked, when he came home with rough hands and a tired back.

"Why, Rosa, if I allow the weeds to grow, the souls of the corn plants will move to cleaner fields. Then what would we eat, my daughter? How could we trade to buy the tools we need, the sandals you wear on your feet?"

hideous: ugly

"Sell the stories Grandmother tells as she weaves on her loom," I said with a laugh.

Father just shook his head, but Grandmother smiled to herself and I knew she would tell me another tale later, when the crickets sang.

That night, Grandmother told me of the great earthquake that leveled our village before I was born. She told me how the houses folded like paper and how giant rocks were tossed from the mountains like pebbles. It was a sad, true story.

"We thought the sun would fall from the sky that time. But it didn't, Rosa," she said quietly.

"Grandmother, when you saw the quetzal in the jungle, did you want to catch him and bring him home?"

"No, Rosa, I knew the quetzal was a bird of freedom. A cage would kill him. There are other ways to enjoy his beauty."

That night, my dreams were troubled. I could not ride the quetzal to the high heavens. I could not hide behind my mother's cooking pots or in the corn of my father's field.

"Where will I go?" I cried. "Where will I go?"

In the morning, soldiers came and burned our village. First, I hid. Then, as the whole sky turned black, I ran and ran. I could not look back.

◆ ◆ ◆

My name is Rosa. Rosa Lucas Paíz. I now live in a place far from where the footbridges dangle above the rushing streams and the mountains stretch green into the sky.

"Grandmother," I whisper, "the cows have fallen off the cliff. The sun has dropped from the heavens and the corn rots."

I miss the corn that gave me life. I miss the pot of water my mother kept boiling all day on the fire. I miss the hoe of my father chopping in time with our people for hundreds of years. I miss the stories my grandmother told and the threads of color she wove on the loom.

"Grandmother," I whisper, "what if I forget the sweet smell of the earth? What if they put all the quetzals into cages?"

This morning, as I walk to the place where I work in the **refugee camp**, I am surprised to hear someone call my name.

refugee camp: temporary shelter for people who have fled their country

"Rosa." The voice is thin, like burnt paper, almost ready to crumble into little pieces.

"Rosa."

It comes to me across the miles that I have traveled while running in the cold night and burning day—fleeing through the cornfields, meeting up with others from distant villages, living pressed up close, finding shelter together from the winter rains. I see again a shared blanket, a cup of water and warm **tortillas** passed around, and these are like sparks of light in the darkness of my memories.

tortillas: round, thin bread

"Rosa, Rosa, is that you, dear?"

And there before me is a shriveled little woman dressed in the **traje** of my village: María Magdalena Rivas, my grandmother's friend. Tears stream down my face.

traje (trä′ hā): style, custom

Here is someone who knew my mother who kept the fire going, my father who lifted the hoe, my grandmother who told the tales and wove the cloth.

And now I sob at my loss, and in the arms of that old, familiar woman from my village, I take comfort.

She reaches deep under the belt that wraps around and around her frail body and takes out a small packet, a packet worn from the journey she has made.

Inside are the sample pieces of weaving, the designs of our people. The pieces handed down by my great-great-grandmother. The ones my grandmother wanted me to have.

As I hold them in my hand, I see the brilliant colors, blue-green, gold, and red—colors of the beautiful bird from the land I love. I know then that I will not forget. I will weave our patterns, designs of light, no matter where I live. I want the world to know and remember too.

"Grandmother," I whisper, "maybe it will keep the cows on the cliffs and the sun from falling. And just maybe tonight I will ride the quetzal, my skybird to the high heavens."

Like Rosa, many people in Central America have seen their lives changed by the actions of dictators and military leaders. People throughout this region have been working hard to build more democratic and more stable governments. The quetzal bird—a symbol of beauty and freedom—is the national bird of Guatemala.

Source: Nancy White Carlstrom, *Light: Stories of a Small Kindness.* New York: Little Brown, 1990.

190

THE OMBÚ

by Luis L. Domínguez, 1843

South America is a continent of stunning beauty. The northern part has vast tropical rain forests, while the southern part has miles and miles of flat, gentle grasslands. These grasslands are called the pampas and are one of the major wheat-growing regions in the world. In 1843 an Argentine diplomat named Luis L. Domínguez (1819-1898) wrote of the pride his people took in the pampas. His patriotic poem, The Ombú, *was named for the tree growing on the pampas that is the national symbol of Argentina. Read two of the stanzas from this poem, either in its original Spanish or in the English translation. How does Domínguez use plants, animals, and other parts of nature to symbolize the beauty of Argentina and South America? How does he feel about the ombú?*

Cada comarca en la tierra	Every region on earth
Tiene un rasgo prominente:	Has a prominent feature:
El Brasil su sol ardiente,	Brazil its burning sun,
Minas de plata el Perú,	Mines of silver in Peru,
Montevideo su cerro,	Montevideo its hill;
Buenos Aires, patria hermosa,	Buenos Aires, beautiful homeland,
Tiene su pampa grandiosa,	Has the grand pampas,
La pampa tiene el ombú....	And the pampas have the ombú....
Puesto en medio del desierto	Placed amid the barren land
El ombú, como un amigo,	The ombú, like a friend,
Presta á todas el abrigo	Willingly offers shelter to all
De sus ramas con amor:	With its branches:
Hace techo de sus hojas	With its leaves it creates a roof
Que no filtra el aguacero,	That no rainstorm can penetrate,
Y á su sombra el sol de Enero	And in its shade the burning rays
Templa el rayo abrasador.	of the January sun are tempered.

For more than 100 years, schoolchildren in Argentina have learned and recited The Ombú. *If you were to write a poem describing your state and your country, what symbols would you use?*

Source: Juan de la C. Puig, *Antología de Poetas Argentinos.* Buenos Aires: Martin Biedma é Hijo, 1910.

INDEX BY *Category*

INDEX BY *Title*

INDEX BY *Author*

INDEX BY *Subject*